DEVELOPING MANAGERIAL COMPETENCE

THIS BOOK IS DEDICATED TO MANAGEMENT,
THE ONLY PROFESSION (TO PARAPHRASE ROBERT
LOUIS STEVENSON) FOR WHICH NO PREPARATION
IS THOUGHT NECESSARY.

DEVELOPING MANAGERIAL COMPETENCE

A Critical Guide to Methods and Materials

❖

William Tate

Gower

Published by
Gower Publishing Limited
Gower House
Croft Road
Aldershot
Hampshire GU11 3HR
England

Gower
Old Post Road
Brookfield
Vermont 05036
USA

William Tate has asserted his right under the Copyright, Designs and Patents Act 1988 to be identified as the author of this work.

British Library Cataloguing in Publication Data
Tate, William
  Developing Managerial Competence:
  A Critical Guide to Methods and Materials
  I. Title
  658.4

ISBN 0–566–07475–3

Library of Congress Cataloging-in-Publication Data
Tate, William, 1942–
  Developing managerial competence: a critical guide to methods and materials/
William Tate
    p. cm.
  Includes index.
  ISBN 0–566–07475–3
  1. Executives—Training of. 2. Management—Study and teaching.
  I. Title.
  HD30.4.T38 1995
  658.4'07124—dc20

95–1073
CIP

Typeset in ITC Garamond Light by Poole Typesetting (Wessex) Ltd, Bournemouth, and printed in Great Britain by Hartnoll's Ltd, Bodmin.

CONTENTS

FIGURES

PREFACE

❖

Junk mail it may be, but the daily postal deliveries say much about the developer's rapidly changing habitat. I receive many unsolicited 'flyers' which fall out of my magazines. Recently three of interest arrived on one day. The first offers *Competence-based Management Development Programmes – the Flexible Way*. It states 'the emphasis of today's training is on developing a person's ability to do the job'. Well, of course! Isn't that what you'd expect? Deceptively straightforward phrases like these invite us to skip blithely over the footings to survey the pretty edifice built upon it. But are we quite sure this is terra firma? What is the implied alternative?

The second flyer offers a conference on *Making Development Pay* and asks 'How can business planning, training and development be integrated?' Again, it sounds an obvious point, yet such integration rarely happens. Why not?

The third flyer offers *Using Competencies to Improve Business Performance*. But don't these competencies sound rather different in nature from those in the first flyer? On closer examination all three flyers represent quite different philosophies and approaches to developing managers.

So developers have to be both sharp in mind and fleet of foot to keep pace with the fast-moving market. The products keep developing, as one would hope. So do the concepts behind them, again as might be expected in a healthy market. But as if this was not enough, root philosophies are being upturned and our values and ideas about organizations and work, about managing and management, and about managerial learning, are being challenged in a more fundamental way than I can ever remember.

Many of the changes are sparked off directly or indirectly by government initiatives, especially the advent of National Vocational Qualifications, which has given rise to the fast-expanding competence market. For purchasers of open learning products, competence is the dominant force behind the activity of sellers who wish to capture this market. Technology is developing rapidly too, beaming learning tools into our homes, networking together isolated learners and tutors, bombarding our senses with multi-media images, driven by ever more powerful chips.

Plenty of choice there may be; but for buyers and users, a shopper's paradise it is not. Not only is the amount of innovation confusing; some of the new options are heavily circumscribed by the new national framework and by political pressures, adding to users' dilemmas – individuals and companies alike. Many feel pressurized to jump on the all-pervasive competence bandwagon; at the very least they need to take a position. When some of the big-name gurus are known to have doubts, and when the information flow and the propaganda are almost entirely one way, finding a way through this particular political minefield is difficult and not without risks. I recently read a newly released book on open learning; it managed not to mention competences once. Now that was taking turning a blind eye to new extremes! Like it or not, there is no way of skirting this issue: we have no choice but to examine the competence route and see if it's safe for managers to tread that particular path. This book is more concerned with illuminating that path than beckoning you down it. Whilst it will suit many, it will not suit all.

Readers' decisions have to be taken with an informed and open mind. To help with that, this book examines the latest methods and the most economic approaches to managers' development, especially the increasingly popular method of open learning in its various forms. But that is only a part of the story. We need to be concerned with learning in an appropriate managerial context – for most people this means their organizational role. The best developers don't simply provide their employees with quality learning packages; they have a deep understanding of the learning context and the ability to manage it. Only in this way can developers embed individual learning in the heart and soul of the organization and give it the best chance of success. Indeed, only in this way can they help the organization itself to change.

That necessary development framework includes being able to decide what kind of learning is and is not appropriate, even when to look for answers to performance problems outside of training altogether. Training and development is never the only possible route to improvement for the organization, and often not the variable with the most leverage. Unfortunately, the means of diagnosing a fuller understanding of the organization's problems and the range of possible development opportunities lies well beyond the scope of this book, which is primarily concerned with individual managers' needs. The companion to this book, *Developing Corporate Competence: A High-Performance Agenda for Managing Organizations*, provides a useful organizational complement to this book's individual manager development orientation.

THE BOOK'S AUDIENCE

Developing Managerial Competence is intended for students of management, in both senses of that expression – consumers and providers, buyers and sellers, clients and consultants, trainers and educators, the developing and the developers.

A prime target is decision makers and practitioners in companies who make choices about, advise on, and conduct managerial development. They may be clients to external providers, but they themselves have client line managers, plus budding managers and supervisors. Help is available in this book with the purchase, application, support, customizing, administrative arrangements, design of learning centres and other considerations needed to allow learning for managers to deliver on its promise. But, more importantly, the client is the company and its top management which needs help to realize and release the full potential of development.

Many readers will therefore be those employed in development, training and personnel departments – in companies and institutions, public and private sector, for-profit and not-for-profit enterprises. (For the sake of simplicity I shall generally use the term 'companies' to describe all such places of employment.)

The book also speaks to external providers of training and educational learning, to suppliers of materials and to those involved in what is sometimes called 'delivery' – offering some ideas and insights from an in-company management perspective borne of long experience.

THE PURPOSE OF THE BOOK

This book has four purposes. The first is to shed light. Heaven knows it's badly needed, especially in the perplexing and controversial world of the competence movement, where the propaganda urges but doesn't answer 'why?' and 'why not?', and doesn't help us choose wisely. So a prime aim is to offer a clarification of the current market.

But the book has much more than a mission to inform. It seeks – somewhat paradoxically – to show how a unifying effect can be found in the plurality of the market. It seems to me that the common ground in the educational and training battlefield is to be found in niche markets, choosing from specific strengths more than seeking a single and comprehensive bill of fare to suit one taste, which anyway doesn't exist. I hope to show why and how.

Third, the book tries to provide a range of ideas and possibilities, which if not all new, certainly don't seem to have been much acted upon and badly need a shove. Coupled with this are pointers to a range of resources and services and indications on what is worth exploring further.

Lastly, the book aims to provoke, but not prescribe. If it helps readers determine or rethink their own position, and even if they then reach a conclusion different from my own, it will have served a useful purpose.

What the book is not is a conventional textbook, even an unconventional textbook. It is neither all-embracing of its subject-matter, nor more than transitory. It constitutes a selective commentary, contribution to debate and source of help with the present volatile state of play.

OVERVIEW OF THE CONTENTS

Developing Managerial Competence is in three parts, with its patchwork woven into a cohesive whole by the developer's thread – the mission of managerial learning.

Part One: The Managerial Context
Part Two: The Competent Manager
Part Three: Open Learning Choices for Managers

The book does not have to be read *en bloc* from start to finish – though there are benefits in so doing. For example, Part Two stands acceptably on its own for developers who have, say, an intense curiosity about the basics of the competence movement but who denigrate the new learning technologies and open learning methods (there are such people, and they are missing something). The reverse can be said for those who have vowed not to get mixed up with competences. But I believe it is hard to move forward in any of these areas without reading Part One, since it is this that gives the rest its purpose, context and hope for a better future.

THE BOOK'S APPROACH

The book tries to make some use of features found in good open learning, within the inevitable constraints of conventional book publishing. For example, in the practical sections you will find important points summarized as Key Tips. More importantly, you are prompted at appropriate points by activities and questions. These allow you to consolidate learning by engaging in health checks, or reflecting and making decisions or analyses of your own. This way I hope you may be better able to capture and record your thoughts and personal learnings. Of course, not all of these activities will apply to everyone – that depends on your individual role and responsibilities – so make use of them only when they appear helpful.

Prospective buyers of learning products will build up the necessary framework through which their decisions almost take themselves. For those expecting to invite providers to tender, completing the activities as you go along will serve to compile the agenda for such meetings.

The management training market is changing for a whole variety of reasons, not all of which have their basis in the current volatility in business and the political and economic environment. This context is challenging our views on the practice and form of managing as well. So any book's contribution at this time on management training and development is bound to be transitory.

The problem is most acute when mentioning products and parties, such as suppliers, endorsing bodies, etc. Given the market turbulence, any book on this subject risks being out of date before it reaches the bookshelves, particularly where technology is concerned. I have done my best to ensure that what goes to print is accurate at that time, but names and addresses rapidly show their age. I apologize in advance if I have failed to report the latest position on any aspect, contact, resource or product.

Though transitory to a degree in these areas, it is important to point out that this book is rather more durable than a directory or a consumers' guide, neither of which it attempts to be. While the book contains examples of products drawn from the market in order to make a point, it does not purport to cover the full range of products in a given field. Nor does it recommend a 'best buy'. In a book like this there is little advice that can be offered on price, since we all want to pay the least, all other things being equal. What can be said for sure is that it is well worth shopping around. One-off programmes on time management, for example, vary from £9.95 to £400!

Appendix 1 lists useful contacts and sources of learning materials and related services. Many are to be found in Pergamon's *Open Learning Directory*, but some of the providers listed in this book are to be found only through advertisements, exhibitions, magazines and the network. To assist with this search, Appendix 2 contains further sources of advice, information and membership.

The author is always interested to hear from readers concerning their own experiences and views in relation to the ideas expressed in this book. He can be contacted at the address given below.

Fernleigh House
The Terrace
Wokingham
Berkshire RG40 1BP
United Kingdom
Tel: 01734 773443

William Tate
June 1995

ACKNOWLEDGEMENTS

I would like to acknowledge the kind advice and help from many friends, colleagues and practitioners in the field of open learning, competences and management development, including Jonathan Chalstrey, Peter Critten, Helen Drummond, Barbara Geary, Fiona Hales-Irving, Helen Murlis, Shafi Parwani, Nicola Peckett, Mike Pedler, Peter Sinclair, Sue Thame, Kaye Thorne, Terry Watts, Lee Wilcock and David Willetts.

I am also indebted to the many providers of learning materials for letting me use samples and quote from their products. They include BBC Enterprises, Executive Business Channel, Lifeskills International, The Hay Group, HDL Training and Development Ltd, Manchester Open Learning, Management Charter Initiative, Flex Training Ltd, MultiMedia Training, TDA Consulting Ltd, The Open College, and Wolsey Hall Oxford. And I would like to thank the numerous fellow authors and publishers for allowing me to quote from their books and publications.

Finally, I could not have completed this project without the help of my ever-patient wife, Pauline, and family, whose support I lovingly acknowledge.

Good learning!

I would like to thank the following for permission to use copyright material.

Butterworth-Heinemann for extract from: Peter Critten (1993), *Investing in People: Towards Corporate Capability*, Oxford: Butterworth-Heinemann.

Gulf Publishing Company for extract from: Malcolm Knowles (1990), *The Adult Learner*, Houston, Texas: Gulf Publishing Company. © 1990 by Gulf Publishing Company. All rights reserved.

John Wiley & Sons Inc. for extracts from: Richard Boyatzis (1982), *The Competent Manager: A Model for Effective Performance*, Chichester: Wiley. © Richard Boyatzis. Reprinted by permission of John Wiley & Sons Inc.

Macmillan Publishers Ltd for extract from: Rosemary Stewart (1991), *Managing Today and Tomorrow*, London: Macmillan.

Pfeiffer and Company for material from: J. William Pfeiffer (ed.), (1991), *Theories and Models in Applied Behavioral Science: Vol. 2, Group*. © 1991 by Pfeiffer and Company, San Diego CA.

Extracts from *Senior Management Standards*, published by the Management Charter Institute, are Crown copyright material and are reproduced with the permission of the Controller of HMSO.

William Tate

PART ONE
THE MANAGERIAL CONTEXT

❖

INTRODUCTION TO PART ONE

This book is in three parts. Parts Two and Three look at various models, methodologies and materials concerned with the occupation of management and its development. But these need grounding in a context. It is the business of Part One to provide that context, comprising a single introductory chapter on management itself, called 'Management – from science to high art'. Crucially, the opening chapter sets the scene for the highly potent work of the competence movement and recent developments in the field of open learning.

In Part Two we shall make a critical examination of the work of the competence movement in the field of management, especially the models developed and promoted in the UK by the Management Charter Initiative (MCI) with its generic form of management standards. Whilst many of the concerns, controversial elements, and perceived problems with the competence movement have to do with principles about competences *per se*, others are concerned with the way competences are used to define management in what seems to many a restricting back-to-basics definition. Others are concerned with what happens when you try to apply competences to management in practice.

It is not my purpose to compete with countless experts by setting out my own account of what does or should comprise management – now or for the future. There are far better qualified writers already doing that, and there are numerous books and journals, from many of which I quote. What I seek to do is highlight issues, contradictions and dilemmas which have to be tackled by any player in the development stakes who wants to be taken seriously. That includes agencies who put forward national models, publishers of development products, consultancies offering their services to companies, and in-house development teams and trainers.

Part One is eclectic rather than comprehensive. Its first purpose is selectively to paint a multi-coloured back-cloth of management reality and management promise against which the various ideas, models of competence, and development products available from providers can be tested for good fit.

Its second purpose is to help you to explore the real nature of management within your own organization – where it is now and where it is going – from your own experience and standpoint, and to think deeply about your own definition and approach to managing. It poses some tough questions to answer, in particular aiming to help you to decide whether a generic approach to management is likely to be appropriate, durable and offer an answer for your own organization's management.

1
MANAGEMENT – FROM SCIENCE TO HIGH ART

OVERVIEW

This chapter describes some of the parameters and variants of managing, helping us to understand that most indefinable of concepts: management. It presents considerations and options of the practice of managing, from the most basic to the most sophisticated.

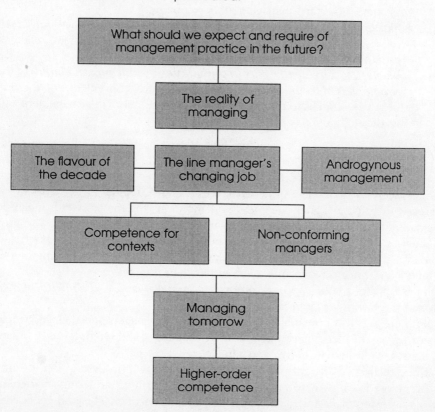

What should we expect and require of management practice in the future?

The reality of managing

The flavour of the decade

The line manager's changing job

Androgynous management

Competence for contexts

Non-conforming managers

Managing tomorrow

Higher-order competence

INTRODUCTION

A quick scan of a few of the more thought-provoking books on current management thinking reveals gurus like Tom Peters,[1] Gerard Egan[2] and Peter Vaill[3] making the following claims:

○ *Management is more an art than a science.* So are we being too logical and analytical?

○ *The manager's job nowadays is equally concerned with creating disorder as order.* Are we still wedded to a model of the manager as the creator and restorer of order?

○ *It is the organization's non-rational 'shadow' which needs managing, as this accounts for its behaviour more than its intended design.* If so, are we being too rational and neglecting the other half of the organization?

○ *Individual managers' ability is not a high-leverage variable in the attainment of increased organizational effectiveness.* Are we being sufficiently imaginative in seeing managers' contributions in context and in perspective?

○ *Today cannot be predicted, let alone tomorrow, we pay people to manage external unpredictability.* Are we recognizing this in our models of competence and management development?

○ *Managing is concerned less with control and more with getting out of the way.* Do we instinctively seek to maximize management, where a minimalist approach might sometimes be desirable?

○ *We need to develop diversity in our management teams and build on the uniqueness of the individual.* Does the practical convenience of 'the one best way' blind us to the joys and choices of pluralism in management and its development?

One could easily loose off a complete belt of armour-piercing bullet points like these – and we shall later. But for the moment, from these few blasts alone we can safely say that the finer art of managing goes well beyond what individual managers can be seen to do and beyond what they can be trained to do. This holds increasingly true the higher one goes in organizations and the more individualistic the nature of the beast, both job and job-holder.

Likewise, the art of developing goes beyond developing managers alone and takes on a direct concern for developing the company's management of the business and organization – the game rather than the players – as I show in my companion book *Developing Corporate Competence: A High-Performance Agenda for Managing Organizations.*[4]

But here we shall primarily confine ourselves to managers and their individual needs – from the elementary and junior to the strategic and senior levels in organizations, as indicated by levels 1 and 2 in Figure 1.1.

The direction of this chapter's own development is from description towards prescription, from today towards tomorrow. It begins by considering a variety of ways of viewing managing, such as the distinctions between all-round generalists and specialists, gender differences, how the line manager's job is changing, and

FIGURE 1.1 HIERARCHY OF MANAGEMENT COMPETENCE

MANAGERIAL COMPETENCE				*CORPORATE COMPETENCE*
1 **WHAT A MANAGER DOES**	→ **2** **THE HIGHER ART OF MANAGING**	→ **3** **INTACT UNIT TEAMWORK**	→ **4** **COLLECTIVE MANAGEMENT TEAMWORK**	→ **5** **MANAGEMENT OF THE ORGANIZATION AND BUSINESS**
A foundation of generic management skills. Centred on the individual. Initial focus on national initiatives on individual managers' competence and discussion on national training targets for managers. Assumed major problem area in the national debate on the country's poor economic competitiveness. Certificate level and Diploma level primarily. Many companies' development interest limited to this level and assumed sufficient, particularly where a heavy orientation towards skill training and competences.	The less tangible meta-qualities, attributes and sensibilities which differentiate excellence from competence, particularly at higher levels, and which complement fundamental skills. Should hope to find uniqueness and capitalize on it. Involves acquiring experience and wisdom. Requires an understanding and managing of the non-rational aspects of the organization as well as the rational. Concerned with managing career plans and sound leadership appointments. Relevant to development activity at higher educational levels/qualifications.	The handling, composition and intra-group performance of intact teams within functions. Not simply concerned with individuals having good team skill and understanding, important though that is. The most commonly found focus for team-building and team-development activity.	How the wider company management team works together for a common corporate goal. Concerned with interdepartmental purposes and relationships, and cross-functional working and collaboration, and how the vertical and horizontal team together deliver business results and continual renewal. Relatively neglected.	The full range of options available to senior managers for improving the management of their part of the organization and business. Has implications for developing organizational capability (via the management climate, systems, rewards, etc.) and not just personal capability, and for directly assessing management competence at the corporate level.
manager development	*manager development*	*management development*	*management development* and *organization development*	*management development* and *organization development*

7

other trends and fashions. We shall see how what managers bring to bear in their jobs has to make a good fit with where their organization lies in its own phase of development. We shall consider various examples, themes and arguments in favour of looking for unique strengths – even eccentricities – in a few key managers, and where these may make for an acceptable trade-off against shortcomings elsewhere. We shall end with an examination of various prominent writers' thoughts on what comprises the grey area beyond tangible skill and knowledge that makes the difference between managing as a well-defined science and managing as a rarely glimpsed form of high art.

THE REALITY OF MANAGING

Volumes have been written over the years about the nature of managing. As far back as 1916, Henri Fayol introduced the language of 'planning, organizing, co-ordinating and controlling' into the managerial vocabulary. Most attempts at describing managing portray it as scientific, and make it appear reflective, rational and systematic. Managing comes across as a set of discrete activities. But there are voices which say that the reality is very different: that folklore is very different from fact; that the world of what managers *should* do disregards the realities of what managers *actually* do. For example, Henry Mintzberg,[5] John Kotter,[6] Rosemary Stewart[7] and others make the following arguments:

- O Managing is less predictable than claimed.
- O Managers have little free time to think, plan and organize themselves.
- O Managers are not strategic, reflective or proactive, and seem to prefer live action and interacting with others at a fast, non-stop pace.
- O Managing is a highly interactive, flowing process, not a neat structure of cause and effect.
- O The success of managing depends more on the individual person than the tasks performed.
- O The days of the middle manager are gone.
- O The manager's job is primarily oral and most information is stored in the head.
- O There are wide differences in the manager's job as practised and required. Influences are the industry, the company, the environment, current situations and temporary issues.

Some readers might find the above list unsettling, particularly those already firmly wedded to MCI's highly rational model of generic management standards (explained later in the book). It is of little comfort to realize that Mintzberg *et al.* are mainly concerned with *describing* what managers actually do, whereas MCI's model and many other devices and tools for management development are intended to be *prescriptive*: they express what managers *should* do. But the two different perspectives cannot simply be left unconnected; management development activities will only be acceptable, useful and implemented if they acknowledge reality.

TOO MUCH PRESCRIPTION

Edgar Schein commented that:

> My recent enquiries into organization culture have consistently shown how idio-syncratic organizations really are and how difficult it is to prescribe what managers should do.[8]

In his excellent summary of 'What Managers Really Do', Alan Mumford expresses the anxieties shared by many when he observes that,

> one can only be surprised and saddened by the apparent continuing failure of many authors, or business schools and management training centres, to define and implement their offerings in terms of what managers really do.[9]

Some challenging research was undertaken in 1989 by the Ashridge Management Research Group. Companies taking part in their survey believed strongly that the 'competitive edge went to those who had the degree of flexibility to relate the competences required to the needs of their market ... an approach appropriate to one is not necessarily appropriate to another'.[10] The conclusion included an HR manager's call for a 'deliberately under-developed system of development'. Compare this with the intent underlying most approaches to management development.

MANAGEMENT AS A CAREER

It is difficult for those embarking on a career to picture what the job of a manager involves. It is hard enough for those who have been practising it for years!

Some, like Peter Wickens, are concerned that management is currently being portrayed as a distinctive career (let alone an occupation), rather than a senior position on a technical ladder or hierarchy of responsibility.[11] This can mislead aspiring managers. It may result in many inexperienced, frustrated and highly qualified generalists. And it might be at the expense of more widescale employee access to development.

Those involved in management development must be concerned with not only the reality of managing, but also the image and impression it conveys.

SENIOR SPECIALISTS OR GENERAL MANAGERS

Most managers' careers develop from a base of technical expertise and to a greater or lesser degree retain everyday working connections with that specialism and a general orientation towards that function, technology or discipline. They may lose touch with the detail, especially in the fast-moving world of IT, but they are required to keep close enough to retain a strategic grasp and to be able to perform credibly as a manager of that function. Very few managers are truly 'general' managers (irrespective of title), spending the bulk of their time performing the purely managerial functions expected of managers at large. Most of their time is spent on business concerned with their own background specialist function. Many retain a substantial technical or administrative component in their jobs. Indeed, this may dominate at the expense of the generic managerial role.

But this truth generally goes unacknowledged in the kind of development most managers receive. At the junior and middle management level, a manager may wish to develop a greater depth of technical expertise in a particular field. That may serve the interest of the employer too. The alternative option of putting effort into broadening one's managerial base may be less worthwhile. But to obtain a generic national qualification may require just that. There is obviously a risk here that breadth might be at the expense of depth. There is also the possibility that technically oriented managers may not recognize the model of managing they are presented with.

The assumption in some models is that the generic manager always has a marketing and a financial element in the job, and this is particularly problematical. In many organizations these functions are reserved for specialists. Similarly, in many organizations – especially in the public sector – managers may not become involved in recruitment and selection (though that is changing in some areas). This raises two issues. The first is that the training and development may fail to reflect the organizational reality. The second is that learners may lack the means of demonstrating such competence to assessors – a key requirement of the competence movement (CM), as we shall see later.

But, by definition, without such generic competence the award of a truly national and portable qualification is not possible. This may sound inflexible, but to concede on this would strike at the heart of the concept of National Vocational Qualifications (NVQs). Transferability and choice make uncomfortable bedfellows.

This example of the fit between the development of managerial competence and the real practice of managing serves to give a foretaste of the kind of issue that will be discussed in Part Two, 'The Competent Manager'.

ACTIVITY 1.1

In your own organization, consider what words sum up the image of a job/career in management, e.g. struggle, pinnacle, reward, super-technician, administrator, sinecure, etc.

- How does this compare with what you consider to be the reality?
- How do people progress to management positions?
- What proportion can reasonably be called 'general' managers?
- How does development activity contribute to a true or false image?
- How well does development activity address reality?

THE LINE MANAGER'S CHANGING JOB

Some of the current trends concerning the breadth of the management role favour a generic management model. There is a move towards reducing the size of head-office functions and pushing new responsibilities out to line managers. An example of this in some organizations is the delegation of a number of daily operational aspects of personnel management, such as selection and training, plus administrative tasks like staff records. Welfare matters were similarly passed out to the line in many organizations in earlier years.

One current use for a management competence model is for head-office specialists to specify the standards to which the company requires such delegated responsibilities to be performed by line managers. As a way of setting down what is acceptable for newly delegated roles, the management standards appear to help. They also serve to drive training programmes. In the local authority field, Berkshire County Council has developed a competence-based model for decentralized personnel management which is now being followed by a number of other local authorities.[12]

Whether such changes are part of a permanent shift in the balance between specialists' and line managers' jobs remains to be seen. These matters are sometimes cyclical, oscillating between specialists at the centre who need to regain control over professional standards from time to time, but then letting go again for reasons of flexibility or efficiency. Often these matters are the subject of fashion.

The devolution of certain personnel tasks is not without risks, since line managers may perform them inadequately, or it may be felt that they require too much time to be spent on them to the detriment of their operational role. But the current personnel strategy is part of a wider, well-founded move to decentralize tactical head-office activity, thereby placing it closer to the (internal) customer, and making it more efficient, more responsive and more flexibly tailored to local needs. At the same time it frees head-office specialists so that they might concentrate on those key activities that can only be conducted at the centre. This demise of the monolithic corporate structure, built in part on the myth and blinkered search for economies of scale, really does appear to be permanent.

ACTIVITY 1.2

Consider how the general role of managers in your organization is changing; for example, as a result of delegating hitherto specialist activities, delayering, quality assurance, computerization and networked information, etc.

- What are the implications for development?

ANDROGYNOUS MANAGEMENT STYLES

There is increasing talk of an androgynous style of managing being appropriate for the future. The word 'androgyny' derives from the Greek *andro* (male) and *gyne* (female) and refers to a blending of both sexes' characteristics.

In the past, managers have been expected to be analytical, concrete, rational and concerned with ideas. It has sometimes been regarded as unbusinesslike to be preoccupied with cooperation, nurturing relationships, appreciating interdependence, and concerned with people's needs.[13]

These attitudes towards managing have their ongins in the predominantly masculine history of management. Concerns with rationality and analysis are *task-orientations* – primarily male values. Concern for relationships and cooperation, on the other hand, are *support-orientations* – primarily female values. Interestingly, for readers familiar with the Myers-Briggs Type Indicator, only one of the four scales consistently shows a sex bias, but it is the one which measures thinking versus feeling (no need to say which is which!).

The process of socialization locks many people – consciously and unconsciously into their expected sex roles. But with the growing numbers of female managers competing for what were predominantly male jobs, we see more women striving for the stereotypical managerial model.

Many readers will be familiar with the Managerial Grid, the dimensions of which are concern for production versus concern for people. The grid's originators, Robert Blake and Jane Srygley Mouton, suggest that every manager has a dominant style.[14] The general belief is that the ideal manager's dominant style is as a so-called 9,9 manager, someone with both a high concern for production and a high concern for people. The authors associate this with what they call the team approach. One might reasonably conclude that the typical bias present in most people will limit their orientation to something less than a balanced 9,9, and that a blending would help the organization.

Increasingly, the benefits of an androgynous approach to managing are being realized. Along with male managerial elements such as presence, authority, clear goals, power and influence, .society now expects more in the way of helping skills, collaboration, appreciation of others, and the ability to express oneself, to personalize as well as generalize, and to enjoy others' achievements as well as one's own.[15] So our business values are likely to shift over the years to accommodate what some people regard as more feminine traits – in the male population, not just through an increasing number of female managers.

In a sense, a generic model of managing represents an androgynous approach, in so far as such models do not draw any distinctions between the roles practised by male and female managers. Yet in reality, people sometimes have different expectations of the roles and of how male and female managers may fulfil them in different ways.

The Hay Group recently undertook some interesting research on a small population of male and female managers, gaining their own perceptions of how they considered they were managing, plus the perceptions of their subordinates. This was part of Trent Regional Health Authority's Opportunity 2000 project. Six styles were categorized, as shown in Figure 1.2.

Hay's research shows that managerial style is a key factor in determining the organization climate, and that this in turn directly impacts work performance.[6] The results also showed that the male and female managers held fairly similar views about their managerial style, but their staff perceived significant differences:

O   Reporting to a manager of the same gender produced a more positive dimate for staff.

O   People reporting to a female manager appeared to have higher expecta-

FIGURE 1.2 MANAGERIAL STYLES

- **Coercive**. A 'do it the way I tell you' style. Managers using this style provide clear direction by telling subordinates what to do and exercising tight control.
- **Authoritative**. 'Firm but fair'. Managers using this style give clear directions and explain the reasons behind decisions.
- **Affiliative**. 'People first, tasks second'. This style stresses keeping subordinates, happy and avoiding conflict.
- **Democratic**. 'Participative'. When using this style, managers ask staff to participate in decisions and aim for consensus.
- **Pace-setting**. 'Do it myself'. Managers using this style have high standards and lead by example.
- **Coaching**. 'Developmental'. Managers using this style help or show their staff how to improve their performance and develop professionally.

Reproduced by courtesy of the Hay group

tions than those reporting to a male manager.

○ The styles used by female managers were not working as effectively with their male staff – their management style did not appear to be as visible to men.

○ When female managers used a pace-setting style it had a more negative effect on the climate than when male managers used this style.

○ All managers could improve the climate by making greater use of an authoritative style with their staff. This would help improve rewards, clarity, flexibility and team commitment.

Trent Region is considering using these data in a number of ways:

○ To develop managers' ability to make use of the most appropriate style.
○ To influence promotional criteria to favour those with the most effective style (authoritative, affiliative, democratic and coaching).
○ To build different expectations into appraisal and interviewing so that women are not unfairly discriminated against in the assessment of potential and performance.
○ To develop female managers and potential managers in the use of a more visible and authoritative style.

ACTIVITY 1.3

Reflect on how aware and concerned your company is, and needs to be, with gender-driven managerial roles, styles and development?

- How might development be more proactive in this area?

THE FLAVOUR OF THE DECADE

What sort of people are the management superstars today? Would they have been superstars ten years ago? Once we were full of admiration for corporate planners. That esteem subsided in due course, and we now expect more by way of communication skill. Yet at the same time the value of consensus has lost ground to brute power – increasingly boss power, not worker power. We used to require managers to be good at keeping the peace with the trade unions; that's hardly the key skill now, but there are signs that it may return. Possible changes of government and European social legislation could have an impact here.

The lesson is that what we most value in managers changes over time. Some of this simply reflects changing needs with changing times. But it is easy to believe that management and how we want managers to be trained and developed is partly a matter of fashion.

The organization of management activity is also subject to fashion, as we saw when discussing the current decentralization of much specialist head-office activity. Talk of 'delayering' the management hierarchy is another example of fashion.

In idealizing both management and its methods of development, we need to be able to see through what is merely fashionable, and seek out what is objective and likely to prove enduring.

COMPETENCE FOR CONTEXTS

At senior levels in an organization where one needs departmental heads who will give leadership to their functions, there may be benefit to be derived from ringing the changes between contrasting management, rather than a bland continuation of what went before. As the fortunes of departmental functions rise and fall, as organizations pass through their natural life cycle, and as their environment changes, their approach too needs to change.

Too often these contextual variables receive insufficient attention in development, appraisal and selection. Particularly when making appointments, it is easy to concentrate excessively on assumed competence for a largely unchanging job, often as portrayed by a largely unchanging job description. This document in any case makes no attempt to define the present organization context: its phase in its own life cycle, its present climate, its current goals, its boss's predisposition, its economic environment.

The manager's match with this current context is as important as with the job description. My own matching tool *Executive-Match* reaches beyond competence and offers context-based choices to help organizations' leaders make senior managerial appointments which take account of their organizations' needs at that particular time.[17] For example, which of the following do they need:

O   More emphasis on cost cutting, or increasing revenue?

O   A stronger departmental image, or more interdepartmental collaboration and networking?

O   Consolidating recent changes and achievements, or a shake-up and injection of radicalism?

O   Adherence to past norms, or a challenge to the existing norms?

These are just a handful of the choices to be exercised and displayed by senior management if they are to make a good fit with where their organization is and what it particularly needs *at that time*. This dimension of timeliness builds on Rosemary Stewart's observation that management differs in different jobs, organizations and countries. It also needs different management at different times. Horses for courses. Or as one might say, competences for contexts.

ACTIVITY 1.4

Try to characterize the particular contextual factors in your organization (or, if you prefer, in a key unit or job) at the present time, within which your managers need to make a good fit.

● What does this imply for managerial competence and development?

NON-CONFORMING MANAGERS

The process of analysing managers' jobs and defining management to produce a generic model effectively reduces the variety we see to a uniform and widely acceptable core. That way it becomes transferable in employment, trainable and assessable. But to the pessimists this sounds like the creation of an identikit manager. Such critics would instead hope to find an element of the unorthodox in the competent manager, someone prepared to break the mould, take risks and try new approaches.

Peter Drucker has sometimes likened leadership to conducting an orchestra. Putting aside arguments about differences between leading and managing, let's indulge in a flight of fancy for a moment and equate the performance of a top manager with that of the maestro.

What makes a great conductor has always been difficult to discern. What they have in common is their remarkable degree of individuality and the fact that this often correlates with their achieving remarkable results. Fritz Reiner hardly moved, controlling the players with glaring eyes. Herbert von Karajan kept his eyes closed. Leonard Bernstein controlled with his mouth and highly animated body gestures.

This parallel with the idiosyncrasy of top managers is not so far-fetched as it might seem; after all, there are now training courses teaching, for example, baton technique for budding conductors. Why? Leopold Stokowski used no baton! The answer may be simple. In both the musical world and business there is a trend towards greater conformity, perhaps resulting in part from less tolerance of a dictatorial style by those who are managed/conducted, and as a result of more training being expected and available.

In the case of the late conductors mentioned, they had to discover for themselves what worked, and they arrived at personal conclusions. But have we progressed? Will baton training courses produce great conductors? I suspect not. That may not be the purpose. It may only produce competent ones! They say the best is the enemy of the good. Might the reverse be equally true? A budding Stokowski might be denied the chance to display his unique gifts if he failed his assessment against the national baton competence standard.

TRADING STRENGTIHS FOR WEAKNESSES

Apart from what organizations need at any given time, the needs and preferences of those on the receiving end of being managed will also vary. They may benefit from and welcome peculiar strengths – even quirks – while willingly accepting some personality or skill shortcomings in exchange.

Some research on highly successful managers has shown that they don't need to be good at everything. Starting at the very top, our own experience and reading about chief executives bears this out. When one chief executive steps down and another takes over, they are often completely different – not just by chance or personality: they may need to be. Although brilliant in one respect, they may be somewhat weaker in another – even considered quite flawed. One's forte might be in managing the financial markets. Another's strength and interest might lie in managing the internal relationships. Their weaknesses and orientations might be compensated for by the chairman or by the chief financial officer. Yet each chief executive in their own way, and judged against the company's general results, may be held to be equally successful.

But generic management standards seem to presume the following:

O   That we can have – and should aspire to have – all these capabilities in the one person.
O   That by so doing no quarter will suffer.
O   That there are no inherent contradictions in these varying strengths and interests.

It would have been interesting to have the process of competence research examine these basic assumptions and the kinds of managerial options described which face organizations and key senior managers at different times.

ACCOUNTING TO STAKEHOLDERS

Differences at the higher levels are not only explained and tolerated on the basis of individual strengths. They are likely to reflect these bosses' views of their role. According to newspaper reports, the chairman of Marks & Spencer, Sir Richard Greenbury (winner of the 1993 Retailer of the Year award from NatWest Securities) confidently claims 'I am not interested in trying to buff up the share price by spending too much time talking with the financial community' – a more acceptable posture now than would have been the case previously. Some other company chairmen would take a different view. It is arguably entirely legitimate for those managers who have a degree of freedom, to shape their role according to their different conclusions.

This variability also reflects the different type of management structure, for example, starting at the top, whether the chairman and chief executive roles are combined or not. But different models of management continue down the management structure. The most obvious differences are those between public- and private-sector models, especially the matter of who takes decisions. A key variable is therefore the job's environment, and it was this that Sir Richard was having to consider and bring his judgement to bear on. And part of that environment question for a manager to consider is to whom he or she accounts, and whether the pressure to deliver comes mainly from one stakeholder or a number of them.

ACTIVITY 1.5

Consider how conforming or non-conforming your organization prefers or allows its managers to be?

- Are strict codes, rules and overt norms of managerial conduct and style spelt out?
- Is management relatively predictable, systematically structured and generic?
- How tightly controlled from above are managers' work requirements?
- Is personal risk-taking encouraged or discouraged?
- What happens to managers who stand out from the crowd?
- Is your priority need to raise management competence across the board, or selectively to develop an élite of excellent leaders?

MANAGING TOMORROW

If you could identify the essential ingredients for managing today, by tomorrow they would need to be different. Fashion apart, the reasons are to be found in the rapidly changing business, political, social and technological environment. We can't be sure that a definition of competence derived from studying today's jobs will correlate with high performance in the future. The pace of change might simply be too fast to freeze the frame.

RIDING, SMOOTHING OR MAKING WAVES

The more confident say that the vital competence will be the ability to manage in a turbulent environment, as well as the ability actively to manage the change itself. The more realistic argue that one can only hope at best to 'cope' with the increasing chaos in the business environment; any claim beyond that is an illusion or the arrogance of leaders who would like it to be believed that they are in control of the future.

or the arrogance of leaders who would like it to be believed that they are in control of the future.

In his mid-eighties, the revered Peter Drucker is still able to take the radical line that being in control means 'controlled chaos' and 'planned abandonment':

> the modern organization is a destabilizer. It must be organized for innovation, and innovation is creative destruction. And it must be organized for the systematic abandonment of whatever is established, customary, familiar, and comfortable, whether that is a product, service, or process; a set of skills; human and social relationships; or the organization itself. ... Managers have to learn to ask every few years of every process, every product, every procedure, every policy: 'if we did not do this already, would we go into it now knowing what we now know?' ... will have to *plan* abandonment rather than try to prolong the life of a successful product, policy, or practice.[18]

The paradox is that in Drucker's knowledge society, managers must prepare to abandon everything they know.

HANDS OFF, LET GO

Many successful leaders of industry argue that to be fleet of foot means giving staff a bigger role in running the business. No doubt many disempowered managers and supervisors would like themselves included in that. But they are finding out that what their leaders often mean these days is fewer managers controlling less. Power seems to be polarizing, with many unfortunate managers left feeling isolated in the middle.

Whether staff are *given* a bigger say or not, in Drucker's view, the organization of the future is an organization of,

> equals, colleagues and associates. No knowledge ranks higher than another; each is judged by its contribution to the common task rather than by any inherent superiority or inferiority. Therefore the modern organization cannot be an organization of boss and subordinate. It must be organized as a team.

While presented by Drucker as a practical consequence of the advent of the *knowledge worker*, it can equally be seen as a moral argument. Indeed, should not knowledge always have enjoyed this status-free position? And if the reasons why it hasn't are to be found in people's motives as much as in their titles, to what can we look to deliver us from our own natural but base dysfunctional inclinations?

TOMORROW'S COMPETENCES

Managing tomorrow is indelibly bound up with fast-changing environments – coping, reacting and managing. Study and research by Professor Harry Schroder, professor of management at the University of South Florida, has identified eleven such 'high-performance managerial competencies'.[19] (NB: Don't worry about the different spelling of competencies; the significance of this is explained in Part Two.) Their application at NatWest has supported Professor Schroder's own research findings. The competencies are as follows:

○   **Information search**. Gathers many different kinds of information and uses a wide variety of sources to build a rich informational environment in preparation for decision making in the organization.

○   **Concept formation**. Builds frameworks or models, or forms concepts, hypotheses or ideas on the basis of information; becomes aware of patterns, trends and cause/effect relations by linking disparate information.

○   **Conceptual flexibility**. Identifies feasible alternatives or multiple options in planning and decision making; holds different options in focus simultaneously and evaluates their pros and cons.

○   **Interpersonal search**. Uses open and probing questions, summaries, paraphrasing, etc. to understand the ideas, concepts and feelings of another; can comprehend events, issues, problems, opportunities from the viewpoint of another person.

○   **Managing interaction**. Involves others and is able to build cooperative teams in which group members feel valued and empowered and have shared goals.

○   **Developmental orientation**. Creates a positive climate in which individuals increase the accuracy of their awareness and their own strengths and limitations and provides coaching, training and developmental resources to improve performance.

○   **Impact**. Uses a variety of methods (e.g. persuasive arguments, modelling behaviour, inventing symbols, forming alliances and appealing to the interest of others) to gain support for ideas, strategies and values.

○   **Self-confidence**. States own stand or position on issues; unhesitatingly takes decisions when required and commits self and others accordingly; expresses confidence in the future success of the actions to be taken.

○   **Presentation**. Presents ideas clearly, with ease and interest so that the other person (or audience) understands what is being communicated; uses technical, symbolic, non-verbal and visual aids effectively.

○   **Proactive orientation**. Structures the task for the team; implements plans and ideas; takes responsibility for all aspects of the situation.

○   **Achievement orientation**. Possesses high internal work standards and sets ambitious yet attainable goals; wants to do things better, to improve, to be more effective and efficient; measures progress against targets.

Rosabeth Moss Kanter believes that there are seven skills and sensibilities which must be cultivated if managers and professionals are to become true business athletes.[20]

○   **Learn to operate without hierarchy**. Replace the crutch of authority with personal relationships, influence and shared achievements.

○   **Compete in a way that enhances cooperation**. Strive to achieve the highest standards of excellence rather than wipe out the competition. Competitors today may be collaborators in the same team tomorrow.

○   **Operate to the highest ethical standards**. Behave ethically for pragmatic as well as social and moral reasons.

○   **Show humility**. A dose of humility is essential. Accept the guidance of coaches. There are always new things to learn.

○   **Develop a process focus**. Show respect for the process of implementation as well as its substance – how things are done as well as what is done.

○   **Be multifaceted and ambidextrous**. Work across traditional functional boundaries, find synergies and form alliances, connecting with the skills of others.

○   **Gain satisfaction from results**. Be willing to stake rewards on results. Rewards will not come through enhanced status and promotion.

Gareth Morgan[21] suggests tomorrow's competences include the following:

○   Balancing chaos and control.
○   Managing in an environment of equals.
○   A new approach to social responsibility.
○   Making specialist staff user-driven.

While such statements can sound idealistic and read like a wish list, there is wide agreement on these themes to be found among the various management philosophers. Where disagreement is to be found is in the best way to help managers make the journey.

Later chapters of this book and its companion, *Developing Corporate Competence*, expand on these recurring themes and discuss their implications for developers, e.g. results versus processes, career management, rewards, collaboration, cross-boundary working, ethics, learning, etc.

There are two further observations worth making. If management is continually evolving, or should be, in the manner suggested by Moss Kanter and others, how can trainers, developers, open learning publishers, MCI's management standards, etc. get a firm enough grip on a definition of management at any one time to pin it down for teaching and assessment purposes? The trick has to be an ability to accept this fluidity and help learners understand it, yet still appreciate the practical value of a snapshot to give you something concrete to act upon for now without being too locked into it.

My second observation is not to worry about the first. It is the least of our worries. Of far more concern is that it doesn't seem to be a problem because many of those who should be struggling to respond to this evolving future seem trapped in the past. Most offerings still paint a rather safe, traditional, humdrum and anodyne picture of what we want from our managers and management. Now that *is* something to be worried about.

ACTIVITY 1.6

Take a look at what you are developing your managers to be.

- How forward-looking is this?
- How imaginative is it?
- How does it compare with forecast requirements advocated by various writers?

HIGHER-ORDER COMPETENCE

A belief that skill and knowledge combine to provide ability to perform effectively is insufficient. In examining the finished content of MCI's management standards, Sir Derek Hornby, erstwhile Chairman of Rank Xerox (UK) Ltd summarized the feelings of many when he said:

> We have arrived, not surprisingly, at a list which will be very familiar; it is difficult to criticise a specification which says a competent manager needs to communicate verbally, in writing, individually and in groups. That he or she needs financial and analytical skills, understands a PC and can handle a keyboard, understands the customer and the market-place and has a good understanding of the legal, financial and social environment in which he or she works and so on. My instinctive feeling is that however vital all that is, we are leaving a number of tricks on the table.[22]

What are these extra 'tricks' that go beyond the mere demonstration of applied skill and knowledge and which combine to produce all-round management performance? Quite apart from the obvious questions about motivation and energy, there are so many other personal qualities that are difficult to observe, let alone find.

C.J. Constable[23] identified a more intangible set of attributes:

- Ability to make sound judgements
- Creativity
- Willingness to take risks
- Decisiveness
- High energy level
- Ability to take initiatives
- Results-orientation
- Tenacity
- Ability to take independent action
- Integrity
- Adaptability
- Resilience
- Ability to deal with detailed information
- Lateral thinking

To this list Constable added his categories of skills:

○   **Self-management skills**: learning skills, communicating skills, time management.
○   **To manage other people**: selection procedures, appraisal systems.
○   **For managing and controlling**: Setting objectives, forecasting and planning, budgeting.
○   **To manage relationships outside the organization**: dealing with other organization cultures, language skills.

Some of what Constable offers is rudimentary and easily captured by a competence model. Other items are peculiar to particular situations or roles. And several are plainly pitched at a higher level of abstraction. John Burgoyne distinguishes such higher-order abilities[24] and over-arching competencies,[25] suggesting that they are concerned with the ability to do the following:

○   Learn, and learn to learn
○   Show judgement
○   Adapt
○   Forecast and anticipate
○   Handle and create change
○   Possess skills of analysis, synthesis, balance and perspective which transcend contextual limitations

Beyond these abilities are claimed to lie professional virtues and various further so-called 'meta-qualities' such as:

○   Diligence
○   Tenacity
○   Perseverance
○   Patience
○   Integrity

More recently there has been discussion involving MCI about managerial concepts like:

○   Ability to think globally
○   Vision
○   Courage
○   Create focus
○   Organizational awareness
○   Strategic thinking

Echoing Drucker, and perhaps, most thought provoking of all, Vaill[3] claims as the most strategic competence:

○   The capacity to shelve one's competence in favour of an openness to the new.

It is easy to assume that these higher-order competences become relevant only for those who have mastered the basics, or to assume that they apply only to senior managers. But there is a school of thought which says that certain of these should come first. In the words of Reva Bernman Brown, the argument runs that such 'managerial capacities as judgement, intuition and acumen ... are a prerequisite if managers are to undertake their managerial tasks competently ... without which any demonstration of competence is a meaningless, hollow and ultimately self-defeating activity'.[26] Once armed with these attributes, managers are in a better position to decide what skills they need to acquire and how and when to apply them. In the case of those items mentioned – and I would suggest sensibilities and qualities such as integrity, courage, and organizational awareness – that appears to make good sense. What is the point of learning *how* to delegate, for example, without the judgement of *what* to delegate or without first learning to trust, let go and get out of the way?

ACTIVITY 1.7

Consider what level of management competence you are currently directing development at, from basic practice through to higher art (see Figure 1.1).

● Who in your organization might benefit from some of the above higher-order or meta-competences?
● Which of these competences seem particularly relevant to your company at this time?

Higher-order abilities seem to hold one of the keys to real management – now and for the future – as distinct from merely what managers can be seen to *do*. But is this, as Hornby puts it, the only missing trick?

Richard Pascale suggests in a video on organization transformation that this condition is about changing what you are *being*, not just what you are *doing*. If we are to find the missing ingredient perhaps we should stop asking the question 'What should managers *do*?' and consider instead 'What should managers *be* and what should they become?'

In the race to be better or best do not miss the joy of being. (Anon)

REFERENCES

1. Tom Peters (1992) *Liberation Management: Necessary Disorganization for the Nanosecond Nineties*, London: Macmillan.
2. Gerard Egan (1988) *Change Agent Skills A: Assessing and Designing Excellence*, San Diego: University Associates.

3. Peter Vaill (1989) *Managing as a Performing Art: New Ideas for a World of Chaotic Change*, Oxford: Jossey-Bass.
4. William Tate (1995) *Developing Corporate Competence: A High-Performance Agenda for Managing Organizations*, Aldershot: Gower.
5. Henry Mintzberg (1989) *Mintzberg on Management: Inside our Strange World of Organizations*, New York: The Free Press.
6. John Kotter (1982) *The General Manager*, New York: Free Press.
7. Rosemary Stewart (1976) *Contrast in Management*, New York: McGraw-Hill.
8. Edgar Schein (1990) 'A General Philosophy of Helping: Process Consultation', *Sloan Management Review*, Spring.
9. Alan Mumford (1988) 'What Managers Really Do', *Management Decision*, **26** (5).
10. Edgar Wille (1989) 'Managerial Competence and Management Development', *Training Officer*, November.
11. Peter Wickens (1991) Oral Presentation to IPM National Conference.
12. Judy Ratcliffe (1992) *Specification for Human Resource Responsibilities*, Royal County of Berkshire.
13. Roger Harrison (1987), *Organization Culture and Quality of Service: A Strategy for Releasing Love in the Workplace*, London: Association for Management Education and Development.
14. Robert Blake and Jane Mouton (1964) *The Managerial Grid*, Houston: Gulf Publishing Company.
15. J. William Pfeiffer (ed.) (1991) 'Androgyny', *Theories and Models in Applied Behavioral Science*, San Diego: Pfeiffer & Co.
16. Margaret Rock (1993) 'Men and Women as Managers', *People & Performance*, London: Hay Management Consultants Ltd.
17. William Tate (1993) *Executive-Match: A Self-Completion Selection Planning Guide*, Wokingham: Prometheus Consulting.
18. Peter Drucker (1992) 'The New Society of Organizations', *Harvard Business Review*, September-October.
19. Tony Cockerill (1989) 'The Kind of Competence for Rapid Change', *Personnel Management*, September.
20. Rosabeth Moss Kanter (1990) *When Giants Learn to Dance: Mastering the Challenges of Strategy, Management, and Careers in the 1990s*, London: Unwin, pp. 361-4.
21. Gareth Morgan (1988) *Riding the Waves of Change: Developing Managerial Competencies for a Turbulent World*, Oxford: Jossey-Bass.
22. Derek Hornby (1991), 'Management Development – The Way Ahead', in Mick Silver (ed.) *Competent to Manage – Approaches to Management Training and Development*, London: Routledge.
23. C.J. Constable (1988) *Developing the Competent Manager in a UK Context*, Report for the Manpower Services Commission, Sheffield: Manpower Services Commission.
24. John Burgoyne (1989) *Management Development: Context and Strategies*, Aldershot: Gower.

25. John Burgoyne (1989) 'Creating the Managerial Portfolio', *Management Education and Development*, London: Association for Management Education and Development, **20** (1).
26. Reva Berman Brown (1994) 'Reframing the Competency Debate: Management Knowledge and Meta-Competence in Graduate Education', *Management Learning*, London: Sage, **25** (2).

PART TWO
THE COMPETENT MANAGER

❖

INTRODUCTION TO PART TWO

❖

You may be wondering: does the book take a stand in the current discussion about whether competences are good or bad? That's not the right question. You need to consider whether the competence approach is right for you, even right for some managers in parts of your organization. Only you can decide that. My job is to help you understand the subject and the pros and cons, and leave you to make up your own mind.

There are already 1800 companies in membership of the Management Charter Initiative (MCI), representing 25 per cent of the UK workforce. The management standards are already used by 11 per cent of companies. We will therefore look at some case examples of those companies' use of MCI's competence methodology. I am not about to condemn something which so many companies are finding ideally suited to their needs; that would be both presumptuous and churlish. But readers will also come to see that there are problems with the competence approach, particularly if applied to the exclusion of other approaches to management development.

My purpose is also to maintain the debate, which is itself developmental in the wider sense. I like to feel that my position is characterized more by balance than fence sitting. Readers will find no wholesale comfort here for their prejudices, one way or the other.

The unavoidable controversies in this subject begin with an examination of the basic competences approach in Chapter 2, 'The Competence Models'. Here we examine the different forms and positions, and we acquire the language of the various models. We need to be able to understand and discuss competence from the standpoint of alternatives before we can see what is happening in detail and in practice in the field of management.

In Chapter 3, 'The Management Charter Initiative', we examine the advent of national vocational qualifications (NVQs) and their Scottish equivalent (SVQs). [Note that all references in this book to NVQs should be taken to embrace SVQs.] We consider the competence movement which NVQs have generated, taken up with vigour by the Management Charter Initiative. For readers looking for sharp advice on what and what not to buy, a rough indication may be found from examining which products have been approved by MCI. Sellers of materials are keen to have their products rubber stamped, so we review an approved product from the buyer's perspective.

Chapter 4, 'Using the Management Standards', is devoted to the practical application of MCI's standards to the four managerial levels: supervisory, first line, middle and senior management. The chapter also examines MCI's Personal Competence Model. Perhaps the best current example of market turbulence in this field is in how to give formal credit for previous and current learning and experience. This so-called Accreditation of Prior Learning (APL) is transforming training and is also discussed here.

On the basis of the understanding built up earlier, we are ready to begin exploring some of the issues and options facing management developers in Chapter 5, 'Making the Most of Competences'.

Then we are ready to bite deeply into the heart of the many controversies surrounding the competence movement. These arguments are brought out in Chapter 6, 'The Competence Controversy'. Some issues concern principles which affect all occupational groups, and these are dealt with first. We then examine some serious practical problems with competences when applied specifically to management.

Finally, Chapter 7 pursues another popular subject for developers, 'Getting the Best from MBAs'. We investigate what can go wrong with these expensive programmes and expensive recruits. Then we attempt to learn from these lessons so that we produce high-powered managers and not just high-powered headaches.

2
THE COMPETENCE MODELS

OVERVIEW

This chapter explains three basic models of competence, concentrating heavily on that adopted for the UK government initiative.

What do the competence models mean and comprise?

UK versus USA approach

Developing management and competence

Defining competence

Input model   Output model   Process model

Drawing the models together

INTRODUCTION

A nywhere you go in the field of management education, training, development and selection, and more recently appraisal and rewards, you will hear people speaking the language of 'competences'. Not far behind they'll mention 'NVQs' (National Vocational Qualifications).

The idea of competences is considered to have originated in the USA in the 1960s as a response to concern with the quality of American teacher education. As interest grew in measuring and managing performance, the approach attracted increasing interest in the UK and became linked with the government's desire to promote NVQs. The qualifications are now the main driving force behind the fact, form and function of the competence movement in the UK, taken up enthusiastically by the Management Charter Initiative (MCI) for managers – if not quite as MCI's *raison d'être*, then at least as the central plank of its marketing strategy.

In this chapter we shall concentrate on competences as a concept. MCI and NVQs themselves qualify for more detailed discussion in the next two chapters.

To understand competences as a concept we first have to master a new language. As competence has grown into something of a boom industry, those engaged in furthering its cause have, true to form, developed their own jargon to describe it. Much of this chapter is devoted to explaining the nuances of the nomenclature in the context of the main and subsidiary models of competence.

This present high level of interest and debate around competences is healthy in itself, never mind whether you agree with the conclusions and current direction. Even those who take a peek at competences and then reject them for their own companies will probably credit the competence movement with causing them to think hard about how they might make their own training and development more directly relevant for their business. We were long overdue a challenge to our traditional approach to education, training and qualifications, and its effect on the country's economic well-being.

It goes without saying that past (and continuing) approaches to management and its teaching can also be said to have followed a competence model of a kind. This is often called the traditional model, the approach by which universities, business schools and colleges have defined management, broken it down for teaching, delivered the subject matter, assessed attainment and awarded qualifications.

This traditional model of management education and training was for years largely taken for granted by most people. It was hardly seen as one of a number of alternative models. Until challenged by a fundamentally different model in more recent times – especially the laying down of management standards by MCI – the topic was not much discussed in these conceptual terms. So when we speak of 'the competence model' in this chapter, we are referring to the *new* competence model and its variants.

UK VERSUS USA APPROACH

One way of dividing the models is between those which follow the original USA purpose, and those which follow the rather different UK approach to competence and what it is for, as developed by MCI acting as the government's Lead Body for the occupation of management.[1] But it should be pointed out that the alternative USA model is also widely used by consultancies in the UK.

The UK approach establishes a single benchmark of competence, primarily for **assessment** purposes. Using this, a manager can be deemed either acceptable or not. The model can be used in a variety of contexts such as appointments, appraisal and for establishing individual managers' development needs. The model can also drive the design of training programmes where the learners will subsequently be assessed against the model, leading to the award of qualifications. By contrast the USA model is based on the study of the competence of outstanding performers in order to be able to plan for managers' **development**.

We will return to these themes later, where we shall examine each model and its implications. But it should be quickly pointed out that the fact that the published ingredients of managerial performance in the two countries are different and are derived by different analytical processes does not imply that the actual standard of management practised in one country against the other is also different. It is the concept of competence itself, and why it is believed worth having, that is different.

DEVELOPING MANAGEMENT AND COMPETENCE

The new perspective on competence has affected many aspects of education, training and development, including design, delivery, assessment and accreditation. But the object here of this new language of competence – namely, management endeavour – is not automatically changed by the competence movement. Competence technology is separate from management technology. In the case of the occupation of management, we pay MCI to meld the two technologies sensibly, taking the best of both at any given time to produce up-to-date and usable management standards. But to be able to examine critically what is going on here, at times we have to be able to disentangle the two.

So far as the separate development of management practice *per se* is concerned, other forces in society, the economy and behavioural science research will look after that. The continuing parallel development of the art, science or practice of management and our understanding of it has, of course, interacted with the development of the competence approach as a means of representing it for various practical purposes, as analysts have sought to break it down and describe its inherent and fundamental competence.

The surprising fact – indeed the sad fact – is that more energy, radicalism and imagination seem to have gone into pioneering the competence model and how it can be applied to management (irrespective of whether you agree with it or not) than have gone into the managerial content. One might even say that the fundamental message about managing itself – rather than the form chosen to depict it – is boringly familiar and traditional. When examined closely the substance actually appears rather insubstantial. You might almost say it appears to be a case of pouring old (management) wine into new (competence) bottles.

But that is hardly fair. Any highly fragmented analytical model tends to take on that rather unexciting appearance. As behaviour is broken down into its tiny component parts, much of the subtlety of the larger managerial act is inevitably dissipated. But while this may help to explain and excuse the 'old wine – new bottles' syndrome, it does serve to highlight one of the criticisms of the analytical methodology and the ultimate utility of its product. We do, after all, want our managers of the future not simply to be better at what they should have been doing, but to manage in ways more in tune with the spirit and needs of the approaching millennium. Trying to redefine what constitutes management competence with this in mind – whatever model is used – could hardly be more timely.

Our view of what constitutes best management practice at any given time is continually adjusting – because of the changing reality, latest research and understanding, as well as new mechanisms for describing it. The unending supply of new books on management attests to that. The changing world business scene and increasingly competitive economic environment place new demands on managing successfully. Views continue to evolve on what we expect from workplaces, from work structures and from work relationships. That includes relationships with hierarchies and the role of supervision, but increasingly it includes managing relationships with business partners and outsourced resources. It deals with the question of how those responsible for business can best manage their organizations to deliver against their mission and satisfy their shareholders and many others in the wider business and social environment who hold a stake in the enterprises' conduct and success. It has much to say about how organizations 'learn', and it speaks to the need for a new morality in management.

Yet it is hard to find the richness and excitement of this in the management competence model. It is a further irony that one of the chief criticisms of the competence movement is that, while it places what managers do under a microscope and then re-labels it, it also suffers from the unavoidable tendency to freeze the definition of management.

The critical voices of the competence movement are strong and will not be stilled. But the criticism that the competence approach is bound to introduce inflexibility is a shade unfair. Those responsible for developing the new management standards are showing a commendable willingness to re-examine their definitions at very frequent intervals. However, it can reasonably be argued that the processes of precise and detailed definition and promulgation for use by educators, trainers, assessors and accreditors must inevitably put some obstacles in the way of fluid change, both of perception and response. If the scene was always moving, some trainers and producers of materials might claim to be unable to grasp the subject for long enough to be able to make anything of it. This is less of a problem at the higher levels of study, where grappling with a dynamic and ambiguous perspective of what constitutes management is itself part of the educational challenge and learning process.

In later chapters we make a thorough examination of the many problems with the competence approach *per se*, both the underlying principles and assumptions, and the practical issues entailed when applying competences. First, let's examine the official position on competence.

DEFINING COMPETENCE

THE EMPLOYMENT DEPARTMENT'S POSITION

The position taken by the Employment Department, which is the power behind the drive for competence-based approaches to developing improved managerial performance, is set out in this statement:

> The concept of competence ... is defined as the ability to perform the activities within an occupation or function to the standards expected in employment. Competence is a wide concept which embodies the ability to transfer skills and knowledge to new situations within the occupational area. It encompasses organisation and planning of work, innovation and coping with non-routine activities. It includes those qualities of personal effectiveness that are required in the workplace to deal with co-workers, managers and customers.[2]

This definition is expanded in a guide published jointly by the Employment Department and the National Council for Vocational Qualifications. This explains that 'Competence is that which is demonstrated by people who are successfully carrying out all the activities associated with their jobs.'[3] This seems to provide a clear and generous definition in what has become a semantic minefield, as we shall see in a moment.

While the official position outlined above should be broad enough and clear enough to answer many of the problems people have with competences, it cannot be guaranteed to drive all claimed 'competence' learning products, for reasons that will become apparent later. Buyers need to understand the field well enough to know what to look for.

WHAT COMPETENCE IS

O   Competence concerns being **able to perform**, not just know about. The standards of competence expected in employment are not just *training* standards. Competence is about performing complete jobs in the real world – more about the workplace than the classroom.

O   Competence also involves bridging the well-known gap in the perceived value of training in terms of making use of it in the real world of work. Anyone who has been on a training course has experienced this – not only in one's own mind, but often from the tongue of a sceptical boss.

O   Competence-based training therefore does away with arguments regarding the transfer of training back to the workplace. Because success is assessed at the place of work, there can be no dispute regarding competence and, ultimately therefore, the utility of training.[4]

○   Competence-based training shifts attention from the design of training programmes (inputs) in favour of assessing its application in the form of outputs.[5]

○   Competence-based training can also help build these bridges at the level of the organization as well as for the individual learner. In many companies a ring is found round the training department's activity, isolating it from the sharp end of the business, and limiting its role to one of reacting to individual demands. This new way of looking at competence grounds training in the heart of business performance.

The competence movement is increasing the prominence given to training by many employers, and raising training's national and public profile. Indeed, the government sometimes appears to give more leadership and take more interest in training initiatives than those employers for whom its words and programmes are intended. But that tide may have turned. A well-managed role for competence-based training and education could take us a long way from that which Eugene Donnelly delightfully described as 'a dubious cocktail of wishful thinking, anecdotal experience, with an admixture of flavour-of-the-month opportunism'.[6]

Most would probably accept the definition of competence and some of the claims made for the concept set out in the Guide to National Vocational Qualifications. But (leaving aside criticisms for the moment) that's the easy bit. Actually recognizing and describing competence in a helpful way is rather more difficult and prone to disagreement among experts. Work done by the NHS Training Division has helped clarify the distinctiveness and usefulness of various models.[7] They boil down to three. We shall look at these in turn, beginning with that which sits most comfortably with the concept described so far.

THE OUTPUT MODEL

The most radical model and by far the most powerful in impacting current managerial education and training is the **output model**. It is at the heart of MCI's work, and therefore the examples given to illustrate the model are drawn from their publications. This model is primarily concerned with:

deciding what *outcomes* you want managers to achieve

In answering this question, MCI has analysed, defined and published generic occupational standards – called management standards – for four levels of management: supervisory, first line, middle and senior. They are what MCI calls 'benchmarks of best practice'.[8]

Other bodies have published occupational standards for different groups of employees.[9] Generically these standards are defined in this way:

> Occupational standards are not descriptions of the performance itself (specific activities or tasks), nor the means of achieving competence (knowledge and skills learned through the training programme) nor the means of measuring quality or achievement (assessment) nor the process by which the achievement is recognised publicly (qualification). Standards are 'benchmarks': descriptions of the

expectations of employment against which the actual performance of individuals will be compared and assessed as competent, or not competent as appropriate.

In the output model, descriptions of competence are derived from a top-down analysis of a job function called **functional analysis** (examined in Chapter 6). This entails a cascade of questions. The first question for each level of management is:

O   What is the occupation's **key purpose**?

According to MCI, for first line and middle managers this is said to be:

> **to achieve the organization's objectives and continuously improve its performance**

O   What **key roles** are entailed in fulfilling that key purpose?

For first line managers, MCI has specified these as:

> **Manage operations**
> **Manage finance**
> **Manage people**
> **Manage information**

O   What are the **outcomes** which must be demonstrated in each of those key roles?

The outcomes are first defined as **units of competence**. These describe in broad terms what is expected of a competent manager in particular aspects of a job. The Confederation of British Industry (CBI) describes a unit as a 'rounded achievement worthy of public recognition'. It is these units which are certificated within NVQs.

To give a simple example, for the key role of 'Manage information' there are two units of competence:

1.   **Seek, evaluate and organise information for action**.
          (Unit of competence)
2.   **Exchange information to solve problems and make decisions**.
          (Unit of competence)

The units of competence are then broken down further into their **elements of competence** (something you are able to *do* as part of that achievement). This is where the tangible meat is in this model. It is elements of competence which are the basis for assessing whether a manager 'has it'. These elements of competence are defined in the ED/NCVQ Guide like this:

> An element of competence is a description of something which a person who works in a given occupational area should be able to do. It is a description of an *action, behaviour or outcome* [my italics] which the person should be able to demonstrate.[3]

For the second of the units of competence mentioned above ('Exchange information ...'), there are three elements of competence:

2.1   **Lead meetings and group discussions to solve problems and make decisions.** (Element of competence)

2.2   Contribute to discussions to solve problems and make decisions.
(Element of competence)

2.3   Advise and inform others. (Element of competence)

(NB: These are the same words but not the same numbers used by MCI in its own published breakdown.)

O   Each element of competence is backed up by **performance criteria**.

These are the means of knowing 'how well' a manager is performing. They are defined as follows:

> Performance criteria are statements against which an assessor judges the evidence that an individual can perform the activity specified in an element.[3]

O   Onto the performance criteria are tagged **range statements** or **indicators.**

These suggest the areas and circumstances within which employees must be able to perform satisfactorily against the elements of competence and provide evidence of achievement. They are defined formally as follows:

> Range statements elaborate the statement of competence by making explicit the contexts to which the elements and performance criteria apply. Also they put limits on the specification to ensure a consistent interpretation. In particular they should be used to define the breadth of competence required, and may also act as a reminder of conditions under which competence is expected but not immediately obvious.[3]

Again, to illustrate the concept, and using the example of 'Advise and inform others', there are five performance criteria, one of which is:

> **Information given is current, relevant and accurate**. (Performance criterion)

O   Covering the five performance criteria are four range indicators. One of these is:

> **Advice and information is given to:**
>   **immediate manager;**
>   **colleagues, specialists, staff in other departments;**
>   **customers**
>   **suppliers.** (Range indicator)

O   The elements of competence are complemented by assessment guidance.

This sets down what the **performance evidence required** covers, and what forms of evidence are expected, that is, the *what* and the *how*. Using this example again, the performance evidence required in support of 'Advise and inform others' includes among others:

> **Advice and information offered proactively with the manager taking the initiative.** (Performance evidence required)

That completes the basic output model. It may sound over-complicated – indeed redolent of a whole new industry complete with complicated jargon. But MCI has done much to make the management standards accessible, for example, by presenting them in the form of pocket guides. The structure actually masks something very simple, as the words (in bold type above) show when describing the content of managing.

The basic conceptual model itself, illustrated in Figure 2.1, is very straightforward and was first developed by Mansfield and Mathews in 1985 to help the government's Industry Lead Bodies develop their national occupational standards.[10]

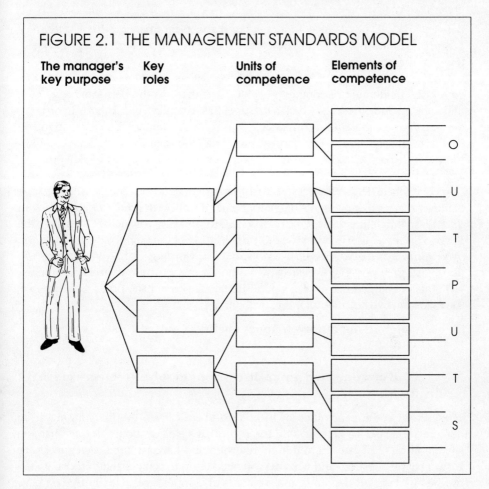

FIGURE 2.1 THE MANAGEMENT STANDARDS MODEL

The manager's key purpose **Key roles** **Units of competence** **Elements of competence**

A FEW ISSUES

Splitting key roles

An intriguing question is whether some of the key roles are truly separate and parallel, for example, the key roles of 'Manage operations' and 'Manage information'. It could be argued that to manage an operation a manager needs to perform such practices as leading meetings, advising others, etc. If you hold that view, the roles are not divisible in this way.

Outcomes or outputs

It is a moot point whether 'outcomes' in some of the above examples should really be regarded instead as 'outputs'. That way we could keep outcomes for the ultimate *consequences, results* or *benefits* for the organization (such as achieving higher production levels) which can be obtained by possessing and demonstrating output competence.

Outcomes or skills

Between the elements of competence and the performance criteria there lies potential confusion concerning outcomes on the one hand, and what gives rise to them on the other.

While the ED/NCVQ Guide includes 'outcomes' as part of its definition of what comprises an element of competence, MCI says that it is the performance criteria that 'indicate the outcomes which a manager has to achieve consistently in order to demonstrate competent performance'. To resolve this apparent contradiction you have to appreciate that the performance criteria (and their associated range indicators) are all part of the element of competence and not a further level of dis-aggregation.

Second, the BTEC (Business & Technology Education Council) Guide to the Standards states that elements of competence '... reflect the *skills, knowledge and abilities* that first line managers are expected to possess.' [my italics][11] whereas the ED/NCVQ Guide (as we saw in the basic description of the model) speaks of *action, behaviour or outcome*. The ED/NCVQ and BTEC wordings imply different orientations, and they possibly explain why we find a mix of these expressions for the elements of competence in MCI's published management standards. For example, the following two seem fundamentally different:

> **Maintain operations to meet quality standards.**

and

> **Lead meetings and group discussions to solve problems and make decisions.**

These examples appear different in both kind *and* level, the first hinting at an outcome (I would say output) and the second at a skill or input. This can happen when you disaggregate the different key roles and have to force each successive answer to the question 'and what do you need to do to achieve that?' into a limited two-tier strait-jacket (i.e. units and elements of competence). Otherwise you have to cope with multiple levels of skills-behind-skills. One has some sympathy for the job analysts. More levels in the model might be even more confusing. In any case, the term 'skill' itself has always been a problem word for analysts, since it is a rather loose umbrella term for a range of personal attributes:[10]

O   **Task skills**: the routine and largely technical components that make up any job.

O   **Contingency management skills**: the ability to recognize and deal with irregularities and variances in the immediate working environment.

○   **Task management skills**: the skills to manage a group of tasks and prioritize between them.
○   **Job role environment skills**: the skills to work with others and cope with specific environmental factors.

Limitations in the model's simple structure and language seem unable to cope easily with some of the subtleties like skills-behind-skills. It helps explain why we find 'skills and knowledge' (i.e. inputs) and 'outcomes' (I believe they mean outputs) mentioned in the same breath (i.e. 'competences'). The important thing to remember, in spite of these nuances, is that we are concerned with the *application* of skill and knowledge, not with their mere *possession*. For anyone to be truly competent they have to possess this range of skills *and* be able to demonstrate performance in their working environment. So we should not become sidetracked by these apparent inconsistencies as we might fail to see the wood for the trees.

Clearly this is a linguistic minefield. It also leads us prematurely to some of the more controversial aspects of competences, such as whether management can be meaningfully viewed only as an integrated activity, rather than in these broken-down elements. That issue and many others will have to wait until a later chapter.

OTHER MODELS

There are two other models: the input model and the process model. They have dominated the traditional field of management in the past, for practical as much as conceptual reasons. In the absence of a challenge by the output model, most users concerned with performance probably adopted these models unthinkingly, rather than as a conscious choice. In any case, serious discussion of what constitutes 'competence' began only in the 1970s, and it is actually much more recently that many practitioners have become aware of the debate.

THE INPUT MODEL

The **input model** is concerned with:

> **deciding what *qualities* you want in managers, who the manager *is* and what the manager *knows*.**

Here competence is thought to depend on the possession of a combination of personal characteristics, expressed in clusters, such as the following:

○   **Intellectual** ability, knowledge, logic, creativity, etc.
○   **Social** language, ability to relate to others, etc.
○   **Emotional** stability, confidence, motivation, etc.
○   **Physical** prowess, dexterity, keen senses, etc.

Work undertaken by the McBer Corporation in conjunction with Harvard Business School[1] has also resulted in a widely used model. Hayes[12] and Boyatzis[13] include references to the following:

O   **Knowledge:** content knowledge, e.g. facts or procedures, technical or interpersonal.

O   **Motive:** the underlying need or thought pattern that drives an individual's behaviour.

O   **Trait:** a general disposition to behave or respond in a certain way.

O   **Self-concept:** attitudes or what people value or are interested in doing.

Items in the input model such as these are sometimes called 'soft skills', compared with the tangible outputs required from the output model. When selecting or developing managers, these factors lead to questions about the kind of person they are, their level of education and what skills they have. This model of competence is the prevalent approach in the USA.

MCI has developed its own **Personal Competence Model** akin to an input model as an adjunct and complement to its sets of management standards, which by comparison are effectively functional competences. The MCI model is discussed further in later chapters.

The need to distinguish between output competences (*doing*) and input competences (*being*) is common to all occupational standards, not just those developed by MCI for management. In some instances, the input variety are termed personal 'qualities' rather than competences; this is the case with the standards developed for the personnel profession. Sometimes they take the form of a stand-alone complementary model (as with MCI) and have no place in the formal assessment process; in other cases elements of both models are dovetailed, as is the case with the personnel standards. MCI began by regarding the Personal Competence Model as an adjunct, but are slowly giving it greater prominence as an inherent part of the standards.

(Note that the use of the term 'input' in the input model is concerned with what people put into their work. It should not be confused with 'input' meaning what is provided during tuition or from learning-materials.)

THE PROCESS MODEL

The **process model** takes the model of personal inputs a step further. It is concerned with:

deciding what *tasks* you want people to carry out.

Some people equate this model with what skills or abilities you want people to display in recognizable *activities*. They are still inputs of a kind; but they can be thought of as *job* or *work* inputs rather than *personal* inputs. They may be best thought of as *throughputs*.

This process model is easily recognizable in the design of many traditional training and selection activities, but nowadays it is the least discussed of the three models at this level, being more relevant for low-level, mass occupations.

DRAWING THE MODELS TOGETHER

Some people feel that an emphasis on inputs is now beginning to creep back into official favour – witness the development of MCI's Personal Competence Model. This was probably inevitable. There is a natural point where the input and output models merge together. For example, MCI's management standards for managing people includes 'managing oneself'. That includes the element of competence 'Develop oneself within the job role', which would seem to dovetail naturally with the idea of personal competence.

The trend towards a blurring of the previously sharp distinction between the two main models (output and input) is probably taking place from both ends. While the output model is giving more recognition to personal qualities, so the input model becomes more interested in purposeful and demonstrable application. Yet the use to which the two models are put remains somewhat different.

At the moment MCI's personal competences, and the knowledge and understanding specifications, are not a formal requirement for assessment – though that could change. MCI's belief is that competence should be verified by performance evidence alone. Only where this is not possible should learners' *possession* (rather than *application*) of essential knowledge and understanding be assessed in order to underpin their claim to competence.

Companies which are wedded to this assessment philosophy are already training their senior managers – in their capacity as bosses – in the skills of assessing their managers' learnt competences at the workplace. (Chapter 5 examines this assessment process.)

The Personal Competence Model for managers is, for the moment, still only bolted on to the output model's management standards, which continue to make the running. Many people use the term competence only with reference to this output model; competence has largely become synonymous with it.

The output model has gained in popularity because competences defined in this way are less abstract than the mere possession of skills or personal attributes, and are more readily observable. The model is less prone to unspoken assumptions and prejudices about people and who can be expected to be able to do what. And it is more clearly concerned with results in a bottom-line business culture.

The growth of nationally recognized standards-based qualifications for vocations is strongly associated with the output competence model. In particular, most of the changes currently taking place in the open learning market are in response to it.

ACTIVITY 2.1

If you have a decision to make about what stance your company should take towards the use of output-based competences for managers' development, you may find it helpful to work through the criteria in Figure 2.2.

FIGURE 2.2 CRITERIA FOR CHOOSING THE OUTPUT MODEL COMPETENCE APPROACH

1. If your company believes that developing managers' individual competence is a significant way to improve your organization's effectiveness, and wants to put considerable time and effort into this field.

2. If your company has a strong management culture which is definite about what it expects from its managers.

3. If your company drives managers' performance top-down to achieve results, rather than giving them considerable freedom to decide what and how they manage as individuals.

4. If your company believes in the benefits of a unitary approach to managing, rather than welcoming the diversity in a pluralistic model.

5. If your company shows considerable concern for how consistently work is undertaken within laid-down frameworks.

6. If your company looks for tangible evidence of managers' demonstrated capability in the workplace.

7. If your company seeks to keep up with national UK initiatives.

8. If your company wants its managers to be able to acquire nationally recognized generic management qualifications at NVQ Levels 3, 4 or 5.

9. If your company considers it has the disciplines and resources to manage the process of workplace assessment.

10. If your company's organizational environment is fairly stable and predictable.

REFERENCES

1. Shirley Fletcher (1993) *Competence-Based Assessment Techniques*, London: Kogan Page, p. 17.

2. Training Agency (1989) *Development of Assessable Standards for National Certification*, Sheffield: Employment Department.

3. Employment Department and NCVQ (1991) *Guide to National Vocational Qualifications*, Sheffield: Employment Department.

4. Linda Miller (1991) 'Managerial Competences', *Industrial and Commercial Training*, **23** (6).

5. Peter Critten (1993) *Investing in People: Towards Corporate Capability*, Oxford: Butterworth–Heinemann.

6. Eugene Donnelly (1991) 'Management Charter Initiative: A Critique', *Training and Development*, April.

7. J. Proctor (1991) *Using Competences in Management Development*, Bristol: National Health Service Training Division/HDL Training and Development Ltd.

8. Andrew Summers (1993) 'Creating Management Standards', *Training Management*, **5** (20).
9. Bob Mansfield (1991) 'Deriving Standards of Competence', *Development of Assessable Standards for National Certification* (ed. E. Fennell), Sheffield: Employment Department, HMSO.
10. B. Mansfield and D. Mathews (1985) *Job Competence – A Description for Use in Vocational Education and Training*, Blagdon: Further Education Staff College.
11. BTEC (1992) *BTEC Certificate in Management: NVQ Standards*, London: Business & Technology Education Council.
12. James Hayes (1979) 'A New Look at Managerial Competence: The American Management Association Model of Worthy Performance', *Management Review*, November.
13. Richard Boyatzis (1982) *The Competent Manager: A Model for Effective Performance*, Chichester: Wiley.

3

THE MANAGEMENT
CHARTER INITIATIVE

OVERVIEW

This chapter outlines the background to MCI's work and its connection with other national initiatives. It then explains MCI's Product Approval Process, and what approval does and does not signify for buyers and users.

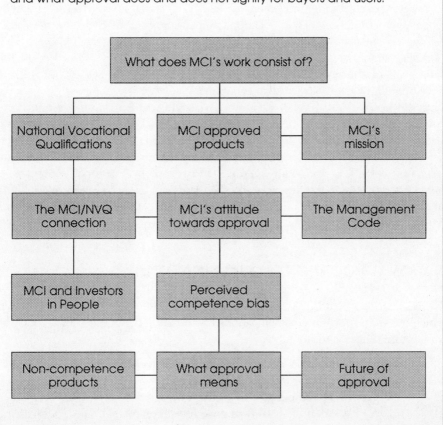

INTRODUCTION

There was widespread concern throughout the 1980s that Britain was failing to compete in the world as a result of poor management education and training. A number of working parties and reports, in particular *The Making of Managers* by Charles Handy *et al.*[1] and *The Making of British Managers* by John Constable and Roger McCormick[2] in 1987 set light to the debate about how best to improve managers' performance.

The discussion actually goes back much further than this. It seems hard to believe, but 100 years ago (in 1894) the idea of business schools was first put forward. The debate about management education escalated in the early 1980s, producing a wave of reports, from NEDO, MSC, DTI and others, about the state of vocational training and education in the UK.

The two reports mentioned led to the launch of the Council for Management Education & Development (CMED) under the aegis of the CBI, BIM and Foundation for Management Education (FME), which became the National Forum for Management Education and Development in 1988, subsequently adopting the shorter label of the Management Charter Initiative (MCI).

This was part of a wider movement affecting all occupations and the processes by which such employees obtain vocational qualifications. 1986 had seen the establishment of the National Council for Vocational Qualifications (NCVQ) to promote National Vocational Qualifications (NVQs), and in Scotland SVQs. We also saw the setting up of the government-sponsored Industry Lead Bodies to oversee the development of standards for all occupations.

At the heart of the Lead Bodies' work was the wish to rationalize and bring coherence to the plethora of standards and awarding bodies involved in offering vocational qualifications which, it was believed, had led to wholesale confusion among employers. For this reason, the Lead Bodies were employer-led. Their main role was to publish nationally agreed standards of occupational competence, understood by employers, learners and their teachers. The Lead Body for the field of management develops those standards for managers.[3] MCI was chosen as this particular Lead Body in 1989.

NATIONAL VOCATIONAL QUALIFICATIONS

The National and Scottish Vocational Qualification system provides a framework in which individual vocational qualifications can be located, so that they are easy to understand. The qualifications are:

○   based on standards, set by employers, which define the knowledge and skills needed in the workplace;
○   a guarantee of competence to do the job;
○   modular so that skills and knowledge common to many jobs can be recognized;   .

○   free from restrictions about the pace, place and method of learning; and
○   accessible to all age groups, from school students to those nearing the end of their careers.[4]

NVQs are acquired through the accumulation of records of achievement for each unit of competence, as individuals build up their portfolios of skills, knowledge and experience in a modular manner. This flexibility is designed to help people manage their continuing education.

The qualifications are awarded by the National Council for Vocational Qualifications – in practice administered by Council-approved bodies. There are a growing number of these bodies for managers. They include BTEC (mainly the service sector) and NEBSM (mainly the manufacturing sector).

As an expression of its determination in these matters, the government has made available tax incentives for employers who offer training leading to NVQs, and rebates for learners. Some TECs (Training & Enterprise Councils) also offer funding for companies running NVQ-related courses.

The Employment Department (ED) compiles a computerized database of NVQ-related open learning programmes (see Appendix 2). There is also an ED-sponsored pilot programme, *Open for Learning*, being managed by BAOL which is intended to make open learning available through large public libraries. And, of course, the ED has sponsored research by MCI into the development of occupational standards, most recently for senior management. Clearly this is a substantial national intervention with much money and push behind it.

To help employers make up their minds about how relevant NVQs are for their own businesses, the ED has published the *Guide to the Business Case Framework*, written by consultants Dent Lee Witte plc.[5] This sets out the pros and cons of three levels of approach – progressive, cautious and passive – and then leaves users to work out for themselves which will suit them best. The guide is written as a do-it-yourself framework to help the manager who is charged by his or her Board with answering such questions as:

1.   What is our industry doing about NVQs?
2.   How do our competitors plan to tackle NVQs?
3.   Given our own business objectives and strategies, what should we be doing about NVQs?
4.   What should be our recommended approach to NVQs?
5.   What are the costs and benefits of our recommended approach to NVQs?

ACTIVITY 3.1

If you are considering whether or not your company, as a matter of policy, should choose to adopt the NVQ approach for its managers, you may wish to work through the questions posed in the ED's publication and produce a business case.

THE MCI/NVQ CONNECTION

There is a hierarchy of NVQs. For what MCI calls 'first line managers' the level is NVQ Level 4, which equates with the certificate level. Some providers have called this award the Certificate in Management or the *New* Certificate in Management. (Note that the names of courses have been changing to distinguish between the pre- and post-NVQ era, i.e. non-competence and competence products.)

NVQ Level 4 is the foundation level at which MCI has developed its occupational standards for management, which it calls 'Management 1', or simply 'M1'. Above this level there is a higher set of MCI-defined management standards called 'M2', pitched at the Diploma in Management level, equivalent to NVQ Level 5.

This middle managerial ground is where MCI began its work, later extending it downwards, and more recently developing definitions of standards upwards. Below M1 level is a Supervisory level, which MCI calls 'M1(S)'. This is pitched at NVQ Level 3, and will qualify for a Certificate in Supervisory Management. Above M2 level come standards for what are called 'senior managers' (M3), for which there is no NVQ equivalent.

Making use of the management standards lies at the heart of MCI's work. The following chapter, 'Using the Management Standards', is entirely devoted to this important subject.

MCI'S MISSION AND CODE

MCI has a widely enabling mission statement:

> To improve the performance of UK organizations by improving the quality of UK managers. Its objective is to increase the quantity, quality, relevance and accessibility of management education and development.

The mission is backed up by a Management Code (see Figure 3.1). Note that this current version of the code is a much simplified version of MCI's original one, though the ideas have not changed.

MCI AND INVESTORS IN PEOPLE (IIP)

MCI is working very closely with another government initiative, Investors in People. Many of the two organizations' aims and values are shared, though MCI is not directly interested in the whole population of an organization. But in MCI's management standards the key role 'Manage people' is highly relevant to a company's ability to satisfy the requirement for IiP endorsement. There are therefore a number of joint promotions and publications that show how the two map together.

FIGURE 3.1 THE MANAGEMENT CODE

1. To improve leadership and management skills.
2. To encourage continuous development.
3. To provide a coherent framework for self-development.
4. To ensure management development is integrated with work.
5. To provide access to training.
6. To encourage managers to gain relevant qualifications.
7. To participate in MCI networks.
8. To strengthen links with providers of management development.
9. To promote the challenge of management in local schools and colleges.
10. To review progress towards all these goals and set new targets.

Reproduced by courtesy of MCI

MCI APPROVED PRODUCTS

Publishers of open learning programmes for managers are rushing to acquire the Management Charter Initiative's sticker on their packages. It's another selling point in this competitive marketplace. After all, MCI is the government-appointed Industry Lead Body for the field of management. But just what does MCI's imprimatur signify? How much notice should you take of the distinctive logo?

Being able to mention in a product's marketing literature that it has been approved by the MCI has cachet. Indeed, some public-sector users will buy only products that state they are 'MCI approved'. But use of the logo is proving quite controversial among publishers, and can be confusing and misleading to consumers too. It does not convey all that some might imagine. That does not diminish its value provided you understand it. You simply need to know what it *does* mean and what it *doesn't* mean.

Choosing approved products is tempting, but you are cautioned to use that indication with discretion. There is no short cut to becoming better informed yourself. Reviews in magazines and journals are helpful in this respect, as are the newsletters and the networks available through membership of the various open learning associations and groups, something well worth contemplating. Names and addresses of some of the relevant suppliers are provided in Appendix 1.

MCI'S ATTITUDE TOWARDS APPROVAL

MCI is keen to encourage those who share its broad goal and who are making efforts to improve their products in its direction. So MCI takes a pragmatic view when it comes to approval, one which recognizes substantial investment in many existing products. It has chosen not to hand out pass/fail pronouncements on publishers and suppliers; instead, it seeks to cajole providers to develop in the MCI direction. In spite of this – perhaps somewhat reassuringly – MCI turns down approximately 30 per cent of applications for approval.

On the other hand, it is important to be aware that MCI is no longer a fully subsidized quango. It has lost its government funding, as was the long-term intention, and has to survive on its income. One means of achieving this is via its approvals, both charging for the initial vetting process and for the subsequent use of the logo on an annual basis. MCI therefore actively solicits producers to encourage them to submit their products.

PERCEIVED COMPETENCE BIAS

The direction which MCI encourages, more often than not, will be towards competence-based learning programmes. The application form for MCI's product approval appears to favour this, lending weight to the view that the die is loaded in the competence movement's favour. Whether or not that is a fair criticism, or even a fair approach for MCI to adopt for learning products at this level of management, is discussed in later chapters when dealing with some of the problems and controversies.

It is interesting to observe that neither the statement of MCI's Mission nor the Management Code makes any mention of competences. Yet, or perhaps because of this omission, there is potential for misunderstanding concerning the connection between competences and approved products. This arises because MCI has become exclusively and indelibly associated in many people's minds with the competence-based route to learning. One of MCI's most important and early decisions was to act as champion for the competence-based approach for managerial learning. It considered that this was an important development which needed a herald.

Politically, MCI probably had no choice, given its shared origins and close association with the NVQ movement, which is wholly based on the competence model. In particular, MCI's role as Lead Body was bound to add to that growing perception and, one has to say, a misconception for which MCI must therefore accept partial responsibility.

The upshot is that as NVQs stand for assessed competence as job outputs (not learning inputs), some consumers believe that any MCI approved product must accord with this approach. This is not always true. But in the minds of some, the pursuit of management competences is now all MCI stands for. Hence the confused perception and marketing problem.

KEY TIP

❖   When you are told that a particular product bears MCI's stamp of approval, make a closer examination. See what you are really being offered.

JUST WORDS

Because competences are fashionable, some publishers find forms of words in their marketing literature to encourage the reader to believe that their products are competence-driven from the outset. They might not be; indeed, few are. Others imply that they directly qualify for NVQs. That might not be the case.

Suppliers sometimes use forms of words like 'equivalent to ...', 'contribute towards ...' or 'lead to portfolio evidence for NVQ Level 4'. The association might be close or tenuous. Some say their product has been 'designed to meet MCI's management standards', but fail to say that MCI didn't approve it! *Caveat emptor*.

MATERIALS ONLY

The other fact to be aware of is that MCI's approval refers only to the materials from the publisher. If we consider open learning materials for example (a leading product category for MCI approval), if produced well these provide an all-round learning experience, but MCI's approval is concerned with only one element of that. It has nothing to say about tutor support, client workshops, work-based assignments, involvement of the learner's boss, and so on. So MCI's approval is not enough to guarantee the learning package as a whole, let alone the learning experience.

WHAT APPROVAL MEANS

Using the 'MCI Approved Product' stamp means that a formal process has been followed. Experts drawn from an independent team of evaluators practising in the world of business have examined the quality of the product and the claims made for it by its publishers. A panel (the Product Approval Group) has considered these views and conferred approval.

In some cases the publisher may have revised earlier programmes to align them with competence statements. An example of this is the NEBSM (The National Examining Board for Supervisory Management) *Super Series 2* programme for supervisors, published by Pergamon Open Learning.

What MCI approval will *not* necessarily mean is that the management standards came first and that learning inputs were then designed in response to them. Some of the best-known MCI approved products on the market have existed for some years and pre-date the management standards.

However, there are some programmes newly designed specifically to meet the requirement for competence-driven learning. The number of these will increase. They may not yet have passed through MCI's product approval process as they are still a relatively recent phenomenon.

Therefore if you want to buy a product designed from scratch as a response to the competence movement, you will need to ask some very searching questions.

KEY TIP

❖   The publishers' product specialists are more likely to be helpful and knowledgeable than their publicity people.

MAPPING

MCI expects publishers to show if and how their product fits with the management standards. The product is expected to contain the necessary 'underpinning knowledge and understanding' (to use MCI's own language) and to have mapped these against the corresponding management standards. Figure 3.2 shows an example of mapping taken from Manchester Open Learning's workbook written for the Chloride Group.

This is a helpful practice, but it is often a post-production measure to fit the selling advantage of competences against an existing product. In other words, the references to 'NVQs' and competences may have been bolted on afterwards. However, in many cases they are still excellent products. Other products will genuinely have been written to address specific competences and the award of NVQs, but this is not a pre-condition for MCI backing.

The product might relate to only a small area within the management standards. It might also be concerned primarily with MCI's Personal Competence Model rather than the output-related management standards. That is not a problem. The question for MCI is whether it constitutes good learning.

MEDIA GLOSS

Given the growing use of computer-based multiple media, one problem is that products increasingly look highly seductive and captivating to learners. But they may not be very good at heart. This type of product also raises the expectation level for future products, which puts solid single-media products at a psychological disadvantage.

APPROVAL CONSIDERATIONS

Among other factors, approval signifies that the product fulfils the following requirements:

○   It is matched to the needs of the target audience.
○   It is appealing and durable.
○   It is easy to use.
○   It is free of cultural bias and/or discrimination.
○   It is identified with its source material and linked with further study where appropriate.

The product evaluators also consider commercial factors such as price; MCI expresses an opinion to publishers on whether the package represents value for money. But such wider considerations are contentious, since it could be argued

FIGURE 3.2 EXAMPLE OF MAPPING KNOWLEDGE INPUTS AGAINST STANDARDS

5 Develop teams, individuals and self to enhance performance
6 Plan, allocate and evaluate work carried out by teams, individuals and self

5.1 Develop and improve teams through planning and activities
5.2 Identify, review and improve development activities for individuals
5.3 Develop oneself within the job role

6.1 Set and update work objectives for teams and individuals
6.2 Plan activities and determine work methods to achieve objectives
6.3 Allocate work and evaluate teams, individuals and self against objectives
6.4 Provide feedback to teams and individuals on their performance

Managing and Planning Training

If you think back to your overview module 'The Nature of Management', you'll recall that a fundamental part of your responsibility as a manager is for the growth and development of your staff both as individuals and as a team.

This responsibility has been reinforced by the previous chapter; appraisal can lead to identification of gaps in performance which can be seen by both parties. These gaps can be caused by lack of knowledge and/or experience and it is your responsibility as a manager to put in place the procedure to correct this situation. It may be that this entails your identifying a training programme or even passing the responsibility on to your training department, but in many cases it will be within your remit to do the training yourself. In any case it will involve you in the identification of resources for training which could have direct impact on other areas of your work such as managing budgets.

Training which can lead to changes in skills, behaviour, motivation and performance is an essential addition to appraisal. By correcting poor practice, developing skills and preparing staff for change, training will affect the efficiency and performance of both individuals and the team in pursuing their and the company's objectives and so contribute to the feelings of confidence and common purpose that mark a cohesive and dynamic team.

3.1   Defining Training

The problem areas that you have identified through the appraisal system may be only temporary lapses in the normal smooth running of the department. But as these breakdowns happen in areas where you have a management responsibility, it follows that you also have a responsibility to correct them.

Decide work objectives
↓
Review performance
↓
Identify areas for counselling or training

fig 3.1

Reproduced by courtesy of Manchester Open Learning

that a product might be very good in terms of MCI's national purpose, mission and standards, yet not sell well through being overpriced. In that case, is it just the publisher who is the loser for making a commercial miscalculation, or is MCI right to try to protect buyers from over-pricing? The problem for MCI, as pointed out earlier, is that buyers tend to equate MCI approval with wholesale endorsement. MCI is therefore trying to respond to that expectation.

Once approved, products receive an entry in MCI's *Directory of Approved Products*. This directory should increasingly prove useful to consumers as the products will show how they map against the relevant standards and can therefore lead towards qualifications.

THE FUTURE OF APPROVAL

MCI is aware of the perception problem, and the product approval process itself is reviewed from time to time to cast maximum light on its product approvals for the benefit of consumers.

There is a problem with the pre-experience managerial market. Many potential managers need learning opportunities before they occupy management jobs. By definition, before they are promoted such managers cannot demonstrate performance against the management standards. They cannot be assessed at the workplace, only at the point of learning the knowledge inputs. MCI considers such traditional, non-output assessable learning valid and wants to encourage good examples of it. At the same time it doesn't want to mislead consumers.

Furthermore, some programmes are wholly designed to improve what MCI calls *personal competences* rather than *management standards*. Personal competences are not directly task-related outputs, but are generic attributes and skills that transcend all managerial activities. A typical example of a personal competence product/course is Time Management. High-quality programmes on subjects such as this may qualify for MCI's stamp of approval. The MCI product approval process rightly includes quality products of this kind.

THE MARKET FOR NON-COMPETENCE PRODUCTS

Some people would have you think that competence-based products are appropriate for everyone. There is a danger that the fashionable nature of the competence movement will drive non-competence products off the shelves – at least for managers. That would be a loss.

Quite apart from any philosophical misgivings some might harbour, there will continue to be a logical place for non-competence products in the marketplace. But the customers will probably influence this less than the providers, and providers may lose interest.

The NCVQ has been keen to promote the idea that the competence route is the only way to a truly nationally transferable qualification – and there is some logic to support this view.

There had been concern, therefore, that the non-competence based Certificate in Management Studies (CMS) would lose its national accreditation via BTEC and NEBSM. Its survival in locally accredited form only could have put its future in doubt. However, a nationally accredited non-competence based course at certificate level has been saved for the time being.

There are plans, however, to redesignate the CMS (as the Certificate in Management) and the NVQ-based Certificate in Management. This may cause confusion in the short term as publishers retitle their products.

Publishers are showing that they are quick to climb on the popular bandwagon of competences. Let's hope they're wise enough to maintain their non-competence offerings in parallel. But why does it matter? There are two markets that arise from purely practical considerations. I hinted at the first when mentioning the practical problems of demonstrating competence before getting promotion to a managerial position.

DEVELOPMENTAL TRAINING FOR FUTURE RESPONSIBILITY

Much management training is provided for aspiring managers to develop their potential to take on management responsibilities. Some argue that much of this developmental training is actually wasted, especially if it occurs long before the opportunity to put it into practice. None the less, it is common.

This training-in-advance approach is found where individuals study in order to obtain a managerial qualification in the hope of enhancing their prospects of promotion. Only then will they attain a responsibility level where they can put their learning into practice. The problem is that until they reach that level they can't demonstrate their ability in terms of achievement on the job against each of the elements of competence – at least not to the satisfaction of an NCVQ-approved external assessor who can award credits. Therefore, competence-based training is excluded to this category of learner on practical grounds. For these learners to qualify, they can be assessed only off the job in the context of what they have learned, not how they have performed as a consequence.

UNDER-DEVELOPED ORGANIZATION CULTURE

The second practical area is where organizations have not (yet) developed their own internal culture to the point where it can cope with the rigours of on-the-job assessment.

A thorough competence-based approach begins with assessment of managers' current competences, called 'profiling'. Then for ultimate certification it is a *sine qua non* of the competence approach that assessment must be against performance at the place of work. The requirement for assessment can only be genuinely satisfied with significant involvement and understanding on the part of the learner's own manager. And it is still somewhat unusual to find a boss who is well informed, sufficiently qualified, genuinely interested, and has the time to devote to subordinates' development in such an active way.

For assessment of competences to work in the way intended requires an organization culture which accepts line-management ownership of training and development. Many companies still find it convenient to delegate such responsibility to the training department. This is therefore a question of readiness within the organization's culture. If it isn't ready, conventional learning programmes will work better. Not surprisingly, there is pressure to water down the insistence on work-based assessment and line manager involvement.

ACTIVITY 3.2

If you are considering buying an MCI approved product, you may find it helpful to work through the buyers' checklist in Figure 3.3.

FIGURE 3.3 MCI APPROVED PRODUCTS: BUYERS' CHECKLIST

1. How much does MCI's approval of your provider's product matter to you? Why?
2. What wording does the publisher use to signify MCI approval?
3. What precisely does the wording convey and what does it leave out? Do the words look suspicious?
4. Have you checked directly with MCI's *Directory of Approved Products*?
5. Can you find out more from MCI about how well the product measured up against their criteria?
6. Does the product claim to comply with the generic management standards?
7. What parts of the management standards does it match against?
8. Does the product match against MCI's Personal Competence Model rather than the standards?
9. How will using the product assist accreditation towards an NVQ?
10. How old is the product?
11. Has the product been developed specifically in response to the competence movement?
12. Does it predate the development of management standards? Has it been revised? How?
13. Does the product identify or map how it fits against the management standards?
14. Will your company be able to make full use of the product to the same level as its written content?

REFERENCES

1. Charles Handy *et al.* (1987) *The Making of Managers*, London: National Economic Development Office, Pitman.
2. John Constable and Roger McCormick (1987) *The Making of British Managers*, Corby: British Institute of Management.
3. Management Charter Initiative (1994) *Management Standards*, London: MCI.
4. Employment Department (1994) *Training in Britain*, Sheffield: Employment Department.
5. Dent Lee Witte (1993) *NVQs/SVQs: Guide to the Business Case Framework*, Sheffield: Employment Department.

4

USING THE MANAGEMENT STANDARDS

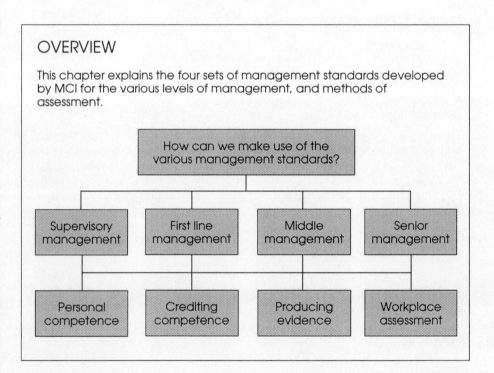

OVERVIEW

This chapter explains the four sets of management standards developed by MCI for the various levels of management, and methods of assessment.

How can we make use of the various management standards?

| Supervisory management | First line management | Middle management | Senior management |

| Personal competence | Crediting competence | Producing evidence | Workplace assessment |

INTRODUCTION

In its capacity as the government's Lead Body for the occupation of management, MCI's best-known role has been to develop and publish occupational standards (which it calls management standards), along with associated means of assessing and accrediting achievement. These may then lead to the award of National Vocational Qualifications (NVQs).

The standards cover four levels of management: supervisory, first line, middle and senior. They comprise the output measures, personal (input) competences or qualities, and required knowledge and understanding. They can be used for a variety of purposes, including development, appraisal, selection and compensation.

In this chapter we shall see what comprises these sets of standards, what to watch out for when using them, and means of assessing managers' competence.

The field of competences is a fast-moving target which shows no sign of reaching equilibrium. It is part of MCI's policy to revise and update the standards at regular intervals. The government's own strategy behind MCI equally comes in for re-assessment. Therefore a book like this can only pass comment on a snapshot. In the case of the senior management standards, the publication date is spring 1995, just as this book goes into print. Thus my analysis and comment is undertaken with an element of risk and the possibility of being overtaken by events.

SUPERVISORY MANAGEMENT STANDARDS

There are three significant problems with the supervisor level in organizations when it comes to applying the supervisory management standards (known as MI(S)) in practice.

What is a 'supervisor'?

There is no agreed meaning across organizations for the word 'supervisory'. The role itself is widely argued about. Job titles cannot be relied upon: many organizations use other sub-manager terms such as foreman, superintendent, officer, etc. Some have several supervisor grades. Some supervisors have a clear technical orientation, others more a human resources one. Some supervisors occupy substantial positions; others are quite obviously below 'first-line manager' level – something also undefined, but we are required to be able to recognize that one too.

Supervisors' changing roles

There is considerable fluidity in a currently changing supervisory role, such as the emergence of team leaders below supervisors and the vastly reduced need for fire-fighting over industrial relations matters.

Matching training to roles

It is difficult to match available training precisely to the breadth of supervisors' roles.

SUPERVISORS' PRESSURES AND PROBLEMS

The role of the supervisor is under pressure and scrutiny. For some it is becoming more demanding as a consequence of the shrinking of staff departments and the devolution of some of their functions, especially those of Personnel, plus the removing of layers of management above them. On the other hand, many workforces are expected to be more self-supervising, select their own team leaders, undertake their own checking and quality control, and be less dependent on supervisors for work allocation, thereby undermining the need for traditional supervision.

Bruce Partridge's thorough analysis of 'The Problem of Supervision' leaves us in no doubt that the role of supervisor is practised in many forms across firms, industries and cultures, and is much misunderstood within companies.[1] This, he believes, 'requires the supervisor to be able to handle complexities, conflicts, ambiguities and uncertainties'. He wisely advises that 'this cannot be handled solely through training; training will only be effective if the appropriate attributes are already there to begin with, which emphasises the careful need for recruitment and selection'.

Partridge's data suggest that promotional channels are being blocked to supervisors which, he says,

> means that fewer line managers above the first line supervisor will have had first line experience which, in turn, means that senior managers are becoming increasingly dependent upon the supervisors as the only managers who have had practical experience with the production technology.

Statements like these concerning the role itself, the degree to which it is already understood, and career paths are, of course, generalizations which may or may not apply in specific organizations. We are probably on firmer ground concerning the supervisors' usefulness in respect of rapidly changing shopfloor technology. Managers are probably becoming increasingly dependent on supervisors to have this technical grasp because of the pace of technological change.

It used to be said that 'the uniqueness of the supervisors' position is that they are located at the interface of the management control system and the shopfloor: they are the ones who have to translate plans and policies into action'.[1] But even this might be changing as companies experiment with less rigid reporting relationships, and sources of communication and information become both more flexible and automated.

The role of the supervisor is accordingly in transition. For the moment I suspect we can say less about the future of supervision than we can about management. In this context it is therefore bold of MCI to publish generic supervisory management standards.

APPROPRIATE SUPERVISOR DEVELOPMENT

Within readers' own companies or within particular departmental functions, some of the above observations about supervision may not apply. For some, the supervisors' role may be wholly clear, and managers may, for example, come from the ranks of supervision. But you can meaningfully respond to the supervisory management standards only if you are clear about your own supervisors' role. Only then is it possible to be confident about what formal training to provide for supervisors, especially if it is assumed that the training has to be based on an agreed definition of what a competent supervisor *does*.

Without this detailed understanding, the most one can say by way of advice is that some people who are called 'supervisor' should actually study for the (manager's) Certificate at NVQ Level 4; while others will find this beyond them, not necessarily in terms of their personal learning capability, but for the role they perform, and should aim at NVQ Level 3.

Purchasers of open learning cannot make assumptions about what is appropriate merely by matching job titles with package titles. Some publishers' brochures try to help potential learners choose the appropriate level with expressions like 'new manager' and 'inexperienced manager', but these don't offer that much of a clue. Buyers and learners need to examine offerings at both NVQ Level 3 and NVQ Level 4 and then decide for themselves the appropriate level to match against their supervisors' roles.

It is also a moot point, with so much change occurring, whether training specifically aimed at helping supervisors adjust to company-specific changing roles would be more beneficial than that concerned with compliance against a set of generic competences.

KEY TIP

❖   Before providing mass competence-based training for your supervisors, first ensure that there is all-round clarification and a shared understanding about the role, its changing nature, and what preparation is ideally needed to address those changes.

FIRST LINE AND MIDDLE MANAGEMENT STANDARDS

The distinctions between these two levels, M1 (NVQ Level 4) and M2 (NVQ Level 5), in the management standards are sometimes hard to find. Occasionally the wording is identical. But this should not surprise or concern us overmuch, as it reflects what one finds in organizations and across managerial roles.

To make the point with an example, for MCI's key role of 'Manage information' for both M1 and M2, one of the units of competence is to 'Exchange information to solve problems and make decisions'. But that is so basic you might reasonably expect it to apply at every level of management. So let's examine two more subtle differences at the next level down.

1. The key role of 'Manage finance'

At M1 level it is:

Recommend, monitor and control the use of resources.

This implies a slightly lower level of responsibility than at M2 level, which is simply:

Monitor and control the use of resources.

The difference here is that the higher level doesn't need to 'recommend', but presumably has recommendations made to it from the level below. Let's examine another key role:

2. The key role of 'Manage operations'

This makes a clearer distinction between the two levels. At M1 it is:

Maintain and improve service and product operations.

And at the higher M2 level:

Initiate and implement change and improvement in services, products and systems.

The difference here is that at the higher level there is expected to be more scope for proactivity and initiating change, plus a role in connection with systems. Where there are clear distinctions like these, they are all very well on paper, but how they pan out in practice in a given organization and for a given manager may be less clear-cut. In reality, they will vary according to the following factors:

○ The numbers of management levels in that company's structure.
○ The breadth and depth of given managers' roles.
○ The pressures and constraints on managers from one day to the next.
○ The faith which higher managers have in the competence of subordinate managers.
○ Senior managers' self-confidence in not needing to hang on to decisions for themselves.

This is not to say that the definitions at the various levels are faulty or lack rigour, just that it is impossible to lay down useful and meaningful differences like those above with enough confidence that they can hold for the vast majority of cases. Organization systems contain too many variables. The answer is to be guided by the standards and fit them to the specific context of one's own organization structure and *modus operandi*.

SENIOR MANAGEMENT STANDARDS

Few will question that the higher one goes in the management structure the more difficult it is to generalize and prescribe on best practice. Yet, taken at face value, MCI appears to have succeeded in the tough task of laying down standards for senior managers (M3). But whatever the ultimate value of these standards in practice, and whether or not they will be seen to hold one of the keys to future business success, it would have been politically unacceptable for MCI to admit that the task was not worth doing or do-able. There is much at stake with these standards. That said, what will the senior management standards be used for? How will they move us forward? What will the standards tell us that we didn't already know? How will their publication change the way we select, develop and appraise senior managers?

At the moment the standards are untried in the real world, but it is fair to be a mite sceptical about how many senior managers themselves will want to be assessed or want to use the model to pinpoint their own development needs, or to change the way they manage. No doubt some of the more open-minded ones will do so, though these will be those with the least need. The standards are more likely to be used for selection and career planning purposes and by the designers of programmes.

WHO ARE SENIOR MANAGERS?

MCI's definition of a senior manager, for this purpose, is a member of a company board or someone reporting to that level. While MCI has adopted a well-considered definition for its research, there is no universal definition of a senior manager. Company structures and titles vary widely, as do their size, nature and complexity. Their roles will likewise vary, for example, in how much they specialize.

Potential for confusion is most acute with directors. In parallel to MCI's work is a not wholly dissimilar attempt by the Institute of Directors (IoD) to spell out what company directors do and should do. MCI's remit included directors, but only when wearing their departmental head hat and not their board member hat. Pleasingly, the two studies have been coordinated.

There is another problem of demarcation. Just as we sometimes have difficulty isolating leadership from managing, we now have to isolate 'direction' as well. At the moment, the IoD equates direction with 'what directors do'. But MCI rightly takes a broader view, being loath to concede that senior managers below director level do not also provide direction.

A third issue is that company directors have distinct legal responsibilities, they differentiate themselves from all other managers with their title, and they tend to view themselves as a breed apart. Yet much of their management task is similar.

So there are problems of definition and perception here for the standards-setting work to overcome.

WHAT DO THE SENIOR MANAGEMENT STANDARDS SAY?

The key purpose sounds reasonable at first glance:

> **To develop and implement strategies to further the organization's mission.**

This is probably acceptable to most people, especially those already in positions of power. Likewise, the four key roles have considerable face-validity:

> **Understanding and influencing the environment**
> **Setting the strategy and gaining commitment**
> **Planning, implementing and monitoring**
> **Evaluating and improving performance**

At the next level of breakdown many users may be surprised that nowhere does one find any mention of profit, finance or ethics, for example! But there is a good reason for this. Views on such matters as these are deemed to be judgements to be made by the senior managers themselves in their own business contexts within the generic conceptual framework provided by the standards. For example, profit could find its place in:

> **Develop a mission to give purpose to the organization ...**
> **Formulate appropriate objectives and strategies ...**
> **Develop measures and criteria to evaluate achievement of the organization's mission ...**

But MCI takes the view that it is no part of its role to offer advice on a matter such as profit in a generic framework, not least one which applies to all sectors, including the voluntary sector. Similarly, while a statement of best practice at this senior level might be expected to include some reference to appropriate corporate values for the 1990s and beyond, there is no guidance on this to be found in the model. Again, you could follow the standards and 'develop systems to review the generation and allocation of financial resources', yet misread the market and buy a dud company! Indeed, it seems that it would be possible to do all these, but exercise poor judgement.

In effect, the model provides the equivalent of an outline core curriculum. We have a conceptual framework consisting of areas of competence, which are rather like questions to which the real players have to come up with the right answers for their own businesses.

A COLLECTIVE SENIOR MANAGEMENT MODEL

A healthy development is that the senior management standards are about what senior *management* does collectively, rather than what each senior *manager* does. What we have here is a collective rather than an individual model like those at lower managerial levels. At least this was the original concept, though the latest advice is that the standards can be applied equally to groups and individuals.

The team perspective is an appealing departure from past practice. It is also sensibly realistic. Not every senior manager in a large company can carry out all the elements in the standards, such as setting the company mission. Nor might they want to. People who work in planning and production, for example, work to different timescales and require different attributes. So the model wisely assumes scope for variation of interest, expertise and priorities among members of the senior management population.

But this inherent feature in the design of the standards poses problems for development use, and to a lesser extent for other potential applications.

THE SENIOR MANAGEMENT STANDARDS AND QUALIFICATIONS

There are no plans for an NVQ Level 6 above the current top Level 5, which equates with the middle management standards, and as used by some competence-based MBA programmes. But MCI and awarding bodies are already meeting to consider whether there should be a change of heart here. They are discussing the possibility of a new range of competency based, masters-level degrees. There would be a problem, however. As I have pointed out, the standards are acceptable for *collective management*, but qualifications are awarded to *individual managers*. If managers wanted to acquire the full NVQ, they would presumably need to demonstrate competence across the whole model.

USING THE SENIOR MANAGEMENT STANDARDS TO DEVELOP INDIVIDUALS OR TEAMS

Being all-rounders may be neither desirable nor practical. While a senior management team may need within it the qualities of a corporate strategist to chart the way ahead, it does not need everyone to be good at this. And a corporate strategist may not be good at making the pace. The top team needs to be able to mix 'n' match to achieve the best optimum balance. A corporate planner may be picked for possessing a reflective, long-term orientation, whereas a production director needs a short-term, action orientation. The ideal personality profiles are quite different. For those familiar with the Myers–Briggs Type Indicator, I would suggest a corporate planner should be a strong P and the production director a strong J.

This example shows how the collective approach to competences is not without practical problems, especially for developers. This may explain why the model's application has shifted in favour of equal relevance to individual senior managers. How could developers use a collective model when developing (or selecting, appraising or compensating) an individual senior manager? But how will we prevent individual managers, and their bosses, from believing that it is automatically in a manager's career interest to acquire the full range of competences? At best they might seek to become jacks of all trades, and at worst seek to display directly opposing qualities.

PRESSURE TO CONFORM

There is a clear danger in taking the national model too seriously and applying the standards too rigorously. The answer to the application dilemmas described may be found in using the standards as no more than a guiding framework – a view which MCI encourages. In other words, the standards should be applied with common sense as appropriate in given organizations. The absence of a tie to a qualification makes this kind of interpretation easier.

This flexible approach fits well with tailoring and matching competences to suit particular business situations and local language. The National Freight Corporation (NFC) has gone one step further. Against each of the seven NFC core areas of competence it has produced three levels of scope, A, B and C. According to the seniority and nature of the individual job, it might be allocated either A, B or C.

However, it is not difficult to find staunch adherents to the national standards for whom every element is wholly appropriate for every manager. In this extreme view, the standards do not call on common sense: they represent common sense. These competence zealots favour using the standards for all managers to develop their weak spots in the name of developing all-round competence. They say 'give them all the model and let managers choose if they want to develop their weak-spots and become all-rounders'. But it's not as easy as that. The risk is that the model could come to assume too great importance. When used for selection, succession planning or appraisal purposes, both managers themselves and their bosses might come to believe that anything less than competence across the breadth of the model would be career limiting.

We could therefore slide towards a more unitary view of senior management, rather than healthy pluralism and specialist depth, where weaknesses are accepted as a trade-off for strengths. Fitting the mould may become what matters, yet the organization may need senior managers who break the mould.

The research process fuels this concern. The exemplars for the study were undoubtedly chosen carefully, but they were nominated by their CEOs. The potential views of rebels and norm-busters will therefore have been weeded out by a combination of the 'halo effect' and its opposite, the 'horns effect', and a process of selecting in one's own image. When the CEOs were asked to rank a list of personal competencies, they put *judgement* and *self-confidence* at the top of the list. Good judgement is hardly likely to include 'disagrees with the boss'. And the valuable competence of *doubt* (not the same as self-doubt) probably looses out to *certitude* in the battle to appear positive, supportive and self-confident.

SUCCESSFUL VERSUS EFFECTIVE MANAGERS

There is research evidence to show that being successful as a manager does not correlate highly with being an effective manager.[2] Success is measured by the position reached through a rapid series of job promotions. Measures of effectiveness, on the other hand, take into account subordinate satisfaction and commitment, and perceived organizational unit performance. Managing one's career successfully calls for a different set of skills and qualities from managing one's work effectively. According to the research, executives who are most effective at the latter tend not to succeed at the former. It should not come as a surprise to learn, for example, that successful and effective managers operate to quite different communication patterns and reach different conclusions on who to spend most time with. It follows that choosing exemplars on the basis of position, or based on the opinions of those who have been successful in achieving positions of power, is not a guaranteed method of generating reliable data on true managerial effectiveness.

But how much does this matter? There is a counter-argument that the standards are not a process model for *how* senior managers should manage. According to the researchers,

> the functions represent the components of what it is that senior management is responsible for achieving, however it is done. ... This breakdown attempts to go just far enough to specify, without excessively determining *how* senior managers achieve what they are meant to.[3]

The standards accordingly say nothing directly about appropriate management styles, or how managers should prioritize their work or allocate their time, for example. It is therefore claimed that there is plenty of scope for plurality and difference here. That's the good news. The bad news is this: if the choice of exemplars is not crucial, what can the standards ultimately tell us about truly effective performance? Clearly, any resulting definition of competence, which amounts to a comprehensive role description, falls short of holding the clues to real effectiveness, as opposed to career success. In the next chapter we look at the difference between assessed competence and real performance.

COMFORTABLE CONTENT

It is likely that readers will find the content of the standards self-evidently worth acknowledging. That is the nature of the beast. But that is not to decry them or belittle the effort that goes into producing them. The statements may appear self-evident, but that does not mean that defining them is easy. What we don't find, however, are controversial descriptions of senior management which we might associate with known senior managers' success, based on our own experience of working with individual and individualistic exemplars. The content is not intended to prove especially creative and shed new insights on what competent senior managers should do. We find a thoroughly analysed, professional and well-presented depiction of what we would already hope the majority of senior managers already see as their job. But perhaps I credit existing senior managers with too clear an understanding of their role. In any event, is the problem with their role or with their applied ability and motives?

Most people will also see the role confirming the mythical presumption of management which, as Vaill puts it:

> Given the ambiguity and fluidity of all organizational situations, stability and control are introduced and maintained in the person of the 'manager'. The manager is a creator and restorer of order.[4]

I hope I am wrong! What price 'shaking things up' and 'getting out of the way', for example? Safe role descriptions, and the selection, training, development and appraisal they are intended to promote, sit uncomfortably alongside those who, like Peters and Drucker, are trying to shock us about what the future of managing needs to be.

There is a further irony: the safe and consensual *content* descriptions of senior management sit ill with the radical nature of the changes in the processes by which such roles are to be brought about, assessed and given recognition (namely, the competence model itself). How would we react if it was the other way round? Are we receiving too much new medium and not sufficient new message?

ACTIVITY 4.1

If you are thinking of using the management standards,

- How well do the four levels in MCI's model match your own organization's management hierarchical structure?
- Is it clear what NVQ levels of qualifications would be appropriate for the managers you have in mind?
- Does your potential provider of management training/learning materials appropriately differentiate between levels, and in a way which mirrors your own company's division of responsibilities?

PERSONAL COMPETENCE MODEL

As an extension to its work on the output-based sets of management standards, and for use as a complement to them, MCI has developed a Personal Competence Model.[5] This can be seen to have some conceptual commonalities with other input models, as discussed in Chapter 2. As MCI itself says:

Management is a complex business, it's about developing a range of practical and technical skills associated with day-to-day work itself. But this is just the base line. Being personally effective means calling on a range of other skills that allow you to adapt to situations and get the best out of people. This part of the management jigsaw is as much about **how** we manage as **what** we actually do. ... Although personal competence is implicit in the Management Standards, we decided it was too important to be left at that. Therefore we have developed what we call the MCI Personal Competence Model.

The MCI Personal Competence Model for the lower and middle management levels consists of four **clusters** and against these thirteen **dimensions**. These are shown in Figure 4.1. The next levels of breakdown against these dimensions, **behaviour indicators**, are not shown here. There is a different model for senior managers.

FIGURE 4.1 MCI'S PERSONAL COMPETENCE MODEL

Clusters of personal competence	**Dimensions of personal competence**
1. Planning to optimize the achievement of results.	1.1 Showing concern for excellence. 1.2 Setting and prioritizing objectives. 1.3 Monitoring and responding to actual against planned activities.
2. Managing others to optimize results.	2.1 Showing sensitivity to the needs of others. 2.2 Relating to others. 2.3 Obtaining the commitment of others. 2.4 Presenting oneself positively.
3. Managing oneself to optimize results.	3.1 Showing self-confidence and personal drive. 3.2 Managing personal emotions and stress. 3.3 Managing personal learning and development.
4. Using intellect to optimize results.	4.1 Collecting and organizing information. 4.2 Identifying and applying concepts. 4.3 Taking decisions.

Reproduced by courtesy of MCI

CREDITING COMPETENCE

NVQs are independent of the mode of learning. So long as candidates can demonstrate competence, it doesn't matter whether they have attended a particular course, learned their skills in a different context, studied at home, etc.[6] This overturns the long-accepted tradition that practising managers have had to follow academic courses to achieve management qualifications. No account was ever taken of what they already knew and could do as a result of their years of experience. For the concept to work fully, NVQs therefore have to allow for the **accreditation of prior learning** (APL), the principle underlying **crediting competence**.

APL is doubly useful. Not only does it provide a means for giving formal recognition to managers' existing competence, but it also provides a starting point in individuals' training needs analyses. It specifies the base upon which further competence needs to be developed in discrete modules, and can thereby avoid repeating formal training in already possessed skills.

Where the latter is the sole purpose and managers are not yet ready to seek formal recognition for competence, they can first use the Institute of Management's *SkillCheck* themselves. This is an IBM-compatible software package which allows managers to assess themselves against the national management standards at NVQ Levels 3, 4 and 5 drawn up by MCI, or against the Institute's own interpretation.

This description of crediting prior learning suggests that the status quo holds unless and until training is given, implying that there is no learning *per se* to drive an improvement in performance. If so, the only gain would be a formal acknowledgement of the existing competence, or a qualification without the usual effort of study, or often wasteful re-study of skills you already know but for which you haven't got the necessary piece of paper. Even where there is no training or additional learning, the service still has to be paid for by the organization. One training manager claimed:

> I could spend all my training budget on accreditation of prior learning but this would not result in any additional skills being acquired, rather existing skills would only be recognised.[7]

But that is too narrow a view of the purpose and reality of crediting competence. Research indicates that the mere process of reflecting on present performance against a model of best practice itself generates improved performance. Some companies are so persuaded as to the effectiveness of crediting competence that they speak of it as 'development' itself.

There is now a feeling that the 'prior' in APL is too suggestive of *previous* rather than *current* learning; also that 'learning' is too narrow compared with 'experience'. But the term seems to be established. Interestingly, the acronym is not used by MCI. Their branded product is the process known as 'crediting competence'. Within this, they speak of the accreditation of current experience. This expression is used generously to include APL up to around five years previously.

CASE EXAMPLES

Here are two case examples which I wrote for MCI with publicity in mind, shortened here, to illustrate how the management standards at the various levels can be used, coupled with MCI's Crediting Competence Scheme.

Case Example 1 concerns BOC Distribution Services (BOCDS), which operates a storage and distribution service on behalf of manufacturers across the UK and throughout Europe. Prime customers include Marks & Spencer, handling items as diverse as hanging garments and temperature-controlled foods.

Case Example 2 shows the experience of Frizzell Financial Services, one of the UK's leading providers of insurance, banking and financial planning services. Frizzell employs around 1600 staff in Bournemouth.

CASE EXAMPLE 1: BOC DISTRIBUTION SERVICES

Expertly managed logistics are at the heart of successful companies in this line of business. This is no less true of training, where around 300 supervisors and managers work in 30 depots nationwide. What's more, the peaks and troughs in workload are fairly unpredictable.

Such a dynamic and pressured management environment presents the training department with quite a headache. Its customers are practical, 'hands-on' supervisors, shift and operational managers. Paperwork to them means delivery slips, not directories of competences. How do you get people to sit still long enough – and in one place – to listen? How do you get them to *want* to?

BOC felt it was already ahead of the national game a few years ago when it developed competence statements ('skill lists') for its managers. These were being used to drive the appraisal process, to design relevant programmes and to generate training needs. Prior to this initiative, random training courses had been the order of the day – as in so many companies in the 1980s. The problem then was 'they just stopped there'. So this earlier approach was abandoned in favour of a more structured and strategic approach which was designed to:

- Develop skills.
- Gear training firmly to the business needs.
- Invest in the future.
- Give some areas of training time to bear fruit.
- Use training strategically to help secure the company's position in the marketplace.

Building on the company's own supervisors' training programme, supervisors have studied for certificates offered by the National Examining Board for Supervisory Management (NEBSM). This innovative work to develop a more business-oriented training strategy was recognized and rewarded when BOCDS won a National Training Award.

The natural next step came when the company was chosen to pilot the new MCI supervisory management standards. BOCDS decided to rely on the advice of an external MCI-licensed adviser and official assessor, IPS Training Group, rather than try to become expert itself in this fast-moving world of training, competences, Lead Bodies and NVQ schemes.

The piloting within this industry of the final drafts of the standards went well. The company's own earlier attempts to define competence aligned neatly with the new standards, with no artificial fit needed to mask the join. Even the requirements for supervisors to be able to demonstrate that they could set a budget fitted well: BOCDS had itself identified the need for this skill to be mastered.

There was no doubt that supervisors' appetites had been well and truly whetted. Many had missed out first time around at school and now glowed with their new-found recognition. So it was relatively easy for the language of 'NVQs' to enter the collective consciousness of the company.

Many of the supervisors and managers possessed hard-won experience acquired on the job over many years. Coupled with the NEBSM certificated training, they were already halfway there. The supervisors could aim at NVQ Level 3 and the managers at Level 4.

So the next step was to take on board the MCI Crediting Competence Scheme. This allows the supervisors and managers to collect evidence of competence in portfolios against the management standards.

Current estimates are that the outcome should show that around 80 per cent of the qualification need has been met by a combination of prior experience and the formal training, leaving a further training need of 20 per cent to be met.

CASE EXAMPLE 2: FRIZZELL FINANCIAL SERVICES

In keeping with its mission to remain a high-quality market leader, the Frizzell Board took the decision two years ago to target management training as the key human resource initiative for the 1990s. Success would require a £18m change programme affecting systems, practices and automation. Only managers, they felt, could lead that.

But behind that commitment in principle obviously lay a range of decisions to be made – choices about targeting the effort, qualifications, suppliers, resources, and so on. On the basis of what kind of analysis would the answers rest?

A review of management training showed that managers often attended courses without a clear outcome. Those which had sufficient structure (traditional Certificate, DMS or MBA programmes) failed to capture the imagination of most managers. Considering the investment involved, results within the company were disappointing. In considering suitable programmes, the following criteria were to be addressed:

- A standard level of training leading to a nationally recognized award.
- Training to help managers spearhead the internal change programme.
- Training directly relevant to managers' own work issues.
- A recognition of managers' experience as a valuable asset.
- A programme that could be controlled and delivered by the company.
- Short-term visible benefits to the company, showing in the bottom-line.

Frizzell opted for a large-scale programme aimed at the bulk of its middle and first-line managers and supervisors. A competence-based approach was chosen to focus on consistent and structured outputs, leading to national qualifications in the form of NVQs at Levels 3, 4 and 5 – felt to be an added benefit and incentive for the managers.

MCI's Crediting Competence Programme is used to give experienced managers recognition for what they already know and provide a personal jumping off point for development.

Three external suppliers are used on site to help deliver the NEBSM programme for NVQ Level 3, the Institute of Management for Level 4 and the Henley Diploma Programme for Level 5.

Work-based assignments are used to relate learning directly to managers' own organization problems and provide short-term benefits. In-house managers were trained to be assessors and mentors.

The programme was going to be controversial with many of Frizzell's longer-serving managers. What was in it for them? The answer to the persuasion issue was to sell the Why as hard as the What. That meant articulating the vision of the company. It seemed to succeed. By 1993 85 per cent of managers were on the programme.

Crediting competence is a powerful element of Frizzell's scheme. Managers have to provide firm evidence that they are competent in all relevant areas. For some the only way to provide this evidence is through job rotation – which may sound drastic. But in practice it has proved a blessing. Rotation helps managers obtain a wider appreciation of the business and gives them a better general picture of what management involves. It does wonders for informal networks – nowadays regarded as a cornerstone of internal teamwork, good communication and motivation.

Frizzell chose to become an MCI Licensed Centre and train its own assessors. The benefits to managers of this level of involvement are substantial. Becoming a Licensed Centre does, however, bring with it a significant administrative workload, as Frizzell's small training department discovered. An alternative option is to buy-in this service.

Benefits come in both the hard and soft variety. In terms of bottom-line impact, 1992 was Frizzell's most profitable year yet. There were obviously many contributing factors, but according to Frizzell's training manager, there is no doubt that the new standard of management through competence-based training has made a significant contribution, 'The programme forced managers to do some hard thinking – "do I really want to be a manager or a technical expert?" Tough choices.' The benefits were as follows:

- Company emphasis on best management practice.
- Development of team spirit.
- Projects tackling business challenges,
- Improved company-wide communications.
- Enhanced role for individuals in the running of the company.

PRODUCING EVIDENCE

The process of assessing new competence and giving credit for prior/current experience and learning operates at the workplace. Evidence for managers was initially expected to take the form of observation and, if necessary, simulations. But these methods are fraught with practical difficulties at NVQ Level 3 and above; for example, where there is a need to assess managers' decision-making and problem-solving skills. So evidence is increasingly gathered in the form of dossiers or portfolios and is now MCI's preferred means. However, this evidence-gathering process can seem bureaucratic and may, in turn, produce an adverse reaction in organizations.

There are several products on the market to offer guidance and assist with the gathering of evidence, such as *Portfolio Development: Towards National Standards – A Guide for Candidates/Advisers and Assessors*, published by Development Processes (Publications) Ltd on behalf of SCOTVEC.[8] According to this Guide,

> A 'Portfolio' in the context of National Standards is a personal collection of an individual's performance at work which helps to prove that the performance meets the standards. Rather like an Art Student's portfolio, it is something which one should be proud of and continually supplement as increased ability is recognised and recorded.

The evidence may be direct such as examples of the manager's own work, or indirect such as the comments of appraisers. The portfolio is submitted to an assessor. The whole process is shown in Figure 4.2.

Some open learning programmes now have portfolio prompts built into the text as an aid to compiling the evidence. An example is the *New Career Manager*, published by HDL Training & Development Ltd. A sample illustration from this programme is contained in Figure 4.3.

The move away from observation towards portfolios is seen by some as a concession to the traditionalists' methods of assessment and a move back in the direction of the 'tried and trusted method of written work'.[9]

In terms of the set of open values declared at the start of this book, the degree of learner control over portfolio-based assessment has much to commend it. But there are risks and deficiencies with the portfolio-based approach. Here are three obvious ones.

Biased choice

Candidates are able to choose for themselves the sample material for inclusion, and this will present a biased picture, as only material which offers a favourable view will be seen. Compare this with the annual appraisal of work performance or a traditional examination, where the learner's shortcomings as well as successes may be exposed.

Partial story

Competence in terms of portfolio evidence is only part of the story. It is not difficult to imagine those who qualify on the basis of assessed competence under this method but who, in spite of this, are generally still regarded as poor managers for a variety of reasons:

O   They may simply not be perceived by those within the organization as managing in the way the evidence implies.

O   They may be considered poor managers for a whole range of other reasons outside the areas being assessed.

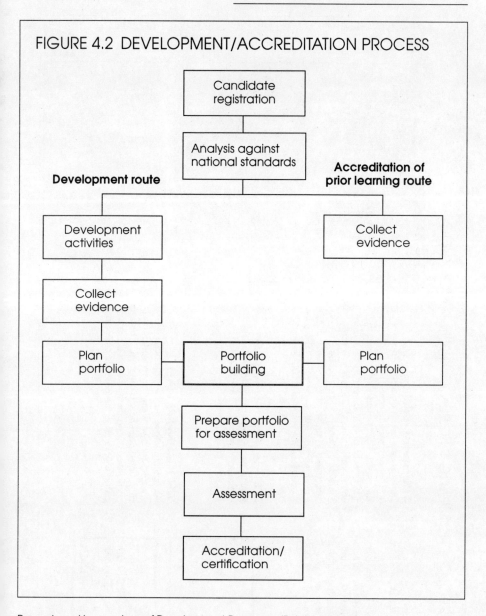

FIGURE 4.2 DEVELOPMENT/ACCREDITATION PROCESS

Reproduced by courtesy of Development Processes (Publications) Ltd

○   However managers *behave*, they may not achieve the ultimate *results* or outcomes the organization is paying them to achieve.

But these assessment problems are true of any process of study and any qualification. The advantage of the competence method is that the criteria have been nationally accepted as the most relevant measures; namely, work-based demonstrated outputs.

FIGURE 4.3 PORTFOLIO PROMPTING IN OPEN LEARNING WORKBOOKS

2 Return on investment

The percentage return on the capital cost over the life of the item.

Again the earnings per month/year are estimated but this time are grossed up over the life of the item. The total return is then expressed as a percentage of the capital outlay, e.g. gross earnings of £30,000 from an investment of £24,000 = 66.6%.

Return percentage

Option 1
(2 years x £10,000		
+ 1 year x £5,000)	=	£25,000
less cost price	=	£20,000
Earnings	=	£5,000
		25%

Option 2
(3 years x £9,000		
+ 1 year x £4,000)	=	£31,000
less cost price	=	£24,000
Earnings	=	£7,000
		29.166%

The obvious choice is **Option 2**.

3 Discounted cash flow

Examines the return against inflation and/or opportunity cost.

This method of appraisal recognises that £100 receivable in a year's time will be of less value than £100 received now. Therefore, future income must be discounted to arrive at its present value, e.g. if inflation is thought to be 10% over a year then the value of £100 is only 0.9091 of £100 (£90.91).

DCF tables (often called Net present value) are readily available and many organisations use built-in computer software calculations.

Which method do I use?

As you may have noticed, methods 1 and 2 represent a very similar approach and discounted cash flow is different. There is no right or wrong method but it is worth being aware of all the possible options.

PORTFOLIO 28

1 Select one major piece of equipment in use in your office and work out the financial implications of replacing it.

   Which methods will you use to analyse the costs and why?

2 Ask your line manager or a financial specialist within your organisation to check your assumptions. Did you, for example, use the organisation's standard amortisation period?

3 Note any amendments you would make to your methodology on another occasion.

Minimizing development

There is a natural wish for individuals to avoid spotting areas of mismatch against the management standards, in the hope of minimizing the need for further development.

WORKPLACE ASSESSMENT

The role of assessors in companies is assuming growing importance. We have to thank the competence movement for that because assessment of acquired and demonstrated competence has, by definition, to be in the workplace, not the classroom. This is, of course, equally true of APL. The Employment Department defines the assessment process in this way:

> The basis of assessment is the generation of evidence by candidates to show that they can achieve the published standards. That evidence is collected by assessors who judge whether it is sufficient to merit accreditation. Their judgements are subject to a system of verification to confirm that they are accurate. Certificates are awarded to the candidates by the Awarding Body on the basis of this assessment.[10]

Naturally, assessors need training. Open learning products are already available for this new market. Then the trained assessors' own performance needs assessing. Against what? Occupational standards, of course! In what to outsiders might sound like a new growth industry, the competence of assessors has been defined, using the same logic and methodology, by the Training & Development Lead Body (TDLB).

REFERENCES

1. Bruce Partridge (1989) 'The Problem of Supervision', *Personnel Management in Britain*, K. Sisson (ed.), Oxford: Blackwell, pp. 203–21.
2. Fred Luthans, Richard Hodgetts and Stuart Rosenkrantz (1988) *Real Managers*, Cambridge, Mass.: Bollinger Publishing Company.
3. Gill Lane and Alan Robinson (1994) *The Development of Standards of Competence for Senior Management*, Henley Management College.
4. Peter Vaill (1989) *Managing as a Performing Art: New Ideas for a World of Chaotic Change*, Oxford: Jossey-Bass, p. 37.
5. Management Charter Initiative (1994) *Management Standards*, London: MCI.
6. Joyce Walmsley (1992) 'Open Learning and NVQs', *Open Learning Today*, British Association of Open Learning, **11** (Summer).
7. Employee Development Bulletin (1993) 'National Vocational Qualifications: A Survey of Progress', *Industrial Relations Services*, April.
8. Janice Marshall (1993) *Portfolio Development: Towards National Standards – A Guide for Candidates/Advisers and Assessors*, Manchester: Development Processes (Publications) Ltd.

9. Rita Johnston and Mark Sampson (1993) 'The Acceptable Face of Competence', *Management Education and Development*, London: Association for Management Education and Development, **24** (3).

10. Employment Department and NCVQ (1991) *Guide to National Vocational Qualifications*, Sheffield: Employment Department.

5
MAKING THE MOST OF COMPETENCES

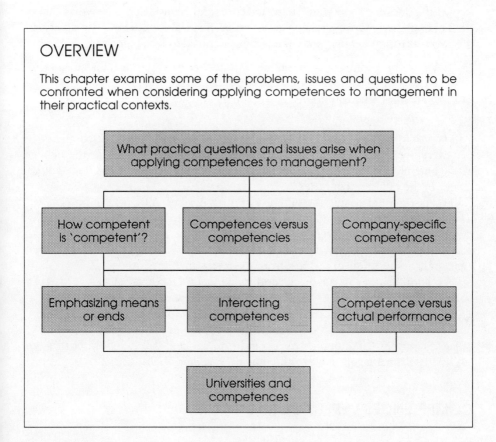

OVERVIEW

This chapter examines some of the problems, issues and questions to be confronted when considering applying competences to management in their practical contexts.

What practical questions and issues arise when applying competences to management?

How competent is 'competent'?

Competences versus competencies

Company-specific competences

Emphasizing means or ends

Interacting competences

Competence versus actual performance

Universities and competences

INTRODUCTION

In the next chapter, 'The competence controversy', we shall tackle some of the complex arguments concerning the competence movement. Many of these points have deep philosophical roots and are concerned with fundamental questions of principle. But, first, in this chapter we shall make a practical investigation of the problems, issues and dilemmas to be faced when applying competences in the real world so that they may be used to best effect.

HOW COMPETENT IS 'COMPETENT'?

To many people, the word 'competent' suffers from the connotation of bare sufficiency or adequacy, as opposed to expertise. It sounds somewhat out of place today when the call is for 'excellence'. The official UK competence movement doesn't intend this mediocre definition at all. It isn't against excellence; it just isn't directly concerned with it. Yet in any training or selection activity we always have to answer the question 'how well?' In the UK competence model, the answer is simply 'well enough' when assessed as competent against a yardstick of acceptability. In the two main approaches, competence can be considered as follows:

○   The threshold level – the minimum necessary to perform effectively (the UK approach).
○   The best – usually arrived at by studying outstanding performers (the USA approach).

The fact that there are two different approaches to the concept of competence and therefore to the subsequent development of detailed models for the field of management, does not imply different standards of *actual* managerial performance in the different countries.

The reason for choosing the different approaches lies in their purpose. The UK has chosen to develop a model of competence that helps with a pass/fail assessment of managers' competence – an output approach. The USA has developed an approach aimed more at developing mastery, arrived at by finding out what characteristics distinguish the best from the rest – an input approach.

Each approach has its advocates and its detractors, its pros and its cons. They both raise difficult questions. How do you agree on what is the minimum acceptable performance? Who chooses exemplars in order to pitch the level of exemplary performance? And who is to say that the most competent couldn't be better?

This dichotomy of approach means that the concept can be about both *what* kind of results managers achieve and *how* they achieve them.

COMPETENCES VERSUS COMPETENCIES

The arguments about competence itself are not helped by the arguments about the language of competence. You will come across two different usages and spellings. One with an 'i' as in 'competencies', and the other without, as used by MCI in its 'competences'.

	singular	*plural*
adjective:	(is) competent	(are) competent

noun:	(demonstrates) competence	(demonstrate) competences
noun:	(has) competency	(have) competencies

Some people don't spot the difference between the nouns or assume alternative acceptable spellings. Few worry about it. Many writers don't observe the nice distinctions, which are in any case not universally accepted. The Hay–McBer Group, for example, which makes extensive use of the personal 'competency' model, also uses the word 'competence' as the singular for 'competencies'. Peter Vaill's extensive quotations talk of 'competencies' where I think they may equally be about the US equivalent of MCI's 'competences'. But for the cognoscenti there is a most important and intentional difference in meaning between the spellings, especially for the plural. Recognizing the different nature of what we are dealing with really does matter, whether or not you accept the utility of the two spellings.

The problem is rather similar to that which we have with the closely related word 'standard'. For example, we hear that the government is concerned with present A-level learners' exam results; if too many pass it is because *the* standards are not high enough. Others defend results, arguing that more learners are passing because *their* standards are higher. The upshot is a paradox: the government may raise the standards (the hoops to jump through) in order to raise the standards (the perceived value of those who qualify). The result: fewer learners will pass! Have standards then gone up or down?

Likewise, competence can be viewed from both ends of the telescope. 'Competences' are what managers are seen to have satisfied if they are competent. 'Competencies', on the other hand, are what the manager must personally possess in order to be able to demonstrate competence in the job. Competences are derived from examining the role, while competencies are a function of the person. Competences are to job specifications what competencies are to candidate specifications.

Interestingly, the dictionary makes no distinction. It is some of the specialists in this field who have chosen to give each of the words its own special meaning to suit their nice purposes. According to these philologists,

> A *competence* is external to the person; it is what he or she *demonstrates* in a job.

By contrast, Richard Boyatzis asserts that,

> A *competency* is what a person *has*; i.e. a characteristic, motive, trait, skill, aspect of one's self-image or social role, or body of knowledge which he or she uses.[1]

Competency then is one of the sets of behaviour that the person must have and be able to display in order to perform the tasks and functions of a job with competence. This view of competency has become associated with soft skills.

However, as the Boyatzis definition suggests, the assumption behind possessing competency is that it will be used. So one can sometimes expect to find similar items both in lists of competencies and competences. There is accordingly plenty of scope, for *skill* items in particular, to become confused as to which they are; they may be both. But there are some clear examples of discrete competencies to be drawn from the government's Information Service to help us see the difference. They include, for example, rapport. Here one may see a clear distinction from applied competences in the output model.

Sometimes we find the term 'areas of competence' being used. This is *job performance related* and is primarily what MCI is concerned with in its management standards. In other words, this has to do with ability to perform against the standards set by the industry. By contrast, 'competencies' are *person related*. They describe the dimensions of personal behaviour behind competent performance. Competencies are thus more developmental than are competences. If someone doesn't demonstrate competence, they need to know why so that they can improve, which means developing their competencies.

> Competences show what potential can do.
> Competencies develop that potential.

Graham Elkin associates competences with a concern at the detailed micro level of performance, and competencies with the less defined and less definable macro level of performance.[2] Hence personal competencies become more important the further one moves up the organization.

Competencies can also be said to concern selection – perhaps more than development. To what extent are such virtues as enterprise and motivation teachable – or learnable for that matter? They may be thought of as largely inherent personal characteristics rather than trainable behaviour. And while competences have to be measurable, measuring many competencies and their application is by no means straightforward. How does one measure judgement, for example? (Relevant executive competencies are captured in *Executive-Match*, an executive selection planning guide.[3])

COMPANY-SPECIFIC COMPETENCES

Is it worth trying to develop one's own list of competences? Many companies have attempted it, such as Manchester Airport, British Airways, BP, TSB, Sun Life, NFC, Wellcome and British Rail, with varying degrees of success and confidence in the outcome. Some companies which undertake their own analysis argue from the position that they want something peculiar to their company's business rather than MCI's unadulterated generic management standards. Some want input competencies rather than output competences. Others go further and say that the generic standards constitute no more than a threshold ('lowest common denominator') level, and that their own version is able to embody best practice. MCI, however, claims its own standards *do* represent best practice.

Interestingly, an examination of the lists of well-publicized cases reveals a high degree of commonality (about 80 per cent), whatever the actual words used to describe the concepts. For some, this throws into question the justification for all the effort entailed, especially if you accept that competence is only one ingredient in the ultimate capacity recipe.

None the less, many such as Julie Hay argue the case in favour of a home-grown approach.[4] What Hay presents, however, is different in nature from MCI's functional offerings: she gives examples of personal 'core characteristics', 'orientations' or 'approaches to situations', rather than skills or knowledge.

The DIY approach may become less frequent as MCI's management standards take a firmer hold and are made more user-friendly and flexible. Paradoxically, it might on the other hand become more frequent, as a wider range of developed models (both output and input) enters the public domain, allowing those who are interested to mix-and-match in a relatively easy fashion, choosing from an options menu rather than conducting their own original research. Courtaulds Textiles has followed this DIY route to developing personal competencies. But to make a success of analysing and defining your own management competences, and proving their unique relevance, still takes considerable skill, plus a significant time and cost commitment. MCI's management standards at least provide a foundation on which to build, offering a format which can shortcut the process.

In some tailoring approaches not only are the management standards adapted to make a good fit with the company, its own product jargon is written into the material. This improves their acceptability, especially at lower levels. A good example is the National Freight Corporation.

Another approach is to textualize the generic management standards by applying additional company-specific ones, which can then be approved by awarding bodies in their own right. One such example is the Open College's work with Severn Trent Water to implement a training programme leading to a specific award issued by the Institute for Supervision and Management. Another example is the Ministry of Defence.

An alternative approach is for the client company to select a set of competencies from a single large databank as being the most important for it to concentrate on as a company, function or job.

MUDDLED LISTS

Both competences and competencies have their place. But Charles Woodruffe, writing in *Personnel Management*, counsels us to watch out for muddled lists which combine aspects of the job and the person as though directly comparable.[5] And in other people's lists, keep an eye open for indiscriminate and confusing use of the two spellings which quite probably signifies an equally confused mind.

Similarly, Ernie Cave and Penny McKeown, in 'Managerial Effectiveness: The Identification of Need',[6] warn us of the need to be clear whether you are talking about:

O   Management areas (e.g. management of resources).
O   Management processes (e.g. communication).
O   Management techniques (e.g. budgeting).
O   Management skills (e.g. negotiating).

AN ETHICAL INTRUSION?

At the ethical level, generic competences might in one sense be felt to be an acceptable subject for open discussion, since they are standards external to the person. By contrast, the idea of generic competencies might sound like an infringement of the individual's composition – certainly in the British culture where wide individual differences are prized.

KEY TIPS

❖   Be clear about whether you are primarily interested in competences for developmental or assessment purposes.

❖   Don't muddle input competencies with output competences. Keep lists separate even if you use both.

EMPHASIZING MEANS OR ENDS

Appraisal schemes are used to having to grapple with the 'means vs. ends' dilemma. Is the company more interested in appraising the achievement of *end results*, or the management practices, behaviours or skills, which are the *means* by which they are delivered? That question is important to us here, because it is in these means rather than in the end results that we find both types of competence.

That last comment can be a source of surprise and confusion. A common mistake is to assume that the output form of competences can be equated with results, and the input form of competencies with management practices. It is not as simple as this. Subsumed under management practices in the typical two-tier appraisal scheme (i.e. divided between means and ends), lie knowledge and understanding, motives and traits, etc., plus certain types of input skill (e.g. prioritizing skill).

You can think of this as a three-level set, beginning with knowledge and understanding, motives, traits, etc. (approximating to personal qualities or competencies) giving rise to demonstrated work behaviours (approximating to functional competences), which in turn hold the potential to deliver the end results which the business needs (see Figure 5.1). Note that skills can be either part of the first or the second level; it depends on what kind of skill they are and where they lie in the skill–subskill chain.

We can see that in MCI's management standards model, the elements of competence, supported by their underpinning knowledge and understanding, equate more closely with *management practices* than with *results achieved*. The *results* in the appraisal scheme are the business *deliverables* hoped for by the company as a consequence of possessing competence in the management standards. (For this reason, the use of the term 'outcomes' to equate with competences that we find in some documentation is misleading, as for example in the MSC's definitions mentioned earlier.)

The fact that competences are not the same as results is not a weakness in defining useful ones. Competences cannot help but fall short of results. There is

FIGURE 5.1 INPUT–OUTCOMES MODEL

1. INPUTS i.e. Learning: means	→ 2. OUTPUTS i.e. Learning: ends	→ 3. OUTCOMES i.e. Real job purpose
Knowledge, understanding, motives, traits, etc. ('competencies')	Demonstrated sample work behaviours ('competences')	Business results, consequences and benefits

WORK BEHAVIOURS/MANAGEMENT PRACTICES
          (i.e. Working means)   (i.e. Ultimate work ends)

no way generic (or even company-specific) best practice can anticipate what a company will want any particular manager ultimately to *deliver*. But as Hales has observed, what is the point of studying what managers do if you don't know either their intentions or the ultimate outcomes that result from their actions?[7]

ACTIVITY 5.1

In the light of the differences between the two types of competence and how they emphasize inputs, outputs and outcomes, check their fit against your company's value system (e.g. how it weights the management appraisal scheme in terms of means versus results).

INTERACTING COMPETENCES

There is a 'new science' principle which argues that the complexity of managerial work cannot be correctly understood by breaking it down into discrete competences using the analytical processes practised by the competence movement, including MCI. The case is that it fails to take sufficient account of the behavioural interconnection in the working relationship between two or more individuals.

Seen this way, neither the process nor the outcome can be predetermined or viewed entirely in terms of the competence of the manager. The behaviour – indeed the *competence* – of the other party is crucial. Good squash players appreciate this: the type of game they choose to play, and are able to play, is dependent on the opponent.

Just as the behaviour and competence of the other person affect one's own, so do their morals and motives. For example, it is not possible for a negotiator to negotiate regardless of whether the other party is equally sincere. Likewise, the process of a manager appraising a subordinate has to take account of the fact that the continual interaction of the one influences the other's behaviour in an unpredictable and unique way.

This interaction dimension clearly places limits on the process of analysis and definition, the nature of training, and assessment of performance. Let's look at how it affects the relationship with one's boss.

MANAGING YOUR BOSS

Managers have to be able to manage upwards – that is, their own boss. Indeed, cynics claim that all a company pays a manager to do is to make the manager's own boss look good! It is certainly true that indifference to this requirement carries a heavy price but, cynicism apart, there are two important points here.

The relationship

One's competence is influenced by the somewhat intangible but powerful interpersonal chemistry with one's own boss, by bosses' values, and not least by their expectations and demands. This affects the following:

O   How competence is defined.
O   Your practical ability to perform competently.
O   How your competence is viewed and assessed.

Consistent performance under one boss might be highly rated and rewarded one year, but under a new boss might receive the thumbs down. The boss may hold a different view from his or her predecessor as to what is required, make it more difficult for the manager to perform competently, or simply take a different view of the manager's performance even if it has not changed.

So the possession of competence must be placed firmly in the context in which performance takes place. There will always be a number of variables, a significant one of which is the evaluating audience including the boss, since, in the view of Annie Pye, competence, seen like this, is not possessed, but 'given' by other people in their evaluation of the actions of others in a particular situation at a particular time.[8]

Meeting the boss's needs

Managing does not only involve managing downwards (i.e. the functional unit and staff for which one is the manager). To be effective also requires the skills to manage upwards. Managers who already understand this often think of 'managing the boss' purely in terms of personal survival or career advancement. And it does work. But managing upwards is needed for reasons of effectiveness as well.

In the competence model too great an emphasis seems to be placed on the possession of competence for and in managing downwards at the expense of other dimensions. What about managing interference at the periphery to give staff a free run, sideways to increase interfunctional cooperative working, and outwards towards partners, customers, outsourced resources and other stakeholders?

In practical terms, managers are limited in what they can do by their own bosses' preferences. For example, the way a manager presents a report for the boss depends on such matters as the boss's liking or dislike of detail. John Gabarro and John Kotter, writing in *Harvard Business Review*, suggest that managers should set out to understand their boss's context as well as their own situation.[9] Figure 5.2 contains what they consider to be the minimum.

FIGURE 5.2 UNDERSTANDING YOUR BOSS'S CONTEXT

- What are your boss's goals?
- What are your boss's strengths and weaknesses?
- What are your boss's organizational and personal objectives?
- What are your boss's pressures, especially those from his/her own boss and others at the same level?
- What are your boss's long suits and blind spots?
- What is your boss's preferred style of working?
- Does your boss like to get information through memos, formal meetings, or phone calls?
- Does your boss thrive on conflict or try to minimize it?

ACTIVITY 5.2

Using Figure 5.2, see how well you understand your boss's context. How can your own approach to managing be modified to take better account of this to benefit both parties?

The boss is only one half of the relationship. Managers have more control over the other half, their own. So they need to understand themselves – their own needs, strengths and weaknesses and personal style, including their predisposition toward dependence on authority figures. In the words of Gabarro and Kotter, they are then able to maintain a relationship which fulfils the following criteria:

○ It fits both parties' needs and styles.
○ It is characterized by mutual expectations.
○ It keeps the boss informed.
○ It is based on dependability and honesty.
○ It selectively uses the boss's time and resources.

Bosses too need to be aware of what is happening. It is easy to feel flattered and allow the 'halo effect' over the relationship to cloud wider judgement about the manager's all-round performance. Bosses need to be able to see when a manager is spending too much effort managing upward. They rarely do. The floor is littered with the bodies of dead subordinates who suffered at the hands of managers who did as they pleased and got away with it by managing their own boss! Seeing through the veneer of upward managing is a key competence that doesn't seem to feature on anyone's list!

ACTIVITY 5.3

Think about subordinates who appear to be managing you well.

- Just what are they doing?
- What seem to be their motives?
- Who is benefiting?
- What would you like them to do differently?

ASSESSED COMPETENCE VERSUS ACTUAL PERFORMANCE

Any assessment of competence involves some degree of inference. Whether a particular task is observed being performed on the job, or the relevant under-pinning knowledge is assessed at one remove, future performance can only be inferred, and even then only approximately. One reason is that managerial tasks do not present themselves in a repetitious, predictable way. Circumstances keep changing, as we've seen. So assessment can't provide consistent on-the-job problems for the manager to solve, nor offer guarantees about future performance.

Some elements of performance remain below the surface and don't lend them-selves to observed assessment. Apart from mental processes, there may be impor-tant aspects of the manager's values, motives and disposition, as we have just seen.

Successful performance comes only with a combination of competence and a host of other organizational factors. Even given the best of intentions, among other things, the department's work must meet the following requirements:

O   Be directed towards the company's goals.
O   Be adequately resourced.
O   Possess suitable systems and procedures.
O   Have a positive climate of inter- and intra-departmental relationships.
O   Have good teamworking and communication.
O   Provide relevant information and feedback.

Furthermore, the organization will have unique and unspoken values about what it looks for in managerial performance, what it takes to succeed, please the boss and make career progress. These go well beyond individual competence. They're part of the organization's culture.

THE RATIONAL AND THE NON-RATIONAL

Competence is part of an organization's rational face. But what occurs in organ-ization cultures is *not* rational – though not necessarily negative or irrational. It is part of what Gerard Egan calls the arational or non-rational 'shadow' side of the organization's personality.[10] Figure 5.3 shows some of the rational and non-rational features to be found in organizations.

FIGURE 5.3 THE RATIONAL AND NON-RATIONAL FACE OF ORGANIZATIONS

Rational	Non-rational
• competence	• departmental rivalries
• mission	• personal jealousies
• goals	• office politics
• codes of practice	• territorial disputes
• organization charts	• ambition
• job descriptions	• greed and self-interest
• people's titles	• fear and insecurity
• published policies	• power struggles
• legal statutes and requirements	• personal friendships
• company rules and regulations	• bosses not on speaking terms
• committees	• in-groups and out-groups

What it means for us here is that there is a host of factors not formally designed into the system (usually where 'who' matters more than 'what'), that have a powerful impact on what happens and on managers' ability to perform in accordance with their competence.

ACTIVITY 5.4

Looking at Figure 5.3:

- Into which side is your organization putting most of its energy?
- Which side is having most effect on your organization's present performance?
- Is most further gain to be found by enhancing the left-hand side (especially developing competence), or by understanding, managing and mitigating the impact of the right-hand side so that the non-rational effect is neutral or positive?

WILL

Then there's 'will'. Here is an apt quotation:

> The difference between a successful person and others is not a lack of strength, not a lack of knowledge, but rather a lack of will. (Anon)

Much overlooked, 'will' is managers' inclination and determination to persist and apply themselves beneficially regardless of circumstances, the system, the climate, the rewards (or their absence) – to achieve and carry through what they believe has to be done. It is more than persistence, perseverance and resilience. Single-mindedness doesn't quite capture the essence either, as it can imply arrogance and roughshod insensitivity as well as being driven. 'Will' is about energy and character.

LIMITS TO COMPETENCE

Competence – even though demonstrated and assessed – merely provides the potential ability to produce the organization's results. But this should not be taken to imply that competence (or the management standards) provides that *total* ability. If, after reading this chapter so far, you accept that the concept of competence cannot paint the whole of the development picture, then it follows that the same is true for other applications such as performance appraisal and selection.

It is important to recognize this because there is a strong trend towards replacing traditional approaches to appraisal and selection with competence-based ones. Given shortcomings in many of the present methods, the pressure to look for better ways is understandable. And competence-based appraisal and selection might provide more objectivity and certainty, *but only for part of the picture*. There is danger in not recognizing these limits to the value of managerial competences and in not understanding what is needed to complement them.

Firstly, in addition to the managerial dimension of the job there will usually be a need to check specialist know-how and competence in some professional or technical field. This aspect may be equally or more important than generic managerial strength.

Secondly, there will be some necessary personal qualities to look for during appraisals and selection which are very difficult, if not impossible, to capture through the normal competence format. This is especially true for senior managerial jobs. In terms of Level 1 in the Input–Outcomes Model (Figure 5.1), personal attributes such as courage and risk-taking may be sought. At the other end of this scale, at Level 3, evidence of achieved beneficial results is likewise important, especially in the appraisal context.

Taking all the above factors into account, successfully assessed competence, even in the most realistic work-based context, is clearly no guarantee of future performance. Having the skills needed to chair a meeting is at best one step removed from taking good decisions. Competence does not equal performance any more than failed performance can be laid at the door of the 'incompetent' manager, however convenient we sometimes find this.

But it is hardly fair to consider this a criticism of the competence-based approach *per se*. Any attempt to define, develop or measure individuals' ability necessarily experiences these shortcomings. It is more a criticism of our tendency to view individuals' capability (even their performance) as the main lever to improve organizational performance at the expense of other levers – both rational and arational. Other levers can be more significant, and pulling them more cost-effective.[11]

DEFINING, DEVELOPING OR APPLYING COMPETENCE

Much effort goes into defining competence, increasingly in a company-specific context. But even the best definition is a step short of realizing improved individual competence and, as we have just seen, is even further removed from realizing improved organization performance. While the most popular question appears to be 'Is it worth developing one's own list of competences?', more important questions are these:

1. In our company's particular circumstances at this time, is the improvement of individual competence the key lever to pull to improve organization performance?
2. How are these defined competences driven by, and rooted in, the organization's current context and the changes it needs to make?
3. Once competences are agreed, what is being done to ensure that they lead to new-found competence in practice?
4. What is the organization itself doing to make sure that it is able to channel and utilize individuals' competence collectively and to the full?[11]

UNIVERSITIES AND COMPETENCES

Universities are now faced with making decisions about where they stand with regard to the competence-based approach to management education and being pressured to take on board responsibility for teaching action-based skills. Many, like Sheffield, are cautious about which aspects can be integrated with their academic approach.

A few of the traditional universities, such as Reading, are enthusiastic. But it is mainly the 'new' universities (ex-polytechnics) which are most readily picking up the challenge thrown down by the competence movement. But even here, this mostly relates to their long-standing involvement in the provision of certificate and diploma courses. For example, South Bank now runs a 100 per cent competence-based Certificate in Management but cannot contemplate a competence-based MBA.

Whatever their various misgivings, there can be no doubt that the universities feel the pressure in the market (employers and employees) for management qualifications which are directly concerned with ability in the place of work and can be pursued there.

One of many problems is that the competence-based approach is synonymous with workplace assessment, though this is changing. It is not very practical, and arguably not the role of universities to award a qualification for assessed achievement at work.

One response to this is for the universities to be influenced by the motives of the competence movement rather than to adopt its methodology. Rita Johnston and Mark Sampson at Sheffield argue that:

> Management degrees cannot afford to ignore the real world. The knowledge must relate to genuine problems and situations learners will encounter in their professional role. And maybe the standards of the MCI and TLDB and other relevant Lead Bodies can help academics check that their theories are not simply 'academic' and that they are perceived as hard professional currency.[12]

The result is that Sheffield offers a Certificate level course, run within a client company's organization but under the aegis of the University, to ensure that 'pragmatic work based decisions had an underpinning of theoretical knowledge and research'.

The issue is how to integrate the external and more conceptual level of study with practical skill development that can be directly used to solve identifiable problems.[13] An outside-in view has to be balanced with an inside-out view. The total training and education experience must consider the individual's needs from the perspective of what is happening in the business's and person's environment, as well as considering the learners' own needs, past experience, interests, and approach to life. It will also include fresh development ideas from outside the organization, rather than be limited by what the company sees as its present problems from its own internal perspective. Too local a perspective, and the learning will be myopic and insular; too remote a perspective, and employers will consider the learning insufficiently relevant – one of the criticisms in the late 1980s that led to interest in competences.

One way of achieving the necessary balance is to contain both dimensions within the one programme. Lancaster University Management School and the Impact Development Training Group have set up a new Diploma in Business Administration that combines academic study and vocational training. It is designed to provide managers with the ability to understand the key issues affecting their organizations, as well as improve their practical capabilities. It hopes to attract managers faced with the consequences of down-sizing, delayering and decentralization.

The problem of university involvement can be solved in this accommodating manner at the practical and lower 'training' levels, perhaps up to the Diploma. But where higher-order managerial competences and qualities are called for in what is more clearly a *management education* process rather than a *manager training* one at master's degree level, then many universities will find themselves unable and unwilling to accommodate competences.

It may sound arrogant on the part of the universities, but one way of conceptualizing this distinction is to regard the competence model as being about *managers* and the traditional model at MBA level about *management*.

Some, like Mick Silver, sensing 'a direct attack on knowledge-based skills', fear too strong a movement in the direction of a more applied orientation will produce a *prescribing* role rather than an *understanding* one.[14]

Where there can be compromise it will help the universities with a practical staffing problem. Influenced by Mintzberg, Colin Talbot at South Bank points out that

> [management skills] have been traditionally the main province of in-house management trainers, developers and consultants. ... all the people who are good at teaching this sort of thing are out there working for employing organisations either as staff or consultants. They are not usually hanging around in universities teaching and researching. This is undoubtedly problematic for competence based programmes in higher education.[15]

Mintzberg himself states bluntly that:

> The fact is that our management schools do not generally hire people capable of teaching true managerial skills. The PhD is the license to teach in a business school. But that degree neither preselects nor trains for skill in pedagogy, certainly not of the experiential kind. The PhD is a research degree, and in good part it attracts introverts, people who want to bury themselves in a library or under a stack of data. ... There are certainly academics who are great teachers, even some who are great at skill teaching. But that is purely coincidental, and in any event, these are few in my opinion.[16]

This is possibly a greater problem in the UK than North America where teaching roles are not so neatly defined and the faculty is more likely to comprise a number of part-time top-notch consultants and writers. But as the reward system and the market changes, that distinction may be becoming less marked, with the USA management experts cutting back on their university commitments, and those in UK universities getting out more.

A sign of the times might be the formation of the Management Verification Consortium (MVC) comprising a growing number of university business schools in the UK (37 at the last count) which have banded together for the purpose of being an MCI-endorsed NVQ awarding body.

REFERENCES

1. Richard Boyatzis (1982) *The Competent Manager: A Model for Effective Performance*, Chichester: Wiley.
2. Graham Elkin (1990) 'Competency-Based Human Resource Development', *Industrial and Commercial Training*, **22** (4).
3. William Tate (1993) *Executive-Match: A Self-completion Selection Planning Guide*, Wokingham: Prometheus Consulting.
4. Julie Hay (1990) 'Managerial Competences or Managerial Characteristics?', *Management Education and Development*, London: Association for Management Education and Development, **21** (4).
5. Charles Woodruffe (1991) 'Competent by any Other Name', *Personnel Management*, September.
6. Ernie Cave and Penny McKeown (1993) 'Managerial Effectiveness: The Identification of Need', *Management Education and Development*, London: Association for Management Education and Development, **24** (2).
7. C. Hales (1986) 'What do Managers do? A Critical Review of the Evidence', *Journal of Management Studies*, **23** (1).
8. Annie Pye (1988) 'Management Competence in the Public Sector', *Public Money and Management*, **8** (4).
9. John Gabarro and John Kotter (1993) 'Managing Your Boss', *Harvard Business Review*, May–June.
10. Gerard Egan (1993) *Adding Value – A Systematic Guide to Business-Driven Management and Leadership*, San Fransisco: Jossey-Bass, pp. 88–132.
11. William Tate (1995) *Developing Corporate Competence: A High-Performance Agenda for Managing Organizations*, Aldershot: Gower.

12. Rita Johnston and Mark Sampson (1993) 'The Acceptable Face of Competence', *Management Education and Development*, London: Association for Management Education and Development, **24** (3).
13. William Tate (1992) 'Low Marks for Management Education', *The Independent*, 3 March.
14. Mick Silver (ed.) (1991) *Competent to Manage – Approaches to Management Training and Development*, London: Routledge, p. 82.
15. Colin Talbot (1993) 'Twin Peaks? MBAs and the Competence Movement – A Tale of Two Courses', *Management Education and Development*, London: Association for Management Education and Development, **24** (4).
16. Henry Mintzberg (1989) *Mintzberg on Management: Inside our Strange World of Organizations*, New York: The Free Press, pp. 85–6.

6

THE COMPETENCE
CONTROVERSY

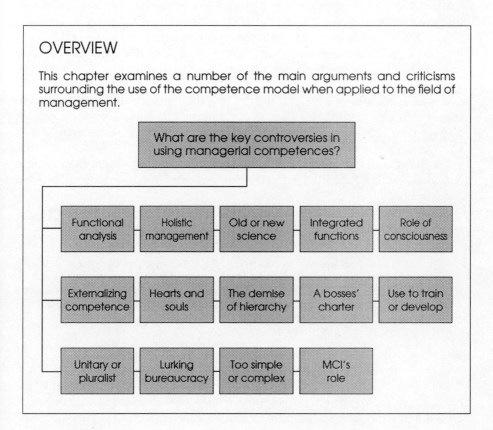

OVERVIEW

This chapter examines a number of the main arguments and criticisms surrounding the use of the competence model when applied to the field of management.

What are the key controversies in using managerial competences?

| Functional analysis | Holistic management | Old or new science | Integrated functions | Role of consciousness |

| Externalizing competence | Hearts and souls | The demise of hierarchy | A bosses' charter | Use to train or develop |

| Unitary or pluralist | Lurking bureaucracy | Too simple or complex | MCI's role |

INTRODUCTION

The competence lobby is a powerful one; it has the ear of government, and in one sense *is* the government. In league with the Employment Department's Training, Enterprise and Education Directorate (TEED) there are a number of large employer interests: the Institute of Management, the Confederation of British Industries and, coalescing around MCI, various providers and accreditors of management training and education.

This coalition of forces has provoked a necessary discussion and generated much interest in management training, education and development. It is also putting new life into open learning products. But is it losing its way? Can the apostles of management competences be accused of following their own path too closely? Have they departed from the thoughtfully expressed concerns and causes espoused primarily in the 1987 reports by John Constable and Roger McCormick, and Charles Handy *et al.*? Or was it reasonable to expect their followers to put a unique stamp on what was initially no more than a problem definition and a foundation of suggestions?

What is certainly true is that some of the original advocates of a radical rethink of management education and training have begun to have doubts about what is happening. Interestingly, many credit the reports referred to for having led to the growth of the competence movement (CM) in the UK and its having taken centre stage in the debate on the future of management education and training. The impact of those authors mentioned above was undoubtedly catalytic in nature, but that is all. It is worth reflecting on the fact that these reports did not mandate the competence approach. The closest they came was to imply generic models of management. And as we saw earlier, neither MCI's own mission statement nor its management code makes any mention of competences.

To give a trailer to a few of the issues to be examined in this chapter, let's consider what has happened compared with some of the originators' hopes and expectations.

John Constable warns of the danger of 'an over-complex bureaucracy for controlling any new qualification structure' which might result from an excess of enthusiasm. And he argues that:

> Reforming zeal must ... beware of ... the belief that the managerial skills and competences required in all types of managerial roles can be described in one all-embracing structure ... [and] ... that managerial competences can be accurately described and accurately measured. The fascination of management is the fact that apparently very different people, with very differing styles of behaviour, can achieve remarkable results in organisations.[1]

John Constable and Roger McCormick note that 'the diversity of the [present] system can be seen as a strength'.[2] But we have seen a strong converging tendency.

These two authors, as well as Handy *et al.*,[3] recognize that the customers in the marketplace consist of both employers and employees, noting that most decisions to undertake formal study are taken by unsponsored individuals. Yet the much vaunted employer-led reforms are dominated by business interests.

On attempts to define the process of management, Handy comments that:

> Logically, managing is a process, akin to words like seeing or believing or inspiring. Such words describe activities but do themselves elude definition. To pin them down too far is to risk destroying them, a kind of death by reification.[4]

One motive of the reforms was to simplify the structure of awards granted by what some saw as too many confusing awarding bodies. But with MCI's backing, the

NCVQ is endorsing the same old bodies rather than rationalizing them. Whilst this might be excused as an open-minded response to market force reality of one kind, the general effect of the reforms on the products offered to the consumer appears to fly in the face of the market and limits choice.

In spite of the many pluses for the competence approach, and considerable support for it from employers and individual learners, readers cannot afford to ignore these criticisms and problems. They need to understand them, learn from them and develop their own position and make choices for their own managers' development and for their companies.

Bear in mind that these criticisms are concerned with the way the competence model is being applied to management. Some of the problems may or may not also apply to other occupations, but that is not our concern here. It can be argued that the task of defining management is of a completely different order from that of defining other occupations, and that it has been a misjudgement to apply the model too rigorously to this field, or at the very least at the higher levels of the management hierarchy. But before we become enmeshed in examining the controversies and issues as they specifically affect management, let's first run over some of the broad principles involved.

Some problems are inherently part of the competence concept, to whatever occupational group it is applied. Some are concerned with either the politics or the administration of how competences are being applied at the moment in the UK. Others surround its application only with management, as I've just said. Others concern its relevance to higher education. And others involve the (re)definition of 'management' itself.

FUNCTIONAL ANALYSIS

It is claimed that when compared with earlier ways of analysing jobs by examining tasks, the process of functional analysis is a significant advance because it ties every step back to a fundamental purpose. The process begins by identifying the purpose for each occupation and then asks what needs to happen to achieve this. The question is repeated down to a level which ultimately allows individual performance to be assessed – in MCI terms, *elements of competence*.

As a grounded methodology for breaking tasks down, that's fine. But as a basis for reconstructing a whole, it's open to question. This process of functional analysis is behind many of the criticisms of the competence movement and will be mentioned frequently in this chapter.

In his paper 'Creating the Managerial Portfolio', Burgoyne[5] highlighted a range of problems, many of which have their roots directly or indirectly in the assumptions behind the functional analysis approach to understanding a manager's work:

O   The holistic nature of management.
O   The inevitability of a large element of judgement in the assessment of competence.
O   The variability of management across situations.

○   The need to incorporate the moral and ethical elements.
○   The need to acknowledge that effective managing changes the nature of managerial competencies.
○   The recognition that there is more than one way to manage.
○   The belief that management development must attend the whole person in the managerial role.
○   The view that collective competency must be attended to in individual competency.

The process of functional analysis appears to equate 'what does a manager do?' with 'what are all the components of a manager's job?' But they are not the same. However you define the component competences, the totality in qualitative terms of what a manager does is self-evidently more than the sum of the parts.

Philosophers say that this simple way of looking at jobs suffers from a number of analysis–synthesis non-sequiturs. In a riveting exchange of letters between Peter Vaill and fellow academic, David Bradford, published in *Managing as a Performing Art: New Ideas for a World of Chaotic Change*, the argument for and against breaking down wholes into parts is itself given this detailed analytical treatment using the analogy of different ways of learning to ski.[6]

HOLISTIC MANAGEMENT

On his concern with the fragmented handling of the subject of managing, Burgoyne has this to say:

> Research and common sense show clearly that managing is not the sequential exercise of discrete competences. … It follows that using divided-up lists of competences to manage by, to select managers by, or to develop managers against, creates the problem of how the list is reintegrated together again into a holistic management performance. Learning separate aspects of managerial competence one at a time does not guarantee integral managerial performance, nor can a manager who has been identified as having separate managerial competences be guaranteed to be able to use them effectively.[7]

Using the skiing example referred to above, the separate component skills have no existence on their own. Skills such as shifting the body's weight onto the outside ski only make sense when moving and when used in conjunction with other component skills.

A famous Shakespearean actor, given the role of Richard III, told his director that he proposed learning his lines first so that he could manoeuvre on the crutches he was using to emphasize the king's deformity. 'How can you possibly learn the lines before you know the first thing about your character, his relationship to the other characters, the situations of each scene? It's unthinkable!' was the director's response.

This shows the heart of the dilemma. How best to acquire the *elements* of competence and *whole* competence? The actor and Bradford are perhaps being practical, the director and Vaill purist. But perhaps both are correct. We all learn in different ways and take on board competences in a way that suits our own learning skills, intelligence, confidence and ways that have worked for us in the past. Provided the Shakespearean actor recognized that once he had become familiar with the other characters, interrelationships and situations, he would have to adapt how he had originally learned his lines and add finesse to the basic competence he had acquired, what's wrong with that? While it may suit the more gifted to begin with the whole competence, others may prefer to build towards it in steps. The director was at fault in failing to recognize and accommodate the actor's preferred learning style.

OLD SCIENCE VERSUS NEW SCIENCE

Functional analysis is a reductionist technique consistent with Newtonian scientific principles. This is the traditional nineteenth-century 'old science' approach typified by Frederick Winslow Taylor. This 'father of scientific management' believed that 'the motives which influence men can be reduced through scientific analysis and control in the same way that the physical activities of shovelling iron can be'. His own motives were to break down tasks into isolated parts in order to control them better. Not surprisingly, Taylor was against teamwork: 'When men work in gangs, their efficiency falls almost invariably down to or below the level of the worst man in the gang.'

Contrast this with the modern writers on Chaos Theory, who suggest a new paradigm in which reality is more than the sum of the parts. Taylor's scientific principles have been stood on their head. For today's scientists, nothing transfers; everything is always new, different and unique. Their language and their strange new world, according to David H. Freedman, is one of holism, relationships, systems-thinking and inter-connectedness:

> They focus increasingly on the dynamics of the overall system. Rather than attempting to explain how order is designed into the parts of a system, they now emphasise how order emerges from the interactions of those parts as a whole.[8]

In *The Fifth Discipline: The Art and Practice of the Learning Organization*, Peter Senge notes:

> From a very early age we are taught to break apart problems, to fragment the world. This apparently makes complex tasks and subjects more manageable, but we pay a hidden, enormous price. We can no longer see the consequences of our actions; we lose our intrinsic sense of connection to a larger whole.[9]

The pre-chaos scientists believed that they understood the relationship between cause and effect in organizations. Freedman considers that managers still think like this, failing to appreciate that 'the links between actions and results are infinitely more complicated than most managers suspect'.[8]

Chaos Theory is concerned with a phenomenon known as 'Sensitive Dependence on Initial Conditions'.[10] According to this theory, it is never possible to know all of the initial conditions in a system from which measurements are to be made. 'And tiny differences in input could quickly become overwhelming differences in output.'

A number of examples immediately spring to mind: the interaction in an appraisal interview, the jockeying that takes place during a negotiation, and the daily interplay with one's boss. In none of these instances is it possible to consider performance solely in the context of one party's competence. The competence of the other party is directly relevant, and in the latter case the opinion of the boss on the subordinate's competence is a further complicating factor.

INTEGRATING MANAGERIAL FUNCTIONS

We saw in Chapter 2, 'The Competence Models', how MCI's process of functional analysis begins by dividing management into 'Managing operations', 'Managing finance', 'Managing information' and 'Managing people'. And I later raised doubts about the extent to which they could be regarded as mutually exclusive, citing the example of the need to practise the elements of competence entailed in 'Managing information' *in the context of* 'Managing operations'.

MCI's analytical approach is not exceptional; indeed there is a long-standing tradition of breaking down management and other functions in this way. The traditional MBA model has at its heart the various management functions: generally, Marketing, Finance, Operations and Personnel. 'Information' is an odd one out and could be seen as transcending or integrating the others. But the models of management and of its assessment tend not to indicate that integration of managerial functions (let alone integration of individual competences) is an important concern. In the light of this apparent weakness, the question is whether professional competence in separately treated functions is likely to bring a generally competent performance for a given individual or, as a next step, for the company's management as a whole. Some such as Louis Lataif think not:

> 'Professional management' ... is inadequate in a globally competitive environment. Our basic management ideas are functionally oriented. We manage each piece of an organization – design, research, product development, manufacturing, engineering, purchasing, sales, marketing, finance – as if optimizing the pieces optimizes the whole.
>
> The approach is badly flawed. It assumes that all the compromises and collaborations required to optimize the organization's results can be anticipated and incorporated into individual, functional objectives. That, of course, is impossible. All the inherent incentives work against operating as an integrated system. Hence, we experience the all-too-familiar organizational dysfunctions: turf battles, inability to surrender one's personal performance for the good of the whole, grandstanding, unhealthy internal competition. But these flaws become apparent only when we face sophisticated competitors who manage the business process (as the Japanese do, both as a matter of practice and cultural orientation), rather than focusing on individual functions.[11]

My companion book *Developing Corporate Competence: A High-Performance Agenda for Managing Organizations* puts forward ideas for tackling such organizational issues.[12]

THE PART PLAYED BY CONSCIOUSNESS

Vaill believes that teaching elements of competence separately fails to take sufficient account of learners' consciousness. Learners are trying to take on new skill elements while simultaneously having to cope with various internal personal issues that are indirectly and privately drawn into question (values, past experience, self-confidence, relationships, appearance, etc.) about which the teachers are often both unaware and unconcerned. Teachers have, in any case, been led to believe that their task is to generalize about the generic skill element across the whole population rather than concentrate on the uniqueness of each learner.

Vaill speaks of his own empirical evidence:

> the struggles I have watched over the years as learners tried to figure out what such things as 'openness', 'giving feedback', 'being participative', etc., mean for them personally in their own ways of thinking and acting in relation to others. ... You *can't* split consciousness and action. ... They realize that we are messing with their heads as well as their 'hands', as it were.[6]

It is difficult to fault Vaill's basic point. To quote a simple example from my own experience, many appraisal schemes require managers to rate their subordinates annually on a fixed scale. The managers are told what approximate percentage of their subordinates should fall in each category to follow a normal distribution. None the less, when you examine the outcome, most subordinates are scored as 'excellent'.

The explanation has nothing to do with training managers in the skills of scoring or in understanding the appraisal form. It has to do with what Vaill calls 'the intertwining of consciousness and action'. For a variety of reasons (such as wanting to be liked, looking after their own pay rise, unwillingness to face appeals, feeling uncomfortable when giving anything less than 100 per cent positive feedback) the managers consciously choose not to do that which they know they are required to do and know how to do.

Furthermore, the presenting problem is part of a much wider one, affecting career management, the management of bad performers, the management of rewards, the climate, the way complaints and appeals are dealt with, past history, the culture's norms, etc. So the solution lies in an organizational intervention rather than an individual manager intervention.

It should be said that at the centre of MCI's assessment methodology lies the concept and practice of live assessment of competence in the workplace setting. While this may not take full account of all Vaill's concerns about learning in a vacuum, it does try to ensure that learning is grounded in the real world of work – one of MCI's chief points in its management code.

EXTERNALIZING COMPETENCE

One of the controversial aspects of the competence movement is that if one decides to focus on *assessment* of competence more than *development* of competence (at least as a starting point and prime purpose), then 'competence' is effectively redefined as 'demonstrated competence'. Competence only exists when it is measured. This is what has happened in the UK in recent years. The familiar idea of competence as something to be equated with ability has undergone a subtle but significant shift in emphasis. As Holmes points out in *Training and Development*, this places competence outside the person.[13] No longer a quality *of* the person, managers move from *being* competent to *having* competences.

Some people are upset by this purists' view that competence is *external* to the person, that it is something a person *has* rather than *is*. On the other hand, we accept the idea that we can criticize someone's performance or ideas while stressing that we are not criticizing them personally. In TA (transactional analysis) terms, we say that 'people are OK', they have worth, value and dignity, though we may not accept what they *do*. So the separation does have some validity.

None the less, to speak of competence in this external way can appear to some people insensitive, indeed manipulative, even authoritarian. It might imply that a higher authority has found a better answer to performance than people themselves. It also suggests that it's only what you *do* that matters.

HEARTS AND SOULS

If Holmes's observed shift had not taken place and competence was still regarded as something people *are* and not what they *have*, that would remain a worry. It would still suggest a mechanistic view of what comprises a 'good' manager. But when we speak of a 'good' person we do not mean a 'competent' person. A good manager might not be a good person. And a good person might not be a good manager. We have divorced morals and motives from competence. Competence is not negative in this matter; it is merely neutral and arid. If we are to humanize the workplace, we need to find a complement to the management standards.

To use the analogy of smiling, if a customer-service employee's smile is false, we see through it and feel cheated. Although you can physically train your mouth muscles to smile, apparently you can't train your eyes (so I am told). Likewise, consulting, informing, negotiating, coaching and leading need to spring genuinely from the heart, otherwise we see through the outward behaviour and feel cheated. Earlier we saw how Vaill pointed out that learners know that trainers are 'messing with their heads as well as their hands' even though the trainers may imagine otherwise. Not only must we admit to the inevitability of this, but we cannot avoid being overtly and legitimately concerned with their hearts and souls too, that is, their motives, morals and cares.

Some of the CM's staunchest advocates accept this and say that the management standards should be used flexibly as a partial framework where helpful, but that the standards don't and can't purport to provide all the answers. At other times, the standards are promoted as the complete answer for all management development problems, and any suggested weakness brings a quick reposte.

THE DEMISE OF THE COMMAND HIERARCHY

Rather than 'managing' people's performance in the sense of controlling their behaviour, some instead prefer to speak of 'facilitating' it. But whatever the moral arguments, most bosses believe in and, let's be honest, enjoy (in the literal sense of deriving pleasure or satisfaction) a degree of control over their fellow human beings; and they may sometimes find it convenient to overlook the uniqueness of the individual.

But for some, the notion of MCI's key role of 'Managing people' is offensive nowadays. They see it as hierarchical, controlling, presumptuous and arrogant. At the more practical level, it can be argued to be unrealistic: two people with the same job description and identical training will perform differently for a variety of reasons, not least because they will attach different personal meaning to it.

Probably of more significance, behind MCI's 'Managing people' there appears to be an assumption that the future manager will continue to have direct hierarchical control over the people who produce work for that area of responsibility. But it is now widely accepted, and is becoming increasingly apparent, that managers will need to be able to work with people producing work for them but for whom they will have no responsibility (a feature in the collapse of the old-style 'command hierarchy', as Peter Drucker calls it). More and more functions will be outsourced – for reasons of quality more than economy.

Alliances and joint ventures will also require a new kind of people-management skill. Suppliers will need managing as partners not adversaries, Robert Heller asserts in *Management Today*.[14] Perhaps 'relationship management' is a better term for the skill.

Finally, there is still talk of managing a 'workforce'. Success will increasingly go to those with the ability to manage individuals, as their expectation for personal recognition and individual treatment grows, and as the acceptability and power of the collective declines.

A BOSSES' CHARTER

Functional analysis tends to support a top-down view of managing organizations – a cascading of purpose. But no longer is it only the slightly anarchic who might challenge this bosses' charter. Many now admit that organizations' scale, complexity, pace of change, technological evolution, and environmental circumstances, are such that bosses can only pretend to be in charge, know about and influence, let alone direct and control. For example, it is now commonplace in many organizations for bosses to ask their subordinates to propose their own objectives.

Apart from what is merely a practical way of running a business, this implies a degree of democratization of managers' world of work. Even at the strategic level one does not have to be particularly radical to argue that managers could behave more strategically and do not always need to wait for the top management to enunciate its strategy.[8]

In the same vein, many now accept the notion that leadership is something which any manager can demonstrate more of, not the unique preserve of formally recognized 'leaders' as such.

From this modern and value-driven perspective, functional analysis has a slightly old-fashioned 'following/obedient' feel to it more than a 'leading/proactive' one.

COMPETENCE FOR TRAINING OR DEVELOPING

This leads naturally to the question of considering the concerns of developers as opposed to trainers – a much neglected distinction.

Functional analysis seeks out a single, correct and highly defined answer – one which can be acted upon in isolation, be it appraisal, selection or training. It is something programmable. Development, on the other hand, includes extending managers in a personally focused way to be able to tackle their future and that of their business, much of which is unknown. Vaill speaks of managing in 'permanent white water', Mintzberg of 'the strange world of organizations'.[15] and Peters talks of 'chaos', 'turbulence' and 'necessary disorganization'.[16]

How can functional analysis help with such an uncertain future? The protagonists of competences argue that the basic elements of competence remain the same; and if you examine the words, that view appears to make sense. Whatever the changing scene and the particular context there will indeed remain the need to 'offer information and advice', 'lead discussions', and so on. But if you accept the argument that you can only meaningfully acquire and practise competence in the real world of a whole, unique and particular context, then the changes taking place outside *do* matter and must impact on the CM's work.

We may well know managers who possess the component skills (and the qualifications) but who cannot adapt them to the current climate. This requires knowing how to apply them, to whom, in conjunction with what, and at the expense of doing what else instead. In other words, having complete competence raises questions of balance, appropriateness, judgement, sensitivity, recognizing contradictions, assessment of risk, stress levels, the situation's current norms, the amount of time available, and many other considerations, all at the same time.

Training people in some of the basic elements may be relevant as a foundation, but if we fail to see the distinction between development and training, there is a danger that the functionally derived competences may be assumed to meet all needs and all contexts.

UNITARY VERSUS PLURALIST MODEL

Just as there can be more than one way to be systematic about training, there is more than one way to manage. There is no one best way. Any search for a universal truth will be elusive and misguided, as may the search for too definitive a route plan or methodology. This is true of development means and products and of the practice of management itself. Vaill puts it well:

it is not wise to plan too intently on getting to any particular place at any particular time in any particular way. Not only is it certain that these plans will not be realized; more importantly, we won't be able to enjoy or have much influence on the ride we are actually having.[6]

Looking at products, for pre-competence and non-competence packages the field was quite wide for open learning writers and other providers to judge for themselves what content and level was appropriate. Now, the externally imposed management standards for competence-based products are expected to narrow this range. This is arguably a mixed blessing. Yet, aside from the end objectives, there remains considerable scope for differences between two or more providers' views on the content, design and presentation of competence-driven materials.

Of deeper concern than a narrowing in the range of hard and soft products is a narrowing of our definition of management. Yet it can be argued that management has until recently lacked sharpness of definition, and that the setting down of management standards meets a long-standing need. On the other hand, many people are more comfortable with a pluralistic approach to management. For them a wide range of products based on different assumptions about managing offers choice. It may offer sloppy thinking.

Whatever your point of view, the official adoption of one competence model, and within it a single definition of competence in the generic management standards, inevitably implies both a move towards a more unitary view of the competent manager, and a narrowing in the range of training options.

Whether or not there is such a beast as the universal manager, it is claimed that this degree of prescription is needed if one is to achieve a uniform, portable management qualification nationwide – one of the reforms' aims. How else can prospective employers easily weigh the relevance of applicants' qualifications against their own organization's management requirements?

It is an acknowledged truism that the very basics of management remain the same while management is changing rapidly. The point that seems to be missed, as Rosemary Stewart observes, is 'that management is very different in different jobs, organisations and countries'.[17] Without necessarily casting aside parts of the competence model which can handle the basics, we need at the very least to bolt on something more sophisticated to address the variability in the contexts.

LURKING BUREAUCRACY

One danger is that the process of defining, laying down and monitoring the generic standards will become excessively bureaucratic. This is a risk of which MCI is aware and wishes to guard against. It has achieved much by way of presenting the management standards in user-friendly formats. It is also quite clear that the management standards are there only to serve as a guide or framework, which companies can take, develop and build upon as they wish.

Despite these good intentions, the tail could still wag the dog. We saw it in the 1970s with the Industry Training Boards' prescriptions for *systematic training*. In one industry, if you didn't complete 17 steps in a precise order, you had to pay the price. This meant sacrificing your firm's levy!

The fear of a bureaucratic monster in this area seems less likely now than 20 years ago. In spite of the criticisms, there is arguably less dogma associated with defining management standards than there was with past attempts to define systematic training. And – for now at least – it is largely free of an overtly threatening monetary dimension. Pleasingly, Constable and McCormick advised that 'management training should not be financed by special taxation and levy systems on employers'.[2] But in the background there lurk party manifestos, drafted by the more interventionist politicians, encouraged by trade unions, which urge a return to the days of training levies (for the highest motives – the nation's good – of course). If this happens, definitions of what earns grants or exemptions from levy could again be engulfed in bureaucracy.

Those who argue for this type of centralist approach to stimulate training quality or quantity suffer from a naïve and myopic view of training's efficacy. There are a number of rather higher-leverage variables to raising organizational effectiveness, such as the reward system, the working climate, the structure, and so on.[12]

SIMPLICITY MASKING COMPLEXITY

The earlier description of MCI's model showed its apparent simplicity. The statements of what comprises a manager's job when broken down into these component parts seem so self-evident that they are hardly worth stating. Is that really all managing is reduced to?

In a sense, that is the strength of the management standards; like 'motherhood' they are difficult to argue against. But in another sense that is also their weakness and what exposes them to the greatest risk of downfall in the long run. When we experience the best of managers we see (but may have difficulty describing) much more than elements of mere competence. Some of what a good manager does may also be individualistic and is therefore excluded from the list in the name of standardization. We further experience a skilled manager's ability to integrate the whole not into what a *manager does*, but into *management*.

However, notwithstanding the apparent obviousness of the elements of competence, many managers do *not* in fact always comply with simple items like 'advice and information offered proactively' (though they might when assessed!). This is not because they don't know it's expected of them, don't know how, or lack the training. It is because it serves their selfish purposes not to. Machiavelli would have no issue with that. While the standards are employer-led and are what employers want for the good of their companies, that same motivation will not always coincide with how individual managers see their own interests. *Can do* is not the same as *choose to do*.

MCI'S ROLE

Having won the tender to be the government's Lead Body for the field of management, the competence die was cast. In 1988 the then Manpower Services Commission had 'envisaged that future qualifications should be based on the "outcomes" of learning or the expected performance, rather than the "inputs" or what should be taught'.[18] (Note that this was a position with regard to occupations generally, rather than management ones in particular.) That model was accepted by the NCVQ as the basis of awarding the new qualifications, and the MSC (for the Employment Department) retained responsibility for developing the standards; so for the field of management it was highly likely that we would end up with something like the management standards.

But MCI's single-minded espousal of the cause of management competences is one of the controversial issues, as there was and is freedom of manoeuvre within MCI's general role – both alongside competences and how and where energy is focused in developing them. MCI may lay itself open to that familiar accusation of being 'a one-club golfer'.

Another issue is where MCI hands over to the trainers. The original view of MCI was that it was to have no role in carrying out training itself. It was to limit its activities to putting in place the right conditions for management to take advantage of training opportunities and achieve relevant qualifications. But MCI is straying away from that remit, albeit in a quite natural and laudable attempt to develop its own products, and is now effectively selling training materials itself.

For example, MCI produces and markets *The Effective Manager*, which takes the form of a small ring-bound personal organizer. As well as containing all the usual components, there are some quality checklists on good practice. That for 'Leading meetings' is shown in Figure 6.1. This venture into what amounts to training materials is controversial because it brings MCI's products into direct competition with those of other companies whose products pass through MCI's product approval process. But in functional analysis terms, it is very easy to see how MCI's activities have developed in this manner. If you keep breaking down a manager's role by asking the question 'and what would you need to do in order to achieve that?' you eventually have a how-to-do rather than a what-to-do. The two become indistinguishable.

For example, to hold an effective meeting you have to follow all the points listed in Figure 6.1. If you then publish this breakdown as a standard of good practice, you are effectively selling a training aid. As MCI itself says, 'By using this standard, you can expect to save time, make better decisions and improve your communications.' If these benchmarks of good practice are dressed up in bureaucratic jargon they look like management standards; if they are rewritten to be user friendly, they look like training materials. You can hardly condemn MCI for attempting the latter approach.

However understandable MCI's own evolution is, there remain two questions:

1. If other commercial companies are already producing and selling rather similar training materials, is this what the government set up MCI to do?
2. How ethical is this latest MCI activity while it has a hold over its competitors through its product approval process? *Quis custodiet ipso custodes?*

On the other hand, it would be unreasonable to confine MCI to a role circumscribed by the management standards, especially since it no longer enjoys a large government subsidy. Like a commercial enterprise, it has to develop or die. But there are other fields of management development which are crying out for

FIGURE 6.1 MCI GOOD PRACTICE CHECKLIST: LEADING MEETINGS

1. **Be clear about the purpose of the meeting** – do not call a meeting if there is a better way to solve a problem or make a decision.

2. **Invite the appropriate people to attend** – only invite those people who have something to contribute or gain, but make sure you invite all those people who are required to make a decision.

3. **Allow time for preparation** – carefully prepare how you will lead the meeting and talk to the other members; circulate papers in advance so everyone can be well prepared.

4. **Clearly state the purpose of the meeting at the outset**.

5. **Allocate sufficient time** – set a fixed time for the meeting to begin and end and allocate time appropriately for each item under discussion.

6. **Encourage all members of the meeting to contribute**.

7. **Discourage unhelpful comments and digressions**.

8. **Summarize** – summarize the discussion at appropriate times and allocate action points at the end of each item.

9. **Take decisions** – make sure that decisions are within the meeting's authority, that they are recorded accurately and passed on promptly to the appropriate people.

10. **Evaluate the meeting** – allow time at the end of the meeting to evaluate whether the purpose of the meeting has been effectively achieved.

Reproduced by courtesy of MCI

more attention, more strategic issues than purely tactical ones like how well managers run meetings, into which it would be less contentious for MCI to move.[12]

ACTIVITY 6.1

Work out where you stand on each of the concerns and criticisms raised in this chapter about the competence movement.

- How do you consider the practice of management is best learned: by mastering small components or by a more integrated and holistic approach?
- If you are using bought-in services, what approach do your providers take? How do they attempt to overcome some of the problems of the kind identified?
- Does your interest lie in learners acquiring a generic foundation of basic skills, or more advanced managerial artistry and judgement?

REFERENCES

1. John Constable (1991) 'A Management Charter or Chartered Managers?', in Mick Silver (ed.) *Competent to Manage – Approaches to Management Training and Development*, London: Routledge, pp. 228–32.
2. John Constable and Roger McCormick (1987) *The Making of British Managers*, Corby: British Institute of Management.
3. Charles Handy *et al*. (1987) *The Making of Managers*, London: National Economic Development Office, Pitman.
4. Charles Handy (1989) *Times Higher Education Supplement*, 10 March.
5. John Burgoyne (1989 'Creating the Managerial Portfolio', *Management Education and Development*, London: Association of Management Education and Development, **20** (1).
6. Peter Vaill (1989) *Managing as a Performing Art: New Ideas for a World of Chaotic Change*, Oxford: Jossey-Bass, pp. 33–48, 85–6, 143.
7. John Burgoyne (1989) *Management Development: Context and Strategies*, Aldershot: Gower.
8. David H. Freedman (1992) 'Is Management Still a Science?', *Harvard Business Review*, November-December.
9. Peter Senge (1990) *The Fifth Discipline: The Art and Practice of the Learning Organization*, London: Century Business, p. 3.
10. James Gleick (1988) *Chaos: Making a New Science*, London: Heinemann, p. 8.
11. Louis Lataif (1992) 'MBA: Is the Traditional Model Doomed?', *Harvard Business Review*, November–December, p. 128.
12. William Tate (1995) *Developing Corporate Competence: A High-Performance Agenda for Managing Organizations*, Aldershot: Gower.
13. Len Holmes (1990) 'Trainer Competences: Turning the Clock Back?', *Training and Development*, April.
14. Robert Heller (1994) 'The Manager's Dilemma', *Management Today*, January.
15. Henry Mintzberg (1989) *Mintzberg on Management: Inside our Strange World of Organizations*, New York: The Free Press.
16. Tom Peters (1992) *Liberation Management: Necessary Disorganization for the Nanosecond Nineties*, London: Macmillan.
17. Rosemary Stewart (1991) *Managing Today and Tomorrow*, London: Macmillan.
18. Manpower Services Commission (1988) *Introduction to Occupations Standards Programme*, Sheffield: Employment Department.

7

GETTING THE BEST FROM MBAs

OVERVIEW

This chapter examines the current MBA scene and some of the practical problems which companies and students experience with it, including the comments of critics. Employer options are then considered, leading to advice on how best to manage MBAs.

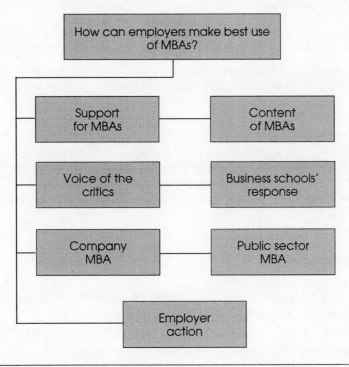

INTRODUCTION

MBAs (degrees of Master in Business Administration) attract more comment – and some say funding – than they deserve, judging by both their actual and potential impact on Britain's economic prospects. Their high profile, under gloom or boom, seems odd when set alongside other performance-enhancing initiatives like Total Quality Management (TQM) and 'empowerment', which imply a need for workforce-wide training – the antithesis of the élitist approach to management education.

But one way or another, MBA programmes are important, and will remain so; and companies have to sort out their response to them, just as business schools have to take up a sensible position in the new market.

It is also quirky that the amount of active support for MBAs for some time appeared inversely proportional to both the amount of criticism the courses (and many of their students) received and the strength of the economy! Perhaps the adage 'all publicity is good publicity' offered an explanation. So too, I imagine, did the acquisitive mood of the late 1980s/early 1990s, enlivened by what seemed for a while to be the only accepted passport to career progress or security.

'More MBAs' was one of the themes of the time. Many of the developments that took place – particularly in volume – we can attribute to the Constable and McCormick report referred to earlier. It called for a rapid expansion in MBA programmes towards a target of 10 000 graduates by the late 1990s. To combat the amateur base and tradition of British management, the report also urged the setting up of a Diploma in Business Administration (DBA), likened to an apprenticeship or articles of management. Access to both courses was to be 'made more easily available to working managers through the provision of part-time, modular courses involving a careful melding of academic and work-based study'.

The main thrust of the various commentaries at the time was that the providers of management education needed to make their product more relevant, and the consumers needed to offer more support. This now seems rather one-sided and unfair. While the business schools clearly could do better, so could employers. This bias appears to be somewhat overlooked; at the end of this chapter, I suggest a set of practical action points for employers.

SUPPORT FOR MBAs

Notwithstanding any partiality, as a result of the upsurge in comment, and following their mauling in the early 1980s, MBAs went from strength to strength if numbers were anything to go by. According to an Institute of Management survey, they increased by 250 per cent as the economy was sliding into recession.[1]

The number of colleagues at work whom one found holding MBAs added a feeling dimension to the hard data, which then had a ratchet effect on the more ambitious ladder-climbers. The race was on to get yourself an MBA, simply to keep up – and *only* an MBA it would appear from the advertisements. MBAs became popular with career-minded students, and with many employers who perhaps never fully understood them or genuinely took them to their heart.

Whether generalists or specialists, and regardless of function, such was the pressure on aspiring managers to acquire MBAs that other higher-education options were being squeezed out and regarded career-wise as a poor second. That was not because of the wonders of an MBA: universities and students alike were mostly responding to what they saw as a competitive market. But in this form it was never in the wider interest. The MBA needed reining in.

For a while it seemed all might be well. Perhaps faults *had* been addressed to the satisfaction of employers, judged by the numerical support. But then realism reappeared. As a result, the phenomenal rate of growth now seems to have passed its peak. In the wake of the recession, and despite the economy picking up, the MBA is in marginal decline and suffering from falling esteem, with around 5–25 per cent fewer student enrolments.

There may possibly be a natural lag in the system operating here – both in slowing down in the late 1980s and in increasing now. But there are other forces at work too. Among them no doubt, a feeling of saturation in the falling middle management job market. Those jobs won't come back at the same rate as the rest of the economy. Peter Drucker points out,

> the world is not in recession but going through a period of transition, and adapting to that transition is one of the greatest challenges facing managers. ... The problem is not that there are too many MBAs in the business world. The problem is, have they really learned anything? [2]

Volume change *per se* is not the most interesting feature in the MBA marketplace. More important, employers have lost some of their faith in MBAs, and they don't do as much as they might to help themselves. And there is confusion about the best way to meet the needs of the future.

There were a number of changes and improvements during the expansion period, such as the growth of the 'company MBA', which we look at in a moment. There were some attempts to strike a better balance between training and education, between theory and practice, between meeting individuals' needs and those of their employers. Yet many of the programmes offered still don't address some of the more fundamental criticisms.

The debate has since moved on and become informed by the power of employers through government initiatives and by the promotion of the alternative competence model. We shall examine the range of views so that you can decide where you stand and what place, if any, MBAs should have in your own company's development strategy.

THE MBA CONTENT

First, very briefly, what is the MBA supposed to be?

There is no fixed curriculum, but there is broad acceptance of what the heart of the MBA should comprise:

O   **Management skills** in the broadest sense, including management science, quantitative methods, accountancy, interpersonal skills and organization behaviour.

O   **Functional management**: human resources, marketing, operations, finance, etc., sometimes with options for specialists.

O   **Strategy**: strategic management, business policy and environment, etc.

As Colin Talbot of South Bank University explains, this model has been under pressure since the late 1980s from government-sponsored agencies and employers to give more recognition to functional management, demonstrable skills, short-term results, modular structures – all part of the so-called employer-led reforms and the competence movement.[3]

WHAT PEOPLE SAY ABOUT MBAs

From both the statistics and the publicity, there seems to be a love-hate relationship with MBAs. Let's remind ourselves of some of the comments that people make about them.

With a deft touch, Tom Lupton, a former director of the Manchester Business School, takes a sideswipe when he observes:

> The curious thing is that when one compares the curriculum of MBA programmes with the work managers actually do, the problems they encounter and their needs for skill and competence to resolve them, one always feels a certain unease at not seeing as many connections as there might reasonably be expected to be.[4]

Peter Vaill echoes one of the most frequently heard criticisms of MBA students:

> They can't manage, aren't interested in managing, think 'management' is essentially a process of rationally analysing 'problems' and deciding on 'optimal solutions' and are generally insensitive to the nuances of organizational cultures and the deep human dilemmas that lie just below the surface of the apparently well-managed organization.[5]

More recently, Louis Lataif, writing in *Harvard Business Review*, offers constructive criticism of both business schools and business itself:

> people and organizations can only accomplish what is permitted by the management control systems under which they operate. So long as the controls are functionally oriented, we will not be fully competitive. Major breakthroughs in time to market, investment, piece cost, and quality come horizontally across an organization, not vertically through individual, isolated functions. And it is our business schools that have not taught how to manage process across functions!
>
> Schools of management must change. They must begin teaching the practice of management as it should be, not as it has been. Certainly, we must continue teaching the basic functions of business, but in a context that produces an understanding of the interdependencies of organizational functions. We must develop the financial control tools and the organizational structures that encourage individual behavior benefiting the entire system.[6]

In 'Training Managers, Not MBAs', Henry Mintzberg offers us:

tomorrow's captains of industry are left with the impression that good managers pronounce from on high based on a quick reading of a pithy report, without ever leaving their offices, while everyone else scurries around down below doing the implementing.[7]

Again, Mintzberg – always happy to paddle alone until others want to join him – is damning in his full frontal assault on the cream of American MBA providers:

> these schools confer advantages on the wrong people. They parachute inexperi-enced people with mercenary intentions into important positions. For the most part, these people are committed to no company and no industry but only to personal success, which they pursue based on academic credentials that are almost exclusively analytic, devoid of in-depth experience, tacit knowledge, or intuition. ...
>
> Stanford takes people, many with a minimum of experience, and pumps them full of theory, which they cannot possibly understand in context, because there is no context, neither personal nor in the professor's head.
>
> That is bad enough. But Harvard goes one step further. It takes people who know nothing about a particular company and then insists, based on 20 pages of verbalized and numerical abstractions, that they pronounce on it in the classroom. The students have never met any of the company's customers, never seen the factories, never touched the products. ...
>
> Out come these students, committed not to particular industries or companies but to management itself as a means of personal advancement. They are para-chuted into companies at middle levels, with authority over people who know the customers, the factories, the products. In effect, two tiers of employees are created, the ones who know the situation but have no MBA, and the others with the opposite credentials – as their bosses![8]

Management Today comments on the findings of Her Majesty's Inspectorate that 'a majority of employers have doubts about the quality and relevance of the MBA offered by a growing number of institutions'.[9] They report on,

> disappointing experiences with MBA employees who failed to fit into the organ-isation, lacked interpersonal skills, proved arrogant, over-analytical, brought little benefit to the company and moved on after a short time.

(These latter observations, of course, also say something about the same employers' selection criteria and organizational arrangements!)

Some of the above comments contain an echo of Harold Leavitt's memorable criticism of the typical business school education, which he said:

> [transformed] well proportioned young men and women ... into critters with lopsided brains, icy hearts and shrunken souls.[10]

Citing the misplaced emphasis on 'strategy' as the prime example, the Institute of Management states that while

> traditional MBA courses have done an excellent job in imparting business knowledge, management theory and analytical tools ... a major mismatch remains between employer wants, student expectations, and the traditional business school fare. The academic content of MBAs has been pitched way beyond the requirements of their average 28-year-old managerial customer, while ignoring his need for the more basic tools of his trade. The tools and techniques which form the basis of the traditional MBA are important, but more so in the long term when a senior position has been attained. In the short term, an employer often finds him-self with an inexperienced, frustrated, expensive employee.

The director of the Judge Institute in Cambridge is reported in *Management Today* as saying:

> Management is about working together with other people to effect the business of an organisation … while analysis is important, it accounts for perhaps 10% of a manager's work. The other 90% is about implementation, about making things happen. Everybody knows this yet institutions do little or nothing to address interpersonal skills and merely provide inexperienced youngsters with a two-year escape from the practical experience they need most.[9]

No wonder we have seen companies trying to take more control and have witnessed a substantial growth in the company MBA. But there are dangers here too, particularly in the eyes of the academics, that 'when companies foot the bill, who can guarantee that academic standards will be maintained'.

AN APPROPRIATE RESPONSE

Universities are now going to amazing lengths to attract custom. Their open-access behaviour is laudable – especially where it means they show more interest in students' worldliness than merely in previous studies. But some university schools of management and business schools appear to be moving downmarket and some people fear that the competence movement could further encourage that process, or at least cause the universities to lose their distinctive educational role.

By way of example, to respond to the new market and try to attract more business, some university courses include modules on 'Finance for non-finance managers' and 'Assertiveness'. Such subjects (often unassessed) have considerable appeal to the world of business. But they are not what universities do best and are not at the heart of a management education. Skills like these are widely available in the open market, and it would be better to leave them there than to try to compete. Managers may need these skills, but the mistake is to assume that the business school, or even the MBA itself, must provide all-encompassing training and education, rather than accept a limited and distinctive remit.

THE COMPANY MBA

The most positive change in the MBA scene in recent years has been the increasing emphasis on company MBAs. In their survey *The Company MBA – Past and Future*, Kim Kennedy and Alex Mason show that 645 managers had graduated from such programmes by 1992.[11] The annual intake had risen from 248 in 1988 to 950 by 1992. The number of programmes on offer had increased from 20 in 1989 to 53 in 1992. The company MBA is a serious trend and many developers will want to consider it for their companies.

The survey covered the four ways of organizing a company MBA programme:

O   The **in-company MBA**: developed and run by an academic institution for the benefit of one specific company.

O The **consortium MBA**: developed and run by an academic institution for a group of participating companies.

O The **hybrid MBA**: with some elements of both the in-company and consortium formats.

O The **company-integrated MBA**: a company's own management development programme, developed and run by internal staff or external consultants, is accredited by an academic institution and provides credit points towards an MBA. This latter option requires participants to attend some form of top-up course in order to qualify for a full MBA.

The pros and cons of these formats are shown in Figure 7.1.

FIGURE 7.1 TYPES OF COMPANY MBA PROGRAMME: ADVANTAGES AND DISADVANTAGES

Model	Advantages	Disadvantages
In-company MBA	The company can make a substantial organizational input to the design and content.	The narrowness of the participant group and business context may limit innovative discussion.
Consortium MBA	A broad perspective (approaching that of the traditional MBA). Lower costs than in-company MBA.	Compromises are needed to make the design and content acceptable for all the participating companies.
Hybrid MBA	Some elements of above.	Some elements of above.
Company-integrated MBA	Can be highly tailored to suit the company. Can draw on teaching staff from more than one institution.	Low transferability value for participants.

The popularity of the wholly externally run in-company MBA and the wholly open traditional MBA programme centred on the business school seems to be in decline, according to the survey, when compared with the company-integrated MBA and the consortium MBA formats. The latter offer some of the external perspective virtues of the traditional MBA, either through other consortium members or the use of consultants sharing the teaching with academics.

Consulting companies which are active in the company-integrated MBA include Harbridge House, the Management Training Partnership (MTP) and TDA Consulting Ltd. Henley Management College dominates the company MBA market.

Some business schools are still wedded to some of the undoubted benefits of the general MBA format, but there is a trend towards tailoring courses to companies. Some offer both formats. It partly depends on your view of the market and who your customer is – the individual or the company. The latter seems to be winning.

The advent of MCI's facility to give credit to prior learning (APL), as discussed in Chapter 4, is an added time-saving bonus and provides a sound and cost-effective basis for identifying and constructing learning based on individual participants' assessed needs. Philip Lowe, writing in the *Professional Manager*, describes the company-integrated package as giving,

> the opportunity to design a management development programme which meets its own internal needs, while at the same time providing participants with the opportunity to obtain an academic qualification, through a combination of assessment of coursework, accreditation of prior learning, and a top-up programme to provide the balance of credit points.[12]

But these modern MBA programmes are not endorsed by AMBA, the Association for MBAs. AMBA requires at least 80 per cent of assessment by examination and will not accept the accreditation of prior learning. As a result, only 28 of the 92 UK providers of MBAs are accredited with AMBA. This penalizes students and favours the classic MBA, since the main high street banks will offer loans only for AMBA-supported programmes.

THE PUBLIC SECTOR

The traditional MBA has offered a broad management education, with the undoubted appeal of mixing managers from different companies and cultures. But this can fail to take sufficient account of either individual companies' needs or those of a given sector. One loser in the past has been the public sector, probably because it has shown very little interest in MBAs and most employers couldn't afford the sponsorship. That is changing a little now: the public sector, including education, is now an area of developing interest for MBA students, representing 10 per cent of qualified MBAs' employment, according to one survey. Given the amount of organizational change occurring in the civil service, in local government, in the health service and in education, that should not surprise us.

But the Local Government Management Board is wary:

> One of the big questions was [whether] a formal qualification, such as an MBA, was desirable for local authorities. The answer seemed to be no. Because local authorities are very different, management and training development is best developed in-house. ... There is also the equal opportunities angle: an MBA might be seen as an option for too few staff. The LGMB is more keen to see competence-based approaches to management development, such as the MCI's levels of achievement. MBAs have a part to play, but don't tell you much about a manager's competence.[13]

There are ways round these two chief concerns.

On the issue of inappropriate content and focus, Henley Management College, for example, offers a course with 25 per cent public service content. The intention is to strike a balance between the interest public service employees show in learning about the private sector, while at the same time recognizing that public sector decision-making and accounting systems are different.

On the lamentable lowest-common-denominator argument ('if we can't all have it, none should'), some companies run a self-nominating 'Open MBA' facility in parallel to the fast-trackers' version.

EMPLOYER ACTION

While the business schools could adapt more quickly to changing needs, many won't, either for reasons of principle or because they lack the teaching skills. Since there is more than one way to skin a cat, employers and students can usually find what they want if they look for it. But my main thesis is that employers themselves have much to do to get their own act together. Here are five practical suggestions.

1. Change the sponsorship criteria

One of the easiest actions would be for employers to reconsider how they select people to join MBA programmes. They should be much more restrictive than they have been hitherto, limiting sponsorship to people who have the following 'qualifications':

O   Substantial organizational and business experience.
O   A senior job which can utilize the more analytical skills.
O   Proven leadership and interpersonal abilities.
O   Demonstrated industry and company commitment.
O   Requisite intelligence.
O   Aged at least 30.

2. Be more flexible when advertising

Look for the above qualities when advertising for MBA-qualified managers. And don't limit yourself to MBAs. Too often we read adverts that *require* an 'MBA', but make no mention of comparable qualifications.

3. Broaden the range of sponsorship

Rather than bemoaning the content and output of the traditional MBA and trying to turn it into something that many universities cannot or will not deliver, compensate for it and complement it with a wider provision of alternative education, including the following:

O   More use of the Diploma in Business Administration.
O   Competence-based programmes leading to NVQ Levels 4 and 5.
O   Alternative master's programmes of a more specialized nature.

For many job-holders, an alternative programme of study is more relevant for their function, offering depth rather than across-the-board breadth.

4. Avoid 'ring-fencing' high-flyer groups

Avoid ring-fencing high-flyer groups so tightly that equally well-qualified current managers are overlooked, disadvantaged or cannot get onto the same career management and development discussion agenda. That is not to say that there won't necessarily be high-flyers, fast-trackers, or such formal schemes; only guard against applying processes exclusively to those people who are externally recruited on such a basis at a young age. The boundary needs to be flexible and the processes seamless. Otherwise, current high-potential managers will consider taking their services elsewhere.

5. Use the full range of MBAs available

Take account of the wide variety of MBAs on offer and tailor the needs of employees who are earmarked for MBA sponsorship accordingly. For some this might include the traditional MBA, company-specific programmes, part-time study, or distance learning.

ACTIVITY 7.1

If your company uses MBAs in one way or another, or is considering doing so, you may like to work through the good practice checklist of decisions in Figure 7.2.

FIGURE 7.2 MBA DECISIONS CHECKLIST

- Will your company have an influence on the design and content of a tailored MBA programme?
- Do you want your managers to study with other companies' managers or with your own?
- Do you want to be able to draw on teaching staff from more than one source, including consultants?
- How important is it that your MBA students have a high transferability through broad study?
- Would you prefer your managers' study to have a narrow single-business focus?
- How important is it to you that your MBA programme is AMBA endorsed?
- Does your organization culture value your senior managers having MBAs or equivalent qualifications?
- On what criteria are you selecting managers for MBA sponsorship and for employment?
- What is your company's record of making full and successful use of MBA recruited managers?
- What is your company's record when choosing to sponsor managers on MBA programmes?
- Are you making full use of alternatives to MBAs?
- Are you managing your high-flyers in a way that avoids adverse reactions?
- Have you considered the variety of MBA programme delivery methods available?

REFERENCES

1. *Management Today* (1992) 'Metamorphosis of the Manager', August.
2. Peter Drucker (1993) 'Drucker: The Change Challenge', *Professional Manager*, September.
3. Colin Talbot (1993) 'Twin Peaks? MBAs and the Competence Movement – A Tale of Two Courses', *Management Education and Development*, London: Association for Management Education and Development, **24** (4).
4. Tom Lupton (1984) 'The Functions and Organisation of University Business Schools', in Andrew Kakabadse and Sureash Mukhi, *The Future of Management Education*, Aldershot: Gower.
5. Peter Vaill (1989) *Managing as a Performing Art: New Ideas for a World of Chaotic Change*, Oxford: Jossey-Bass, pp. 33–4.
6. Louis Lataif (1992) 'MBA: Is the Traditional Model Doomed?, *Harvard Business Review*, November–December.
7. Henry Mintzberg (1989) 'Training Managers, not MBAs', *Mintzberg on Management: Inside our Strange World of Organizations*, New York: The Free Press, pp. 79–91.
8. Henry Mintzberg (1992) 'MBA: Is the Traditional Model Doomed?', *Harvard Business Review*, November–December.
9. Judith Oliver (1993) 'A Degree of Uncertainty', *Management Today*, June.
10. Harold Leavitt (1991) 'A Survey of Management Education', *The Economist*, March.
11. Kim Kennedy and Alex Mason (1993) *The Company MBA – Past and Future*, London: Harbridge House.
12. Phil Lowe (1994) 'The Company MBA – Past and Future', *Professional Manager*, January.
13. *The Independent on Sunday* (1993) 'Along the MBA Way, Public Services Management', 20 June.

PART THREE
OPEN LEARNING CHOICES FOR MANAGERS

❖

INTRODUCTION TO PART THREE

There seem few limits to what modern open learning techniques can accomplish. It was recently reported that a Czech woman taught herself through an open learning course to be one of only 100 fluent speakers of Cornish in the world! Open learners are used to having to talk to themselves during their studies, but to have to continue to do so afterwards is not normally the intended outcome – especially with language studies! Why did this amazing lady *want* to learn Cornish? More astonishing is *how*? (No Czech-lists, please!) And who considered the design of such a course economically viable? Perhaps it was a hoax – you can't believe everything you read in newspapers.

Anyway, here we are not looking at the learning of languages. We are interested only in the world of management. 'Only', he says? Management is neither prosaic nor narrow, as the range of open learning available for this audience testifies. What is on offer embraces single skill subjects like time management at one end of the continuum and several years' educational study towards an MBA at the other end. The range covers off-the-shelf national products and material tailor-made to suit particular companies. We are interested here in all of these.

Those who witnessed the programmed learning boom of the 1960s and 1970s know how 'solutions to all our problems' come and go. But currently many of the changes we see taking place in training themselves result from changing views about management itself and, of course, about economic reality. The axe fell on many large corporate training departments as a result of the early 1990s recession. New means of delivery were sought. In the case of British Telecom, for example, open learning is now the first choice for training. Rover has spent £2m setting up its own open learning mini-enterprise.

Part Three of the book reviews what is currently the biggest growth area in the field of management training and education and the most richly innovative, one in which Britain holds the lead. Did you know that there are now more MBA students using open learning programmes than there are on full- and part-time courses put together? Or that the Open University Business School trains more managers than any other European school of management? Clearly, open learning choices for managers are blossoming.

Open learning's antecedents have a long history in the UK, going back over one hundred years, perhaps because of the country's individualistic culture. In more recent times, information technology has joined hands with educational technology in a big way. IT has transformed individual study into a multi-media networking experience. In turn, educational technology has transformed training films into structured learning beamed into your own home.

Creativity isn't limited to the products' contents: check the packaging to see what is changing; read the seductive advertisements for open learning MBAs. This represents an attempt to create a new learning culture. Open learning isn't just another fad: it holds one of the master keys to today's movement towards a more self-managed learning and continuous development culture.

This Part will help you better understand the choices facing you – both micro and macro – and the basis upon which your decisions should be exercised. Beyond choosing your provider, what are the choices open to you? An important element is what to anchor the learning to. At the micro level the emphasis can be on the individual, in which case it is tactical and transactional. At the other level it can have its roots in the company's agenda for change, in which case it is strategic and potentially transformational.

Five chapters comprise Part Three. The journey starts by providing a foundation of understanding and a common language on the 'what' and 'how' of learning. Those already fully familiar with the field of open learning will find the short introductory Chapter 8, 'The Language of Open Learning', very basic.

The same can be said of Chapter 9, 'The Key Features of Open Learning', which outlines the values and philosophies which drive the open learning approach, movement, method – call it what you will – and explains what it looks like. Readers who are familiar with this field may want to skip parts of it.

Chapter 10, 'Supporting Open Learning', offers advice on the various means and systems used with and within open learning in order to support it and give its users – individual learners and organizations – the best chance of success.

Chapter 11, 'Open Learning Providers', helps readers understand the range of players in the field, how they are differentiated and what they offer, and how to establish their credentials. We cover issues, confusions, dilemmas, needs and risks inherent in any prospective purchase of open learning for managers. Here we examine the choice between a standard product line or specially tailored products; opting for nationally driven initiatives or company specific ones; aiming to obtain qualifications or trying to solve problems.

Finally, Chapter 12, 'The New Technology', discusses how such developments as interactive video and computer-mediated communications are changing the face of open learning, and considers whether they are the equivalent of 'go-faster stripes' or provide real rather than illusory improvements.

8

THE LANGUAGE OF OPEN LEARNING

OVERVIEW

This chapter first explains how the terms training, education and development are given precise meanings. It then helps readers understand the sometimes subtle differences between the various forms of open learning.

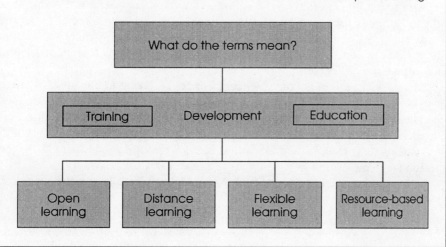

INTRODUCTION

The world of management education is awash with jargon, fashion and slogans. The problem is how to distinguish reality from hype. As a noun, adjective and verb, 'learning' appears unstoppable. Thankfully. As it gradually loses its status as a slightly uncomfortable buzz-word, we now find many applications:

○ Learning from experience
○ Learning without walls

○   Learning throughout life
○   Learning by doing
○   Learning organizations
○   Learning styles
○   Learning environment
○   Learning outcomes

There seems no doubt that 'learning' has at last gained respectability and wide-spread appeal, having real substance, meaning and utility. The word is now firmly rooted in the 'learning business'. Try to imagine the oxymoron 'open training'. That brings home both the power and the sense of the increasing switch from 'training' to 'learning'.

But the language issue reaches well beyond 'learning', so we'll begin by un-ravelling the jargon to help find the way through the labyrinth which educators have such a gift for constructing.

TRAINING

The term 'training' is often used somewhat loosely where people are talking about the full range of learning experiences – either because the word serves better than 'education' or 'development' as a convenient umbrella term where nice distinc-tions don't matter, or because they use 'training' rather casually where they don't appreciate the differences.

Because of its inherent convenience, there are occasions in this book where the use of 'training' in its broad meaning finds favour and avoids long-windedness, paralleling practice in other books. But where the context allows it, the term 'learning' is used in preference. Wherever there is a need to be precise about the form of learning, the use of more distinct terms is clearly desirable, and I have tried to adhere to the meanings given in these introductory pages.

In 'Management Education for Real', Roger Bennett explains the distinctions. He begins by defining training as:

> a process that is concerned with the acquisition of specific skills to do particular activities or jobs. Thus, management training will be geared towards helping a manager carry out a particular function or set of activities within that function.
>
> Management education can be contrasted with this in that it is a process con-cerned with the acquisition of knowledge and skill which fits a manager to take on a role in management. It is thus more general and broad based than management training yet may be concerned with the development of certain skills. It therefore overlaps with training.
>
> Development is seen as a means of fitting and helping an individual to take on jobs at different levels or in different spheres of management in general. It may thus embrace both training and education activities.[1]

The Manpower Services Commission's *Glossary of Training Terms* ('learning terms' might be better nowadays!) defines training as:

> a planned process to modify attitude, knowledge or skill behaviour through learning experience to achieve effective performance in an activity or range of

activities. Its purpose, in the work situation, is to develop the abilities of the individual and to satisfy the current and future manpower needs of the organisation.[2]

Another way of distinguishing training from education and development is to consider training (like teaching) as connoting something *done to* or *available to* people. It generally implies practical, cognitive and skills-based learning intended to produce a relatively short-term payoff for its sponsor. Whereas learning, education and development suggest what is *experienced by* people and hoped-for *beneficial outcomes* with a greater leap of faith required about transfer to the workplace.

EDUCATION

'Education' has a broader and mostly cognitive meaning, more centred on the person than the employer, irrespective of, and rather than, a precise or current job. With education there is more scope for the person to choose why, how and when to apply the learning.

The Manpower Services Commission's own definition supports this, viewing education as

> activities which aim at developing the knowledge, skills, moral values and understanding required in all aspects of life.[2]

The outputs from education (except in the sense of formal qualifications) will generally be less apparent or tangible than with training, and there is generally more freedom to think.

This holds implications for a range of important moral issues. For example, how much do sponsoring organizations actually *want* their managers to feel free to think – and therefore to *challenge* rather than *do*? Which raises the crucial dilemma of whether to train or educate. But such philosophical issues lie outside the scope of what is essentially a practical book. They are, however, tackled in this book's companion volume *Developing Corporate Competence: A High-Performance Agenda for Managing Organizations*.[3] While frequent overuse of the word training, particularly in national debate, has led to some loss of distinction with education, I do not agree with those who regard the distinction as unimportant.

DEVELOPMENT

Some people and some books use the term 'development' to mean processes for enhancing individuals' potential for future jobs. This book rejects that hard distinction between present and future, not least because the present is so fluid that it merges with the uncertain future. As a consequence, no manager's current job and its environment can be regarded as sufficiently static for the job-holder not to benefit from development. That old way of viewing development also implied that the alternative to development for the future was training and education for the present. But that limited role for training and education similarly breaks down.

I take 'development' to encompass a wider range of learning and personal growth experiences beyond formalized learning settings. Whilst it may include training and education, it also embraces planned changes in job responsibilities, assignments, secondments, cultural acclimatization and coaching, for example.

The *aim* of much development (as opposed to its various *activities*) will be to move towards a different state of being or functioning, as Mike Pedler and Tom Boydell conceive it.[4] But I question whether they draw too sharp a distinction when they regard learning as something quite separate from development; namely, 'an increase in knowledge or a higher degree of an existing skill'. As I see the relationship between the two, learning is both a root and also a route concomitant of the development journey.

OPEN LEARNING

An industry, a movement or an ideal?

Two of the best known specialists in this field, Roger Lewis and Doug Spencer in *What is Open Learning?* offer the following definition:

> 'Open learning' is a term used to describe courses flexibly designed to meet individual requirements. It is often applied to provision which tries to remove barriers that prevent attendances at more traditional courses, but it also suggests a learner-centred philosophy. Open learning courses may be offered in a learning centre of some kind or most of the activity may be carried out away from such a centre (e.g. at home). In nearly every case specially prepared or adapted materials are necessary.[5]

The term 'open learning' has tended to become the umbrella term used by most people. It has come to include distance learning, flexible learning, resource-based learning and materials-based learning. The mainland Europe equivalent term is 'open distance learning' (ODL).

Because of this generic practice, many people who use the expression 'open learning' do so loosely, making little or no attempt to distinguish the subtleties between open learning and distance learning which some purists on the provider side try to preserve.

Open learning is inspired by the concept of open access to learning, whatever the means of delivery. Some people do not necessarily associate it with any particular method of conveying information, but think of it as an *objective* or the embodiment of a set of open *values* about learning.

Some companies run what they call 'open learning centres'. In these centres, any of their employees (and in some cases even their families) can access a wide range of learning subjects and sometimes delivery methods. The car industry has led the way, with examples at Rover, Jaguar, Rolls Royce, Ford and Lucas. Rover has reputedly spent £2m setting up its own open learning mini-enterprise, Rover Learning Business. A number of organizations have launched open learning centres just for their managers.

Interpreting open learning in this broad way distinguishes it from the distance learning *method* (discussed later). It allows one to think of open learning as represented by a continuum with *open* at one end and *closed* at the other. Any particular instance of learning can then be placed on this continuum according to how open or closed it is. Figure 8.1 offers some abbreviated examples quoting from Michael Freshwater in *Training and Development*, covering both potential administrative constraints as well as educational ones.[6]

The trend is, of course, from more closed to more open. John Coffey in 1977 defined open learning systems simply as 'those which have removed the constraints which would otherwise make them closed'. So open and closed approaches are not equally balanced options. Closed approaches do not have their own inherently attractive and facilitative features, merely inevitable forms and formats as

FIGURE 8.1 OPEN VERSUS CLOSED LEARNING

	Very open	Very closed
FINDING OUT	Updated information constantly available.	Annual prospectus and leaflets.
GETTING ACCESS	Self assessment. Flexible diagnostic arrangements. Entry at any time.	Set entry requirements. Numbers limited (class, size, etc.). Fixed enrolment.
WHAT	Learning tailored to need. Learner formulates objectives. Modular.	Whole programme only. Objectives prior set. What the tutor decides is needed.
WHERE	Learner chooses (home, work, centre, college, etc.).	By visiting the establishment, i.e. training centre or college.
WHEN	When learner requires.	Fixed attendance times.
HOW	Choice of methods. Variety of media. Learner's pace.	Face-to-face contact with tutor. Classroom. Notes.
SUPPORT	Variety of methods: telephone, face-to-face, colleagues, friends. Guidance. At home or work.	Not during programme. Teachers and specialist trainers. Face-to-face only.
ASSESSMENT	Methods negotiated with learner. May be modular. May be competence-based. Ongoing feedback. Learner decides when.	Methods set by tutor. Overall assessment only. Formal examination. No feedback given. Assessment dates fixed.

a result of practical constraints – coupled with tradition, of course. Programmes and courses that consist primarily of face-to-face tutor contact can be attractive by virtue of this reason alone, even though they are closed.

However, even some face-to-face university courses are now designed to be open to quite a remarkable level (and I'm not referring only to the Open University) – open in access, modular format, timescale, and even elements of self-assessment.

In spite of all this, because the means of delivering the learning material in most cases of open learning is remote from the original source, open learning has for the most part been perceived more narrowly than the table implies, i.e. it has been closely identified with packs of distance learning material. To most people, they have come to mean much the same. The Open University has contributed to this perception.

However, there will be times when distance learning is an inappropriate tool for developing managers, yet the values of open learning will remain pertinent. It is therefore worth holding on to the distinction, while accepting the way 'open learning' is widely used generically, as indeed in this book.

Before we leave 'open learning', it is worth pointing out that devotees of open learning's key attributes – own pace, own time, own way, own place – argue that this is the way real learning inevitably and ultimately takes place, regardless of the mode of delivering new information to the learner within the total process. In other words, we learn our own way regardless of how we are taught. An interesting thought.

This frame of mind may in part explain the prediction, and perhaps also the hope, of some people that open learning will naturally evolve to the point where it ceases to exist only in a separately identifiable form. In other words, their hope is that open learning's *values* will endure and come to predominate.

DISTANCE LEARNING

Strictly speaking, distance learning is a subset of open learning. The term is used to signify a medium or learning methodology that is usually text-based and pursued alone. The material is followed at a distance from the original knowledge source, the teacher, trainer or the educational institution. It is at the opposite end of the continuum from face-to-face tuition.

Again, Lewis and Spencer offer a formal definition:

> Distance learning is a sub-category of open learning. Distance learning usually implies a geographical separation between learner and providing institution. The learner makes contact by post or telephone with the institution and with any tutor.[5]

In the most extreme form, distance learning materials are designed to avoid the need for face-to-face meetings between a tutor and learner, though this is becoming less common and its shortcomings are now well recognized. Distance learning is therefore undergoing change.

Development of learning theory in part accounts for this. The greatest advance in the best applications of distance learning is probably the development of more sophisticated support systems for learners. The term, however, is beginning to sound dated and is losing favour in some quarters.

As to its history, distance learning can be thought of as a natural successor to the correspondence course. But it is a world apart from the simple texts and crude feedback and advice associated with that medium. The use of the printed word is much changed in terms of the interactive component and general style.

Programmed instruction (or programmed learning) is another antecedent of distance learning, though individual learners were often placed in a group setting or classroom to have access to teaching-machines. Technology has moved on from those simple days and is a leading factor dictating the future – perhaps as much what it can do as what learners need or what companies can afford. The talk now is of 'multi-media', which we shall discuss in Chapter 12.

FLEXIBLE LEARNING

Flexible learning is probably currently the term most used in advertisements, because 'flexible' is a popular expression in other contexts such as 'flexible working opportunities', 'flexible contracts', etc. It conveys the implied range of benefits which spring from flexibility. These concern individuals' differing objectives, circumstances, ability levels, learning styles, routes through modular materials, pace, and accessibility to chosen resources.

The term is gaining favour with professional bodies who offer this medium as a route to gaining their qualifications and membership, such as the Institute of Personnel and Development. It is also gaining popularity as a blanket expression, replacing 'open learning' for most purposes and ousting 'distance learning'.

Flexible learning is broader and more diverse than either open learning or distance learning. Flexible learners will not necessarily work in isolation. Flexible learning can also incorporate various learning methods including independent learning, work-based learning, problem-based learning, experiential learning, active learning, etc. In particular, flexible learning describes a way of empowering learners to take more responsibility for their own learning and development.

The Employment Department gives an official definition of flexible learning:

> Flexible learning is the opening up of new opportunities for people to learn; it enables learners to study what they like, when and where they like, using whatever teaching media is best suited to them.[7]

RESOURCE-BASED LEARNING

The term 'resource-based learning', along with others such as 'materials-based learning', is gaining favour. It emphasizes the fact that increasingly diverse materials are replacing the lecturer as the means of input, as Julie Dorrell explains in *Resource-Based Learning – Using Open and Flexible Learning Resources for Continuous Development*.[8]

Resource-based learning is used both generically to embrace aspects of open learning, distance learning and flexible learning; and specifically in the context of library services and centres of open learning. In these centres, staff can learn in their own time and at their own pace, away from the distractions of telephones and colleagues. Such centres usually include video and audio equipment, computers, books and other text-based learning programmes.

REFERENCES

1. Roger Bennett (1984) 'Management Education for Real', in A. Kakabadse and S. Mukhi (eds) *The Future of Management Education*, Aldershot: Gower, pp. 218–36.
2. Manpower Services Commission (1981) *Glossary of Training Terms*, 3rd edn, London: HMSO.
3. William Tate (1995) *Developing Corporate Competence: A High-Performance Agenda for Managing Organizations*, Aldershot: Gower.
4. Mike Pedler and Tom Boydell (1985) *Managing Yourself*, London: Fontana.
5. Roger Lewis and Doug Spencer (1986) *What is Open Learning?*, London: CET Open Learning Guide No. 4.
6. Michael Freshwater (1986) 'How Open is Open?', *Training and Development*, April.
7. Employment Department (1992) 'Open Learning in Industry', *Insight*, **24** (Summer).
8. Julie Dorrell (1993) *Resource-Based Learning – Using Open and Flexible Learning Resources for Continuous Development*, Maidenhead, McGraw-Hill.

9
THE KEY FEATURES OF OPEN LEARNING

OVERVIEW

This chapter describes the most important features to be found in open learning. Some are so fundamental, they define open learning. Others are evident in good quality products.

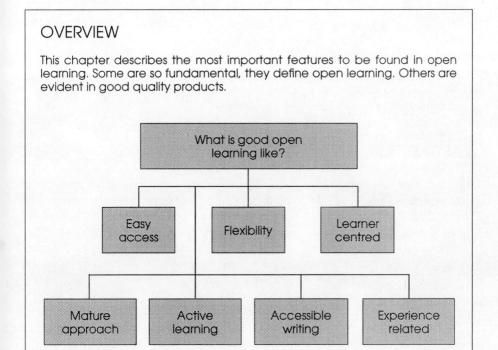

INTRODUCTION

> Open learning enables you to learn
>   what you like,
>   when you like,
>   where you like,
>   at the pace you like.

This says it in a nutshell. The implied values here are those of the learner. Open learning is much more than a medium. Its proponents hold strong values. They are motivated foremost by open learning's accessibility. It is an *including* form of learning.

The values are also those of the marketplace. Our educational institutions are busily acquiring marketing managers to entice learners onto their programmes. Open learning is a world apart from the hurdles which are the business of admissions boards. The modern and 'new' universities can be found advertising higher degrees 'without going to business school'. Want an MBA? Then 'why don't you choose one or two [courses] today to get you started'.

Some university advertisements explain that 'you don't need any existing qualifications, only the ability to learn'. Admission is on the basis of a learner's ability to benefit from the course, rather than on high levels of attainment in some previous examinations.

You want a qualification? 'For certification, buy the course, study, pass the exam and receive the certificate.' In one example, the reader is encouraged to fill in the Freepost reply saying:

> YES! Please send me the Heriot-Watt University MBA course(s) ticked below, at the price shown. Guarantee: if I am not satisfied I can return my course(s) within 10 days of receipt for a full, no quibble refund.

EASY ACCESS

Do such advertisements make you wince? They certainly take one's breath away. Here surely is evidence that the marketeers have taken over from the educationalists. Buying education from the Sunday newspaper supplement has become much the same as ordering a limited edition porcelain figurine for the mantleshelf – probably for around the same price. To cynics these sales pitches represent over-commercial approaches designed to separate fools from their money. But to the more open-minded, they are a breath of fresh air.

So entry to open learning is free of the restrictions and barriers in pre-entry criteria which typify traditional education channels and which can prevent or dissuade potential learners. In particular, open learning allows access to higher education to those who might otherwise be, or have been, denied it – by convention, by circumstance, by ability, by time of life, and so on. Safeguards apart, the spirit which this open approach engenders is redolent of a real learning culture in society – something lacking in the UK in the past.

FLEXIBILITY

Ease of access is made possible by open learning's flexibility with regard to venue and timing, and its ability to accommodate learners' various abilities, styles and needs.

Open learning meets the needs of people who can't attend a study centre for health, distance, transport or shift-work reasons. It appeals to employees who don't wish to take, or who can't take time off during the working day. And it brings a common training approach to nationwide multi-site employers.

Open learning circumvents the problems of conventional fixed-size courses that are over-subscribed, or courses that have already begun.

Key value words in open learning include 'freedom' – not least freedom of time, place and method – and 'choice'. Using an apt analogy, we can say:

> Traditional learning offers table d'hôte.
> Open learning offers you à la carte.

A la carte menus usually carry a premium. You pay for choice. But it seems to be economically attractive to many companies, especially where either very small or very large numbers of learners are concerned. Costs have been judged to be around 60 per cent that of traditional forms of learning, especially when taking workplace release into account.

A study into the economics of open learning was carried out by the Open University and Coopers & Lybrand by examining a number of companies' experiences.[1] It showed the range of savings to be made.

LEARNER CENTRED

Traditional means of learning are centred on the teacher. A teacher's style and pace have to be accepted by the learners. Teachers take the important decisions on behalf of their group. The teaching strategy is that which suits the teacher. The teacher decides the objectives and the learning sequence. And a teacher's natural ego state, when combined with the normal adrenaline flows in the teaching setting, tends to exaggerate the teacher-centredness.

Open learning avoids this. The teacher is no longer the source and channel of knowledge. Tutors are one form of resource among many. Their role switches from being the *sage on the stage* to the *guide on the side*, as one commentator put it. Input comes from a variety of materials. Those who produce the materials constantly put themselves in the position of their learners in order to devise ways of forcing their learners to interact with the material in a personalized way which is appropriate for them.

Open learning in its most flexible form allows learners to choose packages and sequences of learning to suit their pace and requirements, empowering them to be active participants rather than passive observers in the learning process. In other words, the learner takes the lead in establishing the agenda.

However, where professional courses are being followed or national qualifications are sought, then these programmes remain provider-led. As Christopher Bond puts it, they make the assumption that 'all learners require the same knowledge base to function competently and leave little room for creativity and exploration by the learner'.[2]

But there is a negative aspect to this degree of learner-centredness. In a classroom setting good teachers respond in real time to what is happening. They sense the mood, perceive difficulties and change their plans. They recapitulate, intervene and vary speed in a way that is highly learner centred. Particularly in distance learning settings in the home, learners may become stuck and waste considerable time going down a blind alley.

MATURE APPROACH

Traditional teaching can be viewed rather like parent–child relationships. The teacher is expert. The learners are dependent on the teacher to receive the expert knowledge. It is therefore easy to blame the teacher.

Compare this with open learning. The process is very adult and learners take more responsibility for themselves. In part they have to, since most learning takes place without the supervision of the teacher. But in addition to this, open learning encourages learners to identify for themselves what they lack and when learning has been accomplished.

The need to be self-responsible can cause organizations to question whether their employees are ready for open learning. They may be more mature than this patronizing attitude claims. In any case, access to open learning can stimulate a greater responsibility for one's own learning and development.

Assessment with open learning is also different. In traditional education the teacher is assumed to be a better judge than the learner. But it is not difficult to pull the wool over the teacher's eyes. You don't fool yourself, however. We are used to deferring to teachers for assessment, but you are the best source of feedback to yourself.

Learners probably know what grades they deserve better than their teacher does. In open learning much assessment is a form of self-assessment as a result of questions and exercises written into the materials. And unlike conventional approaches to learning, open learners can choose when they are ready for formal assessment.

ACTIVE LEARNING

Open learning is not a passive activity like reading a conventional book. To make progress the learner continually has to take action. The more active the better. The workbook is to a textbook what a workshop is to a lecture.

Professor Phil Race of the University of Glamorgan[3] advises that the tasks which learners may be called upon to do might include the following:

deciding	defending	suggesting	planning
choosing	attacking	illustrating	exploring
prioritizing	backing	explaining	fault-finding
summarizing	proposing	expressing	criticizing
arguing	creating	discussing	evaluating

Figure 9.1 shows an example drawn from *The Learning Delivery System* produced by Lifeskills International.

FIGURE 9.1 EXAMPLE OF OPEN LEARNING WORKBOOK ACTIVITY

In helping and supporting staff a manager can operate in a range of modes. At any one time she or he may be in one of them.

The choice of mode will be to do with the individual's needs in particular situations. In this module we will explore your role in Supporting Development, being someone who motivates and encourages others to take responsibility for their own learning.

The module will:

- offer some insight into learning theory;
- identify strategies we can use to promote other people's learning;
- ask you to reflect on your own competencies as a developer;
- invite you to set up some learning contracts with members of your staff to support their development.

First, let us ask you to explore some of your own values and ideas as a developer of others (✔ the box which fits for you.)

Yes   No

The Role of Developer: Checklist

1 I believe people learn best when they are motivated and can see benefits for themselves from learning.

2 I believe the best way to help people is to help them to help themselves.

3 I recognise that each individual is unique; what works for one may not for another; what makes sense for one may not for another.

4 I believe that approval and recognition for achievement are motivators.

5 I believe that helping is a two-way process; the helper can benefit as well as the one receiving help.

8

THE LEARNING DELIVERY SYSTEM ®
© LIFESKILLS COMMUNICATIONS 1991

Reproduced by courtesy of Lifeskills International

These reader activities help reinforce the learning. They also, of course, break down the reading period into more bite-sized chunks. A reader's attention span is probably no more than 20 minutes, so ways need to be found to try to respond to that and to maintain it as long as possible.

However, this active learning is not the same as the 'having an experience' stage in the natural process of learning (discussed later in Chapter 10) which is ultimately necessary to reinforce the knowledge gained. For this reason, some people argue that distance learning alone is too non-action oriented to win widespread acceptability.

ACCESSIBLE WRITING

To compensate for the relative isolation of learners, the writers and designers of materials have developed ever more elaborate ways of making learning materials attractive, welcoming and easy to follow.

There are still many poorly written workbooks which are little more than textbooks coupled with tutors' notes. But many of the best written workbooks look more like children's playbooks than textbooks. That doesn't mean that the content is less serious, only more easily understood. As well as activities built in from time to time, there are numerous devices available to the writer.

The least obvious technique (or perhaps the most obvious) is the use of white space. It takes considerable discipline, professional skill, and sometimes pressure on the publisher, to leave abundant white space on the page – above, below, to the right and left, often more than the text itself, with blocks of text not seemingly respecting conventional margins or making economic use of the precious paper resource. None the less, it's a technique that works wonders in keeping the reader's attention.

Another technique is the use of signposts to flag or label a particular category of action needed, such as writing an action plan or having a discussion with colleagues. One company's set of signposts appears in Figure 9.2.

Variety of typeface, font style and size, are also used to powerful effect, while seemingly breaking the rules and serious writing conventions.

Another technique. Short sentences. Without active verbs. And short paragraphs. Some beginning with 'and'. Purists blench.

Cartoons are another device to catch the reader's eye and engage and maintain interest. These are a matter of taste. Some find them condescending. They need checking for acceptability with the intended audience. Illustrations of one kind or another, humorous or otherwise, can be relevant and add to readability and memorability, as in the example in Figure 9.3.

The use of colour is less controversial than humour, but is not a cut-and-dried issue. It is an important question if you are commissioning bespoke material for your company. There are ways of appealing subconsciously to readers through the use of colour without great expense. For example, through the use of spot colour for, say, bullet points. Or by using pre-printed coloured footers or brand logo. The cover, in particular, must invite inspection by readers. But colour can obstruct frequent and flexible updating or the minor adaptation of a standard product.

FIGURE 9.2 EXAMPLE OF THE USE OF SIGNPOSTS

The Signposts

We have used eight 'signposts' to highlight necessary actions for you to take as you work through the kit.

Used to identify the exercises themselves.

Used wherever you are requested to carry out a task or complete an exercise.

Used wherever you are requested to complete an action plan.

Used wherever you could benefit from a discussion on the work completed.

Used wherever definitions, additional notes or general information is supplied.

Used wherever you are requested to review and summarise your work.

Used wherever you are asked to complete a checklist.

Used to highlight an end product or a benefit achieved as a result of working through the kit.

Reproduced by courtesy of TAD Ltd

FIGURE 9.3 EXAMPLE OF ILLUSTRATIONS

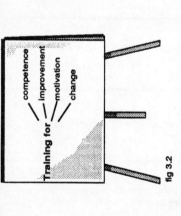

Training for — competence
— improvement
— motivation
— change

fig 3.2

Though we may in fact be training for more than one of these purposes at the same time - training for change or improvement can also be a motivating factor for the trainee - it is important to have clear aims about what we are training for at any time.

The Manager as a Trainer

Although training away from the workplace has an important role to play, the everyday challenges of any workplace are perhaps more important in providing excellent opportunities for learning by experience. Wise managers use these day to day opportunities to encourage and train their staff. In fact, a manager is very well placed to be an excellent trainer because

■ learning situations in the workplace are real and not role-plays or case studies

■ the situation is constantly changing and those on the spot can tackle the problems as they arise

■ a manager knows the people involved and can assess the best way to motivate or help each individual enhance their performance

■ a manager can assess progress and make sure that new skills and behaviours are put into practice

A manager is given many different opportunities to act as a trainer and a skilled manager grasps every opportunity.

fig 3.3

What are Your Personal Training Aims?

What were the deciding factors that led you yourself to begin this training programme? Do you consider yourself training for competence, improvement, motivation or change? All of these or a combination of two of them? Why? Were there any other deciding factors?

Personal competence 3.3 Managing personal learning and development *has the following three behaviour indicators*

■ *take on responsibility for meeting your own learning and development needs*

■ *develop self to meet the competence demand of different and changing situations*

■ *continually set new challenging development needs and take action to meet them*

page 47

144

Publishers use a range of sizes, both landscape and portrait formats, types of binding, built-in bookmarks, etc. to make their products user friendly. Case-studies are often provided separately – a good idea since they are more prone to dating.

Products are sometimes supplemented with inserts for personal organizers and with games. There is scope for creative talent here.

Then there is the option of using other media to replace or supplement the written word. This is more fully discussed in Chapter 12, 'The New Technology'.

EXPERIENCE RELATED

Well-produced open learning material continually relates new knowledge inputs to learners' prior and concurrent experience in their field of work. The opportunity to learn from experience at the workplace is now widely recognized. This is done in both practical ways and through reflection – 'what does it mean for me?' Traditional learning, by contrast, tends to be more academic, remote and less vocationally inclined.

Current open learning developments complement other national developments such as APL, Accreditation of Prior Learning. Here ways are being found to give formal recognized status to prior achievement. Qualifications may be awarded on the basis of employees' hard-won skills and experience, as we saw earlier in Chapter 4.

ACTIVITY 9.1

If you need to assess the presentation quality of potential open learning products, you may like to use the checklist offered in Figure 9.4.

FIGURE 9.4 OPEN LEARNING PRESENTATION QUALITY CHECKLIST

1. Are the materials attractively laid out: white space, variation, typeface, font style, colour, etc?

2. Is the text appropriately illustrated?

3. Is use made of other media, if justified (e.g. visual and aural)?

4. Is the tone of language appropriate for the audience?

5. Is the style lively and interesting?

6. Is the language clear and succinct?

7. Are difficult ideas well explained?

8. Are signposts used well to flag direction and action?

9. Is the material divided into manageable chunks?

10. Does the writer frequently engage learners in the text?

11. How imaginatively does the writer engage learners in the text? (q.v. Phil Race's list of verbs)

12. Does the writer show recognition of learners' past experience and present context?

REFERENCES

1. Employment Department (1988) *How to Profit from Open Learning – Company Evidence*, a study by the Open University and Coopers & Lybrand, Sheffield.
2. Christopher Bond (1993) 'Flexible Learning – A Conceptual Framework', *Training Officer*, July/August.
3. Phil Race (1992) 'Design for Open Learning', *Open Learning Today*, **12** (Autumn).

10
SUPPORTING OPEN LEARNING

OVERVIEW

This chapter offers advice on how best to design and manage open learning so that it offers the learner the maximum support.

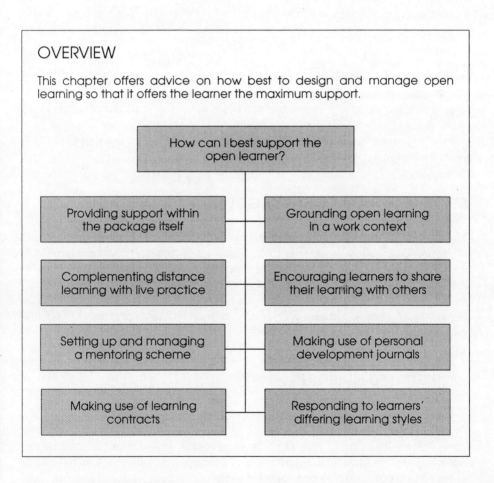

How can I best support the open learner?

Providing support within the package itself

Grounding open learning in a work context

Complementing distance learning with live practice

Encouraging learners to share their learning with others

Setting up and managing a mentoring scheme

Making use of personal development journals

Making use of learning contracts

Responding to learners' differing learning styles

INTRODUCTION

I t has been said that most open learning schemes succeed or fail on the level and quality of learner support provided. In the last two chapters we have spoken of the risk and fear of the open learner becoming isolated. Many features *within* good quality materials themselves try to combat this feeling, particularly in so far as it affects motivation. Technology is able to make a significant contribution too, as we shall see in the next chapter. But the most important ways of supporting open learners are, paradoxically, in personal relationships.

Personal support takes a variety of forms and comes from a number of sources – from fellow learners, bosses and colleagues, as well as members of the company's training department and external tutors. These people provide information, advice, opportunities, resources, encouragement and counselling. Training is now sometimes offered to those in these support positions to help prepare them for their roles.

Support can also take the form of systems and disciplines, as well as complementary forms of learning. One leading user of open learning, the Post Office, claims that while open learning had been chosen because it was timely, easy and appealed to all, and met a limited budget, there was a need to deliver open learning within a support matrix of coaching, benchmarking and conventional courses.

In this chapter we shall examine a variety of approaches to offering support to open learning and open learners.

SUPPORT AS PART OF PACKAGE DESIGN

One aspect of support means surrounding the open learning subject matter with an appropriate designed-in 'structure'. The idea is that the package should not make the question of support dependent on the purchaser. According to Lewis, an internally well-supported package should contain the features listed in Figure 10.1 (in addition to those concerning its written quality in Figure 9.4).[1] Some of the items lend themselves to group discussion at planned seminars, summer schools and special events, alongside individual feedback.

WORK-BASED LEARNING

Open learning is becoming synonymous with work-based learning. But those who sing the virtues of assessing experience and learning in the workplace might be missing some broader aspects of a relevant context. It is the word 'context' that holds the key. For the learning to have real meaning, be motivating and have a real chance of success, it has to be grounded in the local context in a *total* sense. John Coffey, one of open learning's leading innovators, makes the point forcefully:

> At its crudest, the hype tells us that purchase of purpose-designed packages on which one's staff can work unaided (in their own time, of course) will both save employers money and produce competence in the workplace. Nothing could be

---

FIGURE 10.1 OPEN LEARNING PACKAGE SUPPORT STRUCTURE

- An explanation of the content of the training (a map of the ground the learner will cover).
- An explanation of any prerequisite skills the learner needs.
- Clear objectives expressed in terms the learner understands.
- Questions and activities that give the learner a chance to practise skills.
- Feedback, comment and discussion on the learner's performance.
- Hints on how to carry out tasks.
- Chance for the learner to express confusion or to make criticisms.
- Opportunities for the learner to try again, to have another attempt.

> further from the truth... If, for example, the formal training provision gives a different message from that practised in the workplace and if there is no way to examine the mixed message, training will not have beneficial effects, however well packaged. ... Training can no longer work in isolation from the rest of the business to which it is applied, if indeed it ever could.[2]

Nowadays the best open learning handles the problem of grounding learning in a relevant context through such means as company-related projects and assignments of real value to the employer, giving meaningful opportunities to practise what is learned, coupled with a support system that draws on the boss and or a local mentor.

Many higher education establishments are also now bridging the gap between study and the workplace that began to be closed by further education institutions and polytechnics 20 or more years ago. At this leading edge, Middlesex University publishes a *Work Based Learning Bulletin* with the support of the Employment Department. There are over 20 work-based learning projects being run by universities in what probably qualifies for the description of a 'movement'. Quoting David Melville, Vice-Chancellor of Middlesex University, 'we recognise and assess experience and learning in the workplace, as well as at home.'[3] What change from the traditional university approach.

PRIVATE EXCEPTION

One has to recognize an exception to the work-based trend. That is where learners deliberately want to keep their study a secret. One of the attractions for some followers of open learning is just this. For example, if newly promoted managers feel inadequate in a particular facet of managing but don't want to admit it, they may choose the open learning route. It allows people to hide their weaknesses. For some it avoids the feeling of being in a competitive environment alongside other learners. That aside, Coffey's point still holds: however understandable the motivation, the chance of making a success in such circumstances is substantially reduced.

THE MANAGER AS TRAINER

The trend described above reflects a new emphasis on work-based values with, as we have seen, managers and supervisors being trained to be trainers and assessors. As the workbook *Managing and Planning Training* published by Manchester Open Learning explains, a manager is very well placed to be an excellent trainer for the following reasons:

O   Learning situations in the workplace are real and not role-plays or case-studies.

O   Situations are constantly changing and those on the spot can tackle problems as they arise.

O   Managers know the people involved and can assess the best way to motivate them and help enhance their performance.

O   Managers can assess progress and make sure that new skills and behaviours are put into practice.

DEVELOPING PRACTICAL SKILLS

Learning for managers tends to have a higher knowledge component than for lower levels. This makes open learning methodology particularly apt and economic. But it disregards the social element of managing – a problem we shall consider later. Likewise, when it comes to the acquisition of practical skills, the need to link knowledge inputs to real experience is both obvious and fundamental.

If we take the example of making a presentation, we can learn by reading at a distance something of what is entailed. But the knowledge component is only a small part of what is required. It takes a live setting in the presence of others to practise the skill, receive feedback and hone it into true competence.

The distance aspect of open learning can be efficient and make best use of the total available time, dividing it between independent learning and shared learning. In particular, the modern and more flexible form of open learning which includes group experiences makes a balanced whole possible. Some may see this as a corruption of the original concept of distance learning, but the need for it and its benefits for practical skill subjects cannot be doubted.

SHARING LEARNING WITH OTHERS

Open learning has a reputation for being a solitary activity. Much of one's time is necessarily spent entirely in one's own company, especially for self-sponsored learners who simply buy a product from a publisher. There is always considerable reading, and even listening or watching is usually undertaken alone. But to reduce this problem, providers of serious open learning programmes for managers include a mixture of workshops and sessions with tutors. This is important because it gives access to other people's experiences. It also helps keep on track and assist momentum.

Working with others is vital for those people with an extrovert personality who are dependent on interaction to bring out the best work in themselves. These are people of whom it is sometimes said 'they need to think with their mouths open!' or 'they talk to think', as opposed to introverts who 'think to talk'.

The old standard of learning independently is now being challenged. Some designers of open learning encourage shared learning between learners as what has become known as 'learning partners'. To be successful, the quality of the relationship between the partners is crucial (liking, trust and respect) as well as practical considerations such as geographical proximity. In some instances the practice of externally matching two strangers from very different backgrounds has proved motivating and given useful insights.

This trend towards shared learning experiences is not peculiar to open learning; some of the more imaginative management schools encourage learning partnerships and even jointly written and submitted assignments – though this is at the more radical end of the education spectrum.

It is the notion that learning has to be independent (or it's cheating) which engenders damaging competition. Shared learning develops healthy interdependence and promotes collaboration. It also recognizes that for some people and for some forms of insight this is the most effective approach.

MAKING THE MOST OF MENTORS

Recent growth in the use of mentoring mirrors that of open learning itself, in large part because of it. The advent of NVQs based on workplace-assessed competences has given further impetus to line management involvement in support of learning and its practical application. But it is not a soft option for the parties. In David Clutterbuck's analysis of mentoring schemes, data suggest that the failure rate is high.[4] To stand the best chance of success takes careful planning and preparation. Key questions are what should mentors do? What makes for a good mentor? How should they be chosen and briefed? And how do they differ from a good line boss?

WHY BOTHER?

From the standpoint of learners it is well understood that they need to feel supported – particularly those learning at a distance. Open learners frequently feel isolated and neglected by their organization. A mentor meets this psychological need, but also serves a practical purpose; for example, when it comes to career moves. Where trainee managers make a series of rapid experience-building moves as part of a planned development programme, a mentor can provide the continuity which cannot come from the trainee's immediate and short-term line manager. Also the line manager may be too close to the learner in the current working relationship to be objective.

From the company's perspective, as well as predictable benefits such as increased productivity and reduced labour turnover,[5] mentoring bridges the gulf that often exists between the company's opportunities and needs on the one hand,

and the learner's aspirations on the other. Also, there is a wealth of accumulated wisdom which it is in the company's interest to pass on. In these days of high managerial turnover, exacerbated by delayering and early retirement programmes, the advising/guiding/coaching dimension is a way of recycling this otherwise lost experience and know-how, something often underrated.

THE MENTOR'S ROLE

Besides actual job content and both abstract and theoretical knowledge, this transfer process provides support in the context of the organization, especially interpreting the organization's operational, political and social life.

'A good chum, who is not the boss but who can be your godfather in the company', is how one young manager described it. 'Part warm bath, part cold shower', is the view of a personnel director. A 'trusting but critical friendship' where advice may be given in an atmosphere of mutual respect and liking, offered another. The role may comprise the following:

- O Role modelling
- O Advice
- O Information giving
- O Confidential sounding board
- O Coaching
- O Formal sponsorship
- O Informal opening doors
- O Network building
- O Informal assessment
- O Identification of development needs
- O Encouragement to study

CHOOSING MENTORS

To achieve the relationship described, requires choice. No one should be forced to be a mentor or have a mentor chosen for them. Some company mentoring schemes consist of a pool of mentors from which potential protégés can negotiate the mentoring support they need. The pool may be more than a source from which to draw a mentor; members of the pool may be accessed in different ways at different times.

Some mentors will be better at providing psychological support and others practical support. This individual variation is as welcome as it is inevitable. But it means that there is no universally accepted formula based on hard evidence for what makes for success in selecting managers onto a mentoring scheme. However, a high rating against the following factors is likely to increase the chances of success:

- O Influence over others
- O Closeness to the core of the operation
- O Time with the company
- O Knowledge of political ropes

O   Perceived by others as expert or competent
O   Control over resources including people
O   High position in hierarchy

Advice is mixed about whether persons approaching the end of their careers make good mentors. Some believe their interest level and commitment will wane at this time. Others consider that the new role can spark a fresh interest.

Unless the mentoring relationship happens naturally and is working well, mentors should be drawn from outside the direct line reporting relationship. (They may sometimes naturally develop outside the company altogether.) This allows mentoring to operate free of the considerations of the protégé's daily line performance and conduct.

Once selected, mentors benefit from a training programme to prepare them for their role. As there are choices to be made around the design of company mentoring schemes, where possible it is best to design the training and briefing process in-house.

This gives rise to a contradiction. On the one hand, the above says organize your mentoring scheme formally. On the other hand, research shows that mentoring works best when it arises naturally. Perhaps the way of squaring this particular circle is to build upon naturally occurring mentoring wherever possible, and promote it more formally where it otherwise would not get off the ground.

A MENTORING CULTURE

Whether mentoring will occur, will work well, and whether a company will want to develop a scheme, depends on its organization culture. For example, Steve Carter points out that relevant aspects of the culture include the following:

O   Whether managers are encouraged to consider that part of their role is to develop their staff.
O   Whether failing and making mistakes is recognized as part of learning.
O   Whether time spent on non-task activities is recognized as valuable.[5]

If the answer to these questions is No, mentoring is unlikely to feature at all, let alone stand much chance of success.

MENTORS VERSUS LINE BOSSES

As mentioned earlier, NVQs require line manager involvement in the assessment of learners' proven competence. This highlights one of the inherent dilemmas with mentoring: should the learner's own immediate boss seek to couple the supervisory role with that of mentoring the subordinate as protégé?

The combined role sometimes happens naturally where both parties wish it. But clearly the answer to the option should sometimes be No, that is, when the personality of the boss and the quality of the interpersonal relationship is such that the learner would feel unsupported and prefer someone else.

In any case, a combined role cannot fulfil all of the disinterested and confidential functions contained in the earlier list, although some of the functions may be performed better as a result of more direct familiarity and greater relevance. However, assuming that the roles are separate, the problem then is: what should be the relationship and role differentiation between the mentor and line boss?

WHAT CAN GO WRONG?

There are three main areas to watch out for.

The mentoring relationship breaks down

The first and most obvious risk is that of a breakdown in the mentoring relationship. This may happen for a variety of reasons, even resentment by the mentor of the rapid career progress made by the protégé when compared with his or her own earlier career.

Line managers get upset

Mentoring schemes and mentors sometimes incur hostility from line managers who may feel threatened.

Charges of élitism

Mentors can achieve benefits for their individual protégés or for a selected high-flying group of management trainees that bring unwelcome charges of élitism.

KEY TIPS

❖   Discuss the mentoring option with learners, involving their bosses.

❖   Allow learners to choose for themselves.

❖   Prepare mentors for their roles.

❖   Review the mentoring arrangements from time to time.

TYPES OF HELPER

Both a line boss and a mentor may undertake coaching, but there can be subtle differences. The stance of the mentor compared with a coach is likely to be more remote from the job requirements and more centred on the person. You can think of instructing, coaching and mentoring as lying on such a continuum. David Megginson and Mike Pedler, in *Self-development: A Facilitator's Guide*, shows how these distinct roles and styles are manifested in the way they help people to learn, as shown in Figure 10.2.[6] Megginson and Pedler also provide a questionnaire to help people in these roles diagnose their preferred style of helping.

FIGURE 10.2 THREE WAYS OF HELPING PEOPLE TO LEARN

	Instructor	Coach	Mentor
FOCUS OF HELP	Task.	Results of job.	Development of person throughout life.
TIMESPAN	A day or two.	A month to a year.	Career or lifetime.
APPROACH TO HELPING	'Show and tell' – give supervised practice.	Explore problem together and set up opportunities to try out new skills.	Act as friend willing to play 'devil's advocate'; listen and question to enlarge awareness.
ASSOCIATED ACTIVITIES	Analysing task; clear instruction; supervise practice; give feedback on results at once.	Jointly identify the problem; create a development opportunity and review.	Link work with other parts of life; clarify broad and long-term aims and purpose in life.
OWNERSHIP	Helper.	Shared.	Learner.
ATTITUDE TO AMBIGUITY	Eliminate.	Use it as a challenge – as a puzzle to be solved.	Accept as being part of the exciting world.
BENEFITS TO THE COMPANY	Standard, accurate performance.	Goal-directed performance oriented to improving and being creative.	Conscious questioning approach to the mission of the company.

Reproduced by courtesy of McGraw-Hill Book Co.

PERSONAL DEVELOPMENT JOURNALS

The use of journals and logs for recording progress is encouraged. They should be much more than factual progress reports. They aim to capture the learner's reflections, feelings, insights, problems, hopes and concerns, as experience of the learning progresses. Journals are to emotional development what diaries are to factual development. Journals are therefore an invaluable tool for developing self-awareness and for reflecting on values.

A dilemma here for the provider is whether to insist that they are shown and discussed with the tutor. If so, the problem is that they will not be so spontaneous or frank, but will be drafted and rewritten to impress. This largely defeats the point of having them, but at least it ensures that they will be completed.

If journals remain wholly private and for the sole benefit of the learner, not everyone will complete them, but those who do will get much more out of them.

How to handle the vexed matter of journals can be a topic for inclusion in the individual's learning contract, which we look at next.

USING LEARNING CONTRACTS

Where learning is instigated for personal development, the learner can reasonably be expected to plan and carry out the learning on his or her own terms and with minimum formality. But where the learning is of direct interest to a third party, such as an employer or profession, or draws significantly on the contribution of others in the process, then a learning contract may provide clarity and engender commitment – psychologically binding all the parties. In these cases, as Malcolm Knowles explains in *The Adult Learner: A Neglected Species*, 'Learning contracts provide a means for negotiating a reconciliation between these external needs and the learner's internal needs and interests.'[7]

THE PARTIES' ROLES

Contracts are usually between learner and tutor, learner and boss (representing the employer's interest), or may include all three. By the tutor, we mean the range of people or agencies involved in training delivery. This might include colleges, training consultants or in-company trainers.

The process implies that the parties are free to negotiate acceptable terms for provision and study. The tutor and the learner theoretically negotiate as equals; for example, agreeing which topics should be tackled in what order. But some more junior managers and supervisors might be uncomfortable with the idea of negotiating as equals, even negotiating at all. They might expect the tutor to take the lead and decide, adopting the role of expert. They may even be uncomfortable with the idea of learning contracts *per se*.

In practice, there is often relatively little latitude to depart from a structure, especially with professional courses and those linked with qualifications. Here, learning contracts are sometimes pre-printed token documents, which somewhat defeats the object. Schools and colleges are adopting the practice, with their side of the bargain being to provide teaching, for which the learner agrees to attend! This may add little to what would have happened in the pre-contract era. But taken seriously and given individual flexibility, learning contracts can create the right climate for both sides to design appropriate learning and then strive to their limit and honour their obligations.

THE ELEMENTS

Knowles suggests that contracts should contain four key elements:

O   Learning objectives.

O   Learning resources and strategies.

O   Evidence of accomplishment.

O   Criteria and means of validating evidence.

(Note that 'resources' here includes tutors and their expected role and relationship.)

What are referred to here as 'learning objectives' might be better thought of as the learner's ownership of the intended learning outcomes. This is an essential component. Even if the training provision is deficient in some respect, the learner's commitment in respect of the hoped-for results can generally compensate for this. Whereas the reverse is not true.

But this benefit should not be allowed to lead to unbalanced contracts, placing most onus on the learner. John Coffey argues the case for the employer element of the contract to be given more attention.[8] He considers that the main value of learning contracts is between learner and employer, where the aim is to get the employer to commit to the change implied by the learning. The point is that learning can be thought of as 'contracting for change'. Training is not undertaken in order to maintain the status quo. Because of this, the outcome of training is often uncomfortable (for both parties) and can be expected to challenge matters such as working relationships and practices. Coffey advises that this range of issues should be confronted formally beforehand to reduce the discomfort while attempting change and to increase the likelihood of hoped-for benefits being attained.

KEY TIPS

❖   Involve the learner, tutor and boss in the learning contract.

❖   Allow real choice and reciprocation, not tokenism.

❖   Ensure a fair balance between conflicting interests.

❖   Be clear about the confidentiality and role of personal development journals.

LEARNING PREFERENCES

Open learning requires much self-discipline and tenacity, especially for the periods spent working alone. It depends on substantial intrinsic motivation, in other words, motivation from within. Some people find it easier to enter into a commitment to attend a traditional class instead. That at least has the benefit of social pressure on attending, and the visibility of being in attendance, i.e. extrinsic motivation. Classroom regularity is simply easier for some.

This aspect of motivation is just one of a number of factors to take into account when choosing open learning – for oneself or one's employees. Substantial research has been carried out on how people learn. Volumes have been written on learning styles, which we shall look at in a moment. Similarly, the subject of andragogy (adult learning) as opposed to pedagogy (children's learning) has been well explored and written up.[9] Figure 10.3 lists the principles.

Beyond this, we each learn in a variety of ways, and we also have individual preferences in how we learn best – both conscious and unconscious. Alan Mumford captures the point neatly:

> Individuals may react to outdoor training as the most illuminating learning experience in their life, or regard it as a form of damp masochism. One individual may regard reading 140 case studies at Harvard as an intellectually stimulating process which sharpens analytical skills, another may regard it as a form of hypothetical voyeurism.[10]

FIGURE 10.3 PRINCIPLES OF ADULT LEARNING

1. Learning is a process – as opposed to a series of finite, unrelated steps – that lasts throughout the entire life span of most people.

2. For optimum transfer of learning, the learner must be actively involved in the learning experience, not a passive recipient of information.

3. Each learner must be responsible for his or her own learning.

4. The learning process has an emotional as well as an intellectual component.

5. Adults learn by doing; they want to be *involved*. Regardless of the benefits of coaching, one should never merely demonstrate how to do something if an adult learner can actually perform the task, even if it takes longer that way.

6. Problems and examples must be realistic and *relevant to the learners*.

7. Adults relate their learning to what they already know. It is wise to learn something about the backgrounds of the learners and to provide examples that they can understand in their own frames of reference.

8. An informal environment works best. Trying to intimidate adults causes resentment and tension, and these inhibit learning.

9. Variety stimulates. It is a good idea to try to appeal to all five of the learners' senses, particularly those aspects identified by neurolinguistic programming: the visual, the kinesthetic, and the auditory. A change of pace and a variety of learning techniques help to mitigate boredom and fatigue.

10. Learning flourishes in a win-win, non-judgmental environment. The norms of the training setting are violated by tests and grading procedures. Checking learning objectives is far more effective.

11. The training facilitator is a change agent. The trainer's role is to present information or skills or to create an environment in which exploration can take place. The participants' role is to take what is offered and apply it in a way that is relevant and best for them. The trainer's responsibility is to facilitate. The participants' responsibility is to learn.

Reproduced by courtesy of Pfeiffer & Co.

ALONE OR WITH OTHERS

Another dimension is whether individuals learn best alone or with others. It is estimated that around 50 per cent of learners are comfortable with an open learning approach. The others have a preference for, and learn more effectively in, a traditional college-based setting. Clearly, some subjects are more suited to one approach than the other. As a general rule, skills which take place in an interacting context are less suitable for open learning, though there may be aspects within those subjects which are well handled by this medium.

In the era of the *knowledge worker*, there are many people in organizations performing what may be called managerial functions on management grades and titles, though they are in fact specialists engaged in technical fields. Much of their work is information-based, and learning this information can lend itself readily to open learning. But general management – defined as substantially responsible for achieving results through others – is, by definition, a social activity, as, for example, in face-to-face appraisal. In this case it is therefore important to be more selective about aspects of the manager's work which lends itself most to learning via this medium compared with one almost wholly interactive and experiential.

WRITTEN OR SPOKEN WORD

Closely linked with this issue is how well we respond to the written word versus the spoken word in terms of the ability to take in and process information. Many of us know managers who, when being briefed orally on a matter, will say 'I can't take it in like this: please leave me something to read', especially if expected to react in real time. Some make the reverse request, preferring oral sources of information. Such comments can reflect self-awareness about their preferred and most effective process of assimilating information, though they can also have their roots in time management and even shyness.

On this matter of spontaneous or studied reaction is the question of how much individuals need quiet time to reflect on and digest information to make sense of it. A further very basic but important issue is what is our best time of day for learning.

LEARNING MODELS

There is much research available to help designers of learning materials employ the most useful techniques and methods to respond to these variables. There are various models, some covering the general territory of how learning takes place, and some looking at different aspects such as what causes people to want to learn, or how learning is different for adults compared with children. Reassuringly among the theorists there is no widespread disagreement.

Kurt Lewin

An American pioneer in this field, Kurt Lewin portrayed learning as a linear process. He believed that learning begins with some awareness or discomfort about a recognized lack of knowledge or ability. This causes a will to learn, an experience of learning, and a return to a confident and stable state. The initial unsettled state and uncertainty about the ensuing learning process may be threatening and leave learners feeling vulnerable. It may explain some of the unusual early behaviours which learners sometimes exhibit to the consternation of tutors, such as nervousness, contrariness, insensitivity, reticence, absence, etc.

Recognizing and responding sensitively to these ego states is one of the marks of distinction which exemplifies the skilled tutor. One concern expressed about open learning is that the learners may be isolated and their doubts and quandaries may go unrecognized.

There is also a question mark over how much real learning can be achieved alone, if any. The argument is that learning takes hold only in a context in which 'having a go' allows for *interactions* – whether with work, family or a relevant community – and in which other individuals are a source of feedback and a resource to support the learning. Well-designed open learning recognizes this, though at times it falls short of the ideal in terms of enabling a tutor to be present to facilitate the necessary interactive element.

David Kolb

David Kolb's model of the learning cycle is the most quoted general learning theory.[11] This is shown in Stephen Linstead's simplified form in Figure 10.4 and is referred to as the Experiential Learning Model.

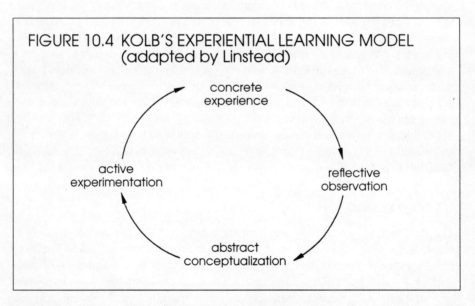

FIGURE 10.4 KOLB'S EXPERIENTIAL LEARNING MODEL (adapted by Linstead)

concrete experience

reflective observation

abstract conceptualization

active experimentation

The idea that we go round this cycle (at least partially) when we learn – and certainly when we learn best – is fairly straightforward. More interesting is the notion that we all have different degrees of comfort with the four stages. The belief is that for reasons of upbringing, type of educational background, personality and habits, we prefer to learn in one way more than in another – a learning preference or style.

This amounts to wanting to dwell more in one area than another, or being more successful if we start our learning process at a particular stage, say, with an experience rather than an abstract concept.

Traditional learning and that conducted in business schools tends to concentrate on the bottom half of Kolb's circle (*abstract conceptualization*), whereas it is suggested that those whom we would term 'streetwise' would have learnt mostly in the top half (*concrete experience*).

Teachers, facilitators and writers often have a choice about whether to begin with the practical or with the theory. One can present a theory, concept or principle and follow it with an example by way of illustration. Or one can offer an example first, from which the theory may be deduced. Bearing this in mind, where possible it is desirable that teachers and facilitators should attempt the following:

O   To exercise their choice on the basis of the actual or considered preference of the learner or group of learners. Where there is a group, this is obviously more difficult, but teachers should avoid simply following their own preferred way or without giving it any thought whatsoever.

O   To construct the learning experience in a way that permits the learners to pass through all the stages (or admit that learning is incomplete).

Peter Honey and Alan Mumford

Peter Honey and Alan Mumford have further developed Kolb's model and gone on to popularize the subject and develop questionnaires (in *The Manual of Learning Styles* and its companion *Using Your Learning Styles*) to help users identify their own preferred learning style.[12] Their own model, perhaps easier to understand than Kolb's, is shown in Figure 10.5.

According to Mumford:

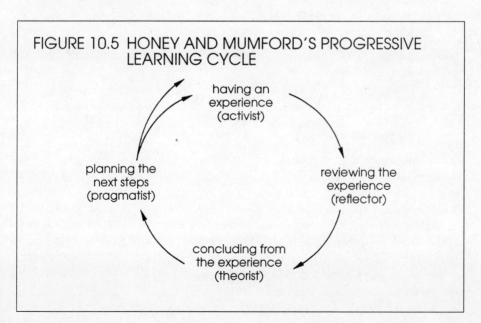

FIGURE 10.5 HONEY AND MUMFORD'S PROGRESSIVE LEARNING CYCLE

having an experience (activist)

reviewing the experience (reflector)

concluding from the experience (theorist)

planning the next steps (pragmatist)

Activists:
- O   try anything once;
- O   tend to revel in short-term crises, fire-fighting;
- O   tend to thrive on the challenges of new experiences;
- O   are relatively bored with implementation and longer-term consolidation;
- O   constantly involve themselves with other people.

Reflectors:
- O   like to stand back and review experiences from different perspectives;
- O   collect data and analyse it before coming to conclusions;
- O   like to consider all possible angles and implications before making a move;
- O   tend to be cautious;
- O   actually enjoy observing other people in action;
- O   often take a back seat at meetings.

Theorists:
- O   are keen on basic assumptions, principles, theories, models and systems thinking;
- O   prize rationality and logic;
- O   tend to be detached and analytical;
- O   are unhappy with subjective or ambiguous experiences;
- O   like to make things tidy and fit them into rational schemes.

Pragmatists:
- O   positively search out new ideas or techniques which might apply in their situation;
- O   take the first opportunity to experiment with applications;
- O   respond to opportunities as a challenge;
- O   are keen to use ideas from management courses;
- O   like to get on with things with clear purpose.

Mumford sharpens our perception of the four styles by amusingly contemplating their ideal epitaph:

> Activists: 'I was fighting this fire and ...'
> Reflectors: 'I'd like more information before deciding whether I like it here.'
> Theorists: 'I believe in the after life.'
> Pragmatists: 'This is better than the other place.'[13]

While the Honey/Mumford model still serves as a basis for examining individuals' preferred learning styles, Mumford states that 'it has become increasingly clear to me that the totally enclosed learning cycle represents better the design of structured learning events than it does the possible routes or progress of the individual learner.'[14] This comment seems to me to be spot on and appears tantamount to suggesting a slightly different *purpose* from Kolb's model, rather than an *enhancement* of it. It therefore renders the two models complementary.

The frequency with which these models are redrawn shows how limited still is our understanding of the learning process.

The models imply that individuals who have a strong preference for staying in one part of the cycle (say, studying the theory) are disadvantaged in terms of complete learning. A group can therefore have an advantage over the isolated learner, since the members of the group can bring their learning orientations to bear in complementary ways to resolve problems. The so-called *action learning method*, which takes place in groups, carries this advantage. But the logical consequence of this is that either individuals have to broaden their styles, or they will always need to be with others who have been carefully chosen to be complementary as well as to provide the necessary dynamic.

Stephen Linstead, in *The Journal of European and Industrial Training*, quotes the problem of learners who become trapped in a narrow style of their choosing, to their long-term growth disadvantage.[15] Good face-to-face facilitators can help with this. Distance learners and distance facilitators are therefore clearly at a disadvantage in this respect.

Phil Race

For those attracted to a simpler and highly practical model, Phil Race offers what he calls his 'one-page universal theory of learning' in 'Designing for Open Learning'. This contains some of Kolb's elements but has a clear start and finish like Lewin. The four stages are as follows:

1.   Wanting to learn (including knowing what to learn and why).
2.   Learning by doing.
3.   Learning from feedback.
4.   Digesting what has been learned.

Race's most interesting observations come at the last 'digesting' stage, which in other models is called 'reflection'. He describes this rather passive sounding process as 'making sense of it, taking stock of it, and allowing it to fit in among all the other things we know'. Some others call it 'giving it meaning'.

Compared with mere reflection, 'digestion' reminds us that much learning amounts to piling on new information that 'fills people up with all sorts of things they don't really need'. We need to face up more to the need for them 'to sort things out, then dispose of the rest'. Somewhat colourfully, Race suggests that some people avoid learning opportunities because it causes the equivalent of constipation! Information overload is something with which most of us can identify.

Other models

Another simple model is to view our chosen learning method as one of the following:

O   Learning by reading
O   Learning by seeing
O   Learning by hearing
O   Learning by writing down
O   Learning by doing

Ultimately, it is 'doing' which cements the understanding firmly in place. As we say (or Confucius he say):

I hear and I forget
I see and I remember
I do and I understand

ACQUIRING TIMELY ADVICE

Many open learning programmes for managers now build in a module on learning styles and learning techniques. This may be treated as part of the induction process, often in booklet form. Mumford argues that it should be handled as a serious managerial topic in its own right:

> [if] we take the overall objective as being that of learning, and if we accept the reasonable presumption that there are skills involved in learning, we are then faced with the extraordinary fact that the learning process is never identified and never discussed with individuals on programmes. It seems to me an absolute paradox that we can presume to engage managers on a process designed to help them learn without actually discussing the learning process.[17]

Advice on learning styles is becoming more frequent, but it is ironic that it always seems to come after the decision has been taken (often in ignorance and by default, or by a third party such as the learner's employer) that the medium of open learning is the appropriate one. This happens partly for practical reasons: only when the decision has been taken can tutors get access to the learners. But to be more blunt, it is not in the interests of the provider to cause potential learners to question whether open learning suits their style.

Some employers also might find this inconvenient, especially if open learning is their chosen corporate approach for logistical or cost reasons. But it is wise to discuss this at the beginning. It has to be said that, for some people, open learning is simply inappropriate.

At the practical level, working in the home environment may not be conducive to learning. It may not suit or fit in with other family members, may conflict with domestic commitments, contain distractions, and so on.

If possible, potential learners should be enabled to give full thought to their learning styles and preferences *before* embarking upon an open learning programme. If this is not possible (let's say where there is a company-wide policy decision to use open learning), then a wide variety of materials, media and shared activities improve the prospects of a good learning fit.

Conversely, a heavy emphasis on learning by oneself through the sole medium of the written word is more likely to be problematical for some learners.

KEY TIPS

❖   Make plenty of choice and variety available to learners.

❖   Help learners understand their preferred style.

❖   Allow learners freedom to influence the shape of the learning process.

❖   Help learners with these choices before decisions are made on their behalf.

ACTIVITY 10.1

You may like to use Figure 10.6 as a good practice checklist of support for open learning.

FIGURE 10.6 SUPPORTING OPEN LEARNING: GOOD PRACTICE CHECKLIST

1. How well are learners supported by colleagues, tutors, line managers and mentors?
2. How well does the open learning package/provider offer a supporting framework?
3. How well are line managers utilized in supportive on-the-job coaching?
4. What use is made of journaling for personal development?
5. Are learning contracts used to good effect?
6. How much advice is given to learners to help them understand their learning styles?
7. How much are people's different learning styles and preferences accommodated?
8. Do learners receive help with their learning styles in good time?
9. How much are learners allowed to influence the choices available?

REFERENCES

1. Roger Lewis (1985) 'Open Learning', *Topics*, January.
2. John Coffey (1990) 'Distance Learning – Efficient and Effective but no Panacea', *Education + Training*, **32** (2).
3. David Melville (1993) 'A University Perspective on Work Based Learning', *Work Based Learning Bulletin*: Middlesex University, **1**, May.
4. David Clutterbuck (1991) *Everyone Needs a Mentor*, Wimbledon: Institute of Personnel Management.
5. Steve Carter (1993) 'Developing an Organisational Mentoring Scheme', *Professional Manager*, May.
6. David Megginson and Mike Pedler (1992) *Self-Development: A Facilitator's Guide*, Maidenhead: McGraw-Hill.
7. Malcolm Knowles (1984) *The Adult Learner: A Neglected Species*, London: Gulf, pp. 222–7.
8. John Coffey (1992) 'Contracting for Quality in Learning', *Education + Training*, **34** (1).

9. William J. Pfeiffer (ed.) (1991) 'Andragogy: Principles of Adult Learning', *Theories and Models in Applied Behavioral Science*, San Diego: Pfeiffer & Co.
10. Alan Mumford (1990) 'The Individual and Learning Opportunities', *Industrial and Commercial Training*, **22** (1).
11. David Kolb (1984) *Experiential Learning: Experience as a Source of Learning and Development*, Prentice-Hall: Englewood Cliffs.
12. Peter Honey and Alan Mumford (1992) *The Manual of Learning Styles*, published privately by Peter Honey.
13. Alan Mumford (1991) 'Learning Style Epitaphs', *Management Education and Development*, London: Association for Management Education and Development, **22** (1).
14. Alan Mumford (1991) 'Individual and Organisational Learning – The Pursuit of Change', *Industrial and Commercial Training*, **23** (6).
15. Stephen Linstead (1990) 'Developing Management Meta-Competence – Can Distance Learning Help?', *The Journal of European Industrial Training*, **14** (6).
16. Phil Race (1992) 'Designing for Open Learning', *Transition*, May.
17. Alan Mumford (1986) 'Adult Learning: How and Why', *Education + Training*, September–October.

11

OPEN LEARNING PROVIDERS

OVERVIEW

This chapter clarifies the roles and credentials of the various parties who together comprise the provider side of open learning. It then explains their approaches and services, helping you assess their credibility.

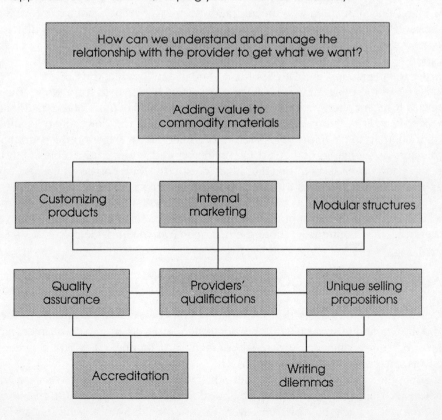

INTRODUCTION

The open learning business is populated by a variety of interested parties. Some are publishers who are household names. For them open learning is just one particular dimension or outlet. Some providers are management or communications companies or consultancies, where again open learning might be one product line, or it might be their whole business to develop and produce open learning materials.

Some providers' products might actually be services. Many providers are organizations which 'deliver' open learning packages to their users – often other people's packages. Their role it is to add value in various ways by supporting and managing their application with learners and with client liaison. Chief among the deliverers are educationalists and trainers, many of whom work for colleges.

In some cases, the various roles may be provided by a total-service organization. Its service can include the analysis and design of appropriate learning materials, the administration of learner services such as written assignments, the arranging of group workshops, the provision of tutors, and the managing of certification by external awarding bodies.

The various providers include private consultancies and companies, possibly working in a consortium with the education sector to provide academic input (e.g. Wolsey Hall Oxford with Oxford Brookes University), not-for-profit FE-affiliated organizations (e.g. Manchester Open Learning), colleges of further and higher education including the Open University Business School, professional bodies (e.g. Institute of Personnel and Development), and institutions like the BBC.

Some of the new universities have been active in this field for a while. But a relatively recent phenomenon is the entrance to the field of more of the traditional universities. For example, the School of Management at the University of Reading decided that the competence-based movement for managers' education and training was so significant that it could not be ignored. It found it was able to buy in ready-made materials and then add its own expertise with corporate clients. This approach suits universities with closely developed links with local businesses.

Appendix 1 contains a list of many of the better known companies and institutions who either supply materials or provide support services. Whatever their role, this chapter talks about them as open learning 'providers'.

ADDING VALUE TO COMMODITY MATERIALS

The providing companies do more than sell-on the publisher's products. They supply the administration and the not insignificant amount of customer care involved in managing a substantial company programme. They run induction events, provide tutors and organize workshops.

Some direct-selling publishers offer a half-way house. They give advice on the necessary workshops, mentoring, etc. but don't set out to provide the resources themselves. So it is possible for buyers to deal directly with a publisher and to provide or arrange their own add-ons.

Sometimes the provider's services are combined in one company with the role of publisher, i.e. writer, designer, printer and distributor.

Sometimes the front organization buys in another publisher's product as a commodity, often rebranding it to disguise the fact to potential clients; it might like you to think that it generated all its own material and that it is different from a competitor's. Sometimes the content might be part bought in and part home grown. Some front organizations will help you choose course materials from a range of publishers.

If you invite two or more open learning providers to tender, you may not immediately realize that their content comes from the same stable. Your choice may not be quite as wide as you thought, and may come down to how value is added to the commodity. There are numerous providers, in one form or another, and they are not all easy to pigeon-hole.

KEY TIP

❖   Check on exactly what role is being played by whom using what.

CUSTOMIZING PRODUCTS

Learning materials can either be off-the-shelf product-centred, or can be tailored to suit the buyer's company. Some publishers of open learning come exclusively from a broad publishing background; their products are usually generic. But increasingly standard published products are subsequently being adapted around a buyer's needs and wishes.

Alternatively, to meet a company's highly specific learning needs (as opposed to those, say, leading to national qualifications) bespoke tailor-made materials are commissioned at the outset.

Some providers such as TDA Consulting Ltd work almost exclusively in the tailoring field. Other providers offer to customize the content of existing products in an appropriate way. It may mean adding client-based case-studies or special workshops. Occasionally it includes rewriting certain parts of the material.

How should you set about deciding whether it's worth the extra time, trouble and expense to commission tailored products? Chris Dunn of TDA offers some rules of thumb (see Figure 11.1).[1]

INTERNAL MARKETING

BADGE ENGINEERING

The most limited form of tailoring is one of the features of an internal marketing campaign, where the external appearance of products is tailored to a client company by giving prominence to the client's own logo on materials and workbooks. This is

---

FIGURE 11.1 DECIDING WHEN TO TAILOR PRODUCTS

When tailoring can be important

- The more strategic in nature the assignment is.
- The more business process related the assignment is (i.e. the greater the need to lock the training into the relevant commercial systems).
- The more senior the target audience is.
- The volume of use justifies the up-front tailoring fee.

When off-the-shelf products are often suitable

- Where there are non-strategic level assignments.
- Where the emphasis is on generic skills.

Reproduced by courtesy of TDA Consulting Ltd

called 'badge engineering'. Some readers might consider this little more than a marketing ploy. But badge engineering is a simple and relatively inexpensive, trouble-free and uncontroversial activity which takes place at a company-wide level. It does, however, fall a long way short of tailoring open learning products and their delivery in a way which genuinely fits the client's own circumstances.

Badge engineering has four motives, meeting the following needs:

O   To make the client company feel good about itself.
O   To make an apparent fit between a nationally available product and a company-specific one.
O   To help 'sell' the company's development programme to its employees.
O   To help the development department's relationship with the company's top management.

Badge engineering has been around for a while. But interest in it, making rather more of it, and going well beyond it, took off with the skill shortages and demographic problems in the labour market, much talked about in the late 1980s. The discussion is now moving on and there is talk of marketing companies to their potential and current employees as brands.

To recruit and retain skilled people, personnel departments are acutely aware of the need to present their company with a favourable image to compete alongside employers fishing in the same pool. With the squeeze on many head-office overhead activities, combined with a spirit of pushing support activities out to line management, a reaction by training departments in the form of wishing to spend money on the internal marketing of their programmes comes as no surprise.

PUBLICITY MATERIALS AND CAMPAIGNS

Campaigns can be an important part of the programme. At the most basic level they help recruit learners onto the programmes. These days training departments usually *do* have to attract volunteers for their programmes. This is consistent with a widespread shift in attitude towards career planning and development, whereby managers are expected to take more responsibility for their own development and show less dependence on their employer. Companies are therefore becoming more loath to dictate who should receive what training.

An exception is where a company embarks on a major programme radically to change its management culture as part of its business strategy. Then it will require all employees to take part, and this of course requires its own special highly planned internal marketing programme, which goes well beyond merely presenting a favourable image in the labour market or selling management learning opportunities.

This marketing requirement brings together expertise in the field of human resources, marketing and public relations, to make both a competent and strategic impact. Strategists recognize that open learning materials can be a powerful vehicle for promoting a new vision by top management.

Management development departments can find themselves starting from a disadvantageous position, suffering from what may be a negative association with Personnel – a history of an administrative role, managing via the rule book, obstructing line managers' authority, and so on. This is a tough image to overcome and can add to the case for the careful marketing of management learning as part of a wider HR programme. David Clutterbuck, writing in *Professional Manager*, suggests such campaigns should be based on the criteria in Figure 11.2.[2]

FIGURE 11.2 CRITERIA FOR INTERNAL MARKETING ACTIVITIES

- Understanding the needs of internal customers and being able to respond to them effectively.

- Linking all the functions' activities closely with the strategic objectives of the business.

- Developing excellent communications with internal customers.

- Developing excellent relationships with internal customers.

- Ensuring internal customers' expectations of HR are realistic.

- Continuously improving the professionalism and capability of HR in line with internal customers' needs.

Reproduced by courtesy of *Professional Manager*

KEY TIPS

❖   Avoid jargon where you can.

❖   Ensure that you produce materials to a high (external standard) quality, and make professional presentations.

Many companies are ruthlessly examining their core businesses and market-testing their internal services on a make-or-buy basis. According to Clutterbuck, 'Unless the staff department can demonstrate measurable benefits from retaining its services within the company, it is in severe danger of being relegated to little more than a purchasing function, acting on behalf of the line.'

But beware! Internal marketing is a two-edged sword. It is a political activity. If not sponsored or supported from the top, it may not receive a sympathetic response from some such as the chief financial officer who might challenge its motives and cost-justification.

ACTIVITY 11.1

Consider whether you need an internal marketing programme for your activities. If so,

- What image do you want to convey?
- Is your target wholly internal or also external?
- Should management training, education and development be all or part of the campaign?
- What assistance can external providers give?

MODULAR STRUCTURES

One form of flexibility to suit the client company may be to offer various routes through a modular structure. With producers' modular structures you first need to see if you share their values about what is core and what is optional. For example, one producer offers a structure in which financial management is core but communications is optional. This would not suit everyone.

You may be able to redefine the elective subjects around a firm, substantial and credible core of modules to suit the biases of your company without compromising a national qualification. But the scope for flexibility is limited where the package is designed to satisfy national standards and lead to the award of NVQs. This reason apart, some clients in any case feel more comfortable knowing that their managers are studying identical programmes to other companies. But as a general rule, tailored products have more appeal to companies because they relate to company problems and change strategies. Generic products appeal more to learners because they may offer a 'ticket' and increase personal marketability and mobility.

QUALITY ASSURANCE

There are various models of quality assurance. Most prominent currently are Total Quality Management (TQM) and certification with ISO 900 (which embraces British Standard 5750). The quality standard was originally developed in a manufacturing context, but it is now being widely applied to service organizations. Some providers of open learning are seeking, or have already obtained ISO 9000/BS 5750 approval, such as Wolsey Hall Oxford and Manchester Open Learning.

Approval means that your provider's organization has the systems and procedures in place to enable it to deliver on its promises. Obtaining such accreditation takes considerable time, effort and cost. It is not a piece of paper, but represents a culture change and a new way of life for an organization, complete with external audits. As the chairman of Wolsey Hall Oxford, Peter Newell said when his company was accredited, 'BS 5750 does not end with accreditation. It begins then; accreditation is simply the tip of the iceberg.'[3]

Some companies have a policy of taking services only from suppliers who have ISO 9000/BS 5750. This is regrettable for two reasons:

O   Some providers are too small to be able to invest in the consultation processes leading to accreditation, yet may have worthwhile products and services.

O   It may encourage providers to seek the quality standard for the wrong reasons, simply to keep up with the competition, rather than genuinely seeking the improvement which accreditation is intended to bring.

PROVIDERS' QUALIFICATIONS

How qualified are your providers? The Employment Department has produced a code of practice for the industry: *Ensuring Quality in Open Learning*.

A measure of whether or not your provider has the necessary formal skills and approaches is possession of one of the formal qualifications. There are three relevant ones, each in turn superseded by a more recent development. They are COLD, ADDFOL and T&D(FOL).

CERTIFICATE OF OPEN LEARNING DELIVERY

The Certificate of Open Learning Delivery (COLD) became available in 1988. It covers the following components:

O   Find and select open learning packages and programmes.
O   Design and develop open learning programmes.
O   Provide advice and direction to learners.
O   Provide tutoring for individuals and groups of learners.
O   Provide administrative services for an open learning scheme.
O   Manage the resources of an open learning scheme.
O   Provide marketing services for an open learning scheme.
O   Evaluate and validate an open learning scheme and its programmes.

There were two problems with COLD. It failed to fit with the strategy for nationally-based qualifications within an NVQ framework. More importantly perhaps, it assumed a strictly narrow definition of open learning which had the effect of excluding people working with 'flexible learning' in a broader way, mixing packages and media from a variety of sources. Nonetheless, provided this background is understood, possession of the COLD qualification remains valid evidence of providers' bona fides.

AWARD FOR THE DEVELOPMENT AND DELIVERY OF FLEXIBLE AND OPEN LEARNING

COLD was superseded by the Award for the Development and Delivery of Flexible and Open Learning (ADDFOL). Whereas COLD was based on the more conventional forms of open learning, ADDFOL recognizes the wider variety of learner-centred approaches featured in later forms of flexible and open learning today. ADDFOL awards cover the following:

O   Learner support.
O   Implementing flexible and open learning systems.
O   Design and development of flexible and open learning.

Unlike COLD, ADDFOL was modified to take account of the then new national standards for training and development produced by the Training & Development Lead Body within the government's programme for National Vocational Qualifications (NVQs) and in Scotland, SVQs. But ADDFOL itself is disappearing, being subsumed within a revised TDLB framework.

AWARD IN TRAINING & DEVELOPMENT (FLEXIBLE AND OPEN LEARNING)

The latest qualification in this area is the Award in Training & Development (Flexible and Open Learning). This is abbreviated to T&D(FOL), sometimes spoken of as 'Tadfol'. This qualification is entirely based on the revised occupational standards developed by the government's Training and Development Lead Body, and published in spring 1995. A number of qualifications will become available to cover the various aspects of open learning under the T&D(FOL) banner, but at the time of writing they are still at a formative stage. They are likely to cover four or five areas, among them advising, tutoring, writing and managing a centre. The awarding bodies will include the RSA, City & Guilds and SCOTVEC.

OPEN LEARNING AWARDS FOR EXCELLENCE

Either individuals or providing organizations may have been granted the OLAFE (Open Learning Awards for Excellence) – a mark of distinction offered by an amalgam of the British Association of Open Learning (BAOL), the Birmingham Open Learning Development Unit (BOLDU), the National Centre for Educational Technology (NCET) and the Open Learning Federation (OLF).

UNIQUE SELLING PROPOSITIONS

Some providers are niche players in the management market, e.g. HDL Training & Development Ltd (formerly Henley Distance Learning Ltd) and Wolsey Hall Oxford.

Other organizations have a broader base which includes management products, e.g. The Open College.

Some providers trade on what they hope and believe is a unique reputation, if not a USP (unique selling proposition). Check on this. Establish their self-image. What business do they promote themselves as being in? For example, do they consider they are in the communications or learning-delivery business, of which open learning is one of their strands? Do they consider themselves to be in the 'creative training solutions' business, again with open learning being one possible service? Do they consider open learning unique or merely a highly accessible form of written information?

Are the providers highly specialized in the open learning field, with the benefits of depth this brings? Or are they players in a number of learning/communication fields, with the benefits of breadth this brings? The field is wide, especially where you are not concerned with lengthy courses of study leading to national vocational qualifications.

Check potential providers' specific reputations. Where do they believe they have particular expertise and a good name? For example, it may be in tailoring materials, responsiveness to individual learners, corporate care with those responsible for the client contract, design of workshops. They will not necessarily be all-rounders.

You might have to sacrifice one aspect in order to buy strength in another. One large corporation made a switch of provider, choosing to forfeit the most attractively laid out learner workbooks in favour of a reputation for quick response times to client problems and speedy marking of learner assignments.

ACCREDITATION

Decide whether it is important for your learners to be accredited with a qualification. This imposes certain constraints and formalities, but it is a strong motivator. It may be the only factor that helps a learner through the mid-term blues.

Also decide whether it is important to you who ultimately accredits the learner's successful completion and awards the appropriate certificate or diploma.

Universities who deliver open learning programmes for managers will continue to issue their own certificates and diplomas.

In the case of private companies in England and Wales the awarding body will probably be among those listed in Figure 11.3, shown with their corresponding NVQ Level. (NB: This list keeps expanding.)

ACTIVITY 11.2

If you are evaluating a number of potential providers, you may like to use checklist provided in Figure 11.4.

FIGURE 11.3 NVQ AWARDING BODIES FOR MANAGERS AND SUPERVISORS

Name of awarding body	Level 3	Level 4	Level 5
British Polymer Training Association Ltd	X		
British Production and Inventory Control Society (BPICS)		X	
Business & Technology Education Council (BTEC)	X	X	X
City and Guilds of London Institute	X	X	X
College of Preceptors		X	
Engineering Construction Industry Training Board	X		
Henley Management College	X	X	X
Institute of Management London		X	
Institute of Motor Industry		X	X
Institute of Personnel and Development (IPD)		X	X
Institute for Supervision and Management (ISM)*	X	X	X
London Chamber of Commerce and Industry	X	X	
Management Verification Consortium (MVC)	X	X	X
Marine and Engineering Training Association	X	X	
National Examining Board for Supervisory Management (NEBSM)	X	X	
Open University Validation Services		X	X
(RSA) Examinations Board	X	X	X
Scottish Vocational Education Council (SCOTVEC)	X	X	X
University of Oxford Delegacy of Local Examinations	X	X	X

The Institute for Supervision and Management is unable to offer MCI-endorsed awards at Levels 4 and 5.

FIGURE 11.4 CHECKLIST FOR EVALUATING POTENTIAL PROVIDERS

1. What are the roles of the various parties? Who is adding value to what?

2. Who compiled the basic learning material?

3. What are the writers' and providers' qualifications?

4. Have the providers got ISO 900/BS 5750? How much does this matter to you?

5. What is the providers' background and reputation?

6. Who else uses these providers? What is their experience of them?

7. What are the providers' claimed strengths, markets, and areas of niche expertise?

8. Do you want your learners to obtain a qualification? What? Awarded by whom?

WRITING DILEMMAS

The task of open learning writers is to convey relevant knowledge and under-standing requirements in an appropriate interactive and exemplified format. This means achieving a fine balance between material which is simple yet challenging, new without being voluminous.

STRETCHING THE LEARNER

The first challenge for the writer is how to strike the right balance between merely spoon-feeding the learner with information to read and absorb, and placing excessive demands on the learner with the response element. The writer then has to make a more significant step change in the kind of approach which is suited to the different levels of management education. For example:

○ At the certificate level the purpose of the interaction is to elicit an answer which is essentially right or wrong.

○ At the diploma level the purpose is to help learners form judgements, to see for themselves and draw their own conclusions.

The more senior managers are, the more they can accept that there are few right answers. Junior management is about learning patterns; middle management about when to break from them. Some go further; Tom Peters says that if you are not confused you are not in touch![4]

OVER-EGGING THE PUDDING

One of the freedoms available to open learning writers is how much material to use to deal with the MCI's knowledge and understanding requirements, as well as how difficult to make it. The minimum level is laid down, but not the maximum.

It is difficult for a highly qualified management expert to put him or herself into the shoes of someone aiming at a lower level. There is a strong tendency to fill out the material to too high a level and at great length, for its own sake, because 'it's there and people ought to know it'. There is also the temptation to impress.

Huge blocks of knowledge like this are the bane of learners. But a more minimalistic approach may present problems for the publishers' marketing people in a highly competitive environment. They might not want to admit that their product doesn't cover such-and-such compared with that of a competitor.

Buyers tend to equate more with better. But the writer's firm aim should be to keep it as short and simple as will meet the minimum requirements. Buyers should examine materials with that in mind. Be impressed by their simplicity, not their complexity.

THE VIRTUE OF SIMPLICITY

Simplicity is different from naïveté. One can be simple without being simplistic. Some non-competence materials which introduce people to management, allegedly at a level equivalent to NVQ Level 3, reflect a naïve view of managing. Such packages are easy to work through, but are fairly misleading. They put the components of managing into boxes. They make it appear as though management is a sequential exercise of discrete skills. Experienced managers know it's a complex whole.

The reality of management was examined in Chapter 1, 'Management – from Science to High Art', and returned to from time to time in Part Two. This enables you to check whether you share the writer's assumptions, philosophy and approach towards management. In particular, you can test your own position against the assumptions behind the competence approach.

ACTIVITY 11.3

If you need to evaluate the quality of written learning materials, you may find the checklist in Figure 11.5 helpful.

FIGURE 11.5 CHECKLIST FOR EVALUATING WRITTEN MATERIALS

Does the writer:

- Share your values and beliefs; e.g. about how learning takes place?
- Strike the right balance between complexity and simplicity?
- Avoid overloading the learner with irrelevant information?
- Stretch learners in an appropriate way for their level?
- Provide a good balance between reading, assignments, workshops and case-studies?

REFERENCES

1. Chris Dunn (1991) 'Training: Off-The-Shelf or Tailor-Made?', *Human Resources*, **2** (Summer).
2. David Clutterbuck (1994) 'Marketing the Staff Departments', *Professional Manager*, January.
3. Peter Newell (1993) 'BS 5750 in Action', *Open Learning Today*, British Association for Open Learning, **15**, July.
4. Tom Peters (1993) 'Hard and Fast Rules for a Soft Economy', *The Independent on Sunday*, 29 August.

12
THE NEW TECHNOLOGY

❖

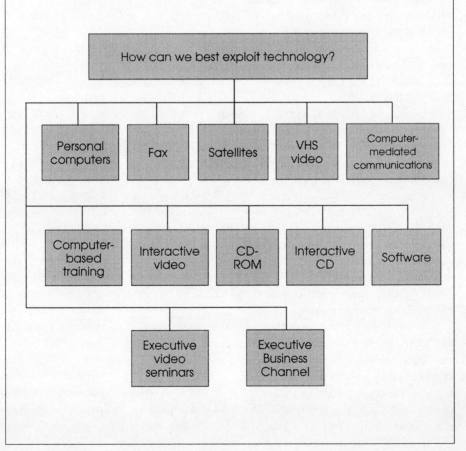

OVERVIEW

This chapter helps you to understand the latest technological trends, and how best to capitalize on technology to deliver and support open learning.

How can we best exploit technology?

Personal computers | Fax | Satellites | VHS video | Computer-mediated communications

Computer-based training | Interactive video | CD-ROM | Interactive CD | Software

Executive video seminars | Executive Business Channel

INTRODUCTION

Technology-based training (TBT) has been around for many years, but it is moving through a number of ever-shorter phases. Most visibly as applied to open learning, technology is fast leaving behind the paper-based image of correspondence courses.

The current technology – 'second generation' as it is sometimes called – has added audio and video to enliven and illuminate the learning process. These now familiar technologies have been coupled with a variety of other features and learner services in the best open learning, such as face-to-face workshops and help-desks.

Both the current and emergent technological developments offer a range of exciting prospects of two kinds:

○   Those which enhance the learning process – both in assimilation terms as well as increasing motivation.
○   Those which widen and introduce greater efficiency between players in the open learning game.

Coupled with this, costs are falling, though the need to equip learners with playback and other user facilities will remain a deterrent for many in the near future. But this is easing too.

Most open learning providers these days include a variety of media along with text. The media most commonly include audio-cassettes and video-cassettes with text, but the range is expanding. Additional media add to the cost but assist learning substantially.

For example, one open learning package on effective presentations uses print to develop organizing skills, audio-cassettes to help with breathing and speaking, and video to show how to set up and use visual aids and arrange the room. But print remains the dominant medium, and the bulk of knowledge inputs for learners of management still comes via text. This is likely to continue. The long-heralded demise of the book (under pressure from the screen) seems a long way off.

However, text is not what it used to be, at least the best isn't. It's a world away from the traditional textbook and the old correspondence course. For a start it's interactive. Text is creatively designed to hook the learner actively into a dialogue.

PC-based desktop publishing (DTP) for writers has dramatically raised the standard of written presentation, thereby further engaging the learner's interest. These developments were explained and examples were shown in Chapter 9 when discussing accessible writing.

The very basic forms of open learning suffer from narrow learner goals which are consistent with their media's limitations. If there is minimum learner-tutor contact, this promotes a low expectation of the open learning process and limited outcomes. Many learners are therefore content merely to acquire information. For many, learning is purely instrumental in orientation, that is, it is seen only as a means to an end, the acquisition of a qualification being the sole aim. Likewise, many companies take a very practical and simple view of what they want open learning to achieve for their managers.

But some of the more recent technological developments claim the possibility of fundamentally changing the feel of the open learning experience, thereby moving it to a different learning paradigm. At its most imaginative and varied, learners can seek deeper meaning for themselves or have what Peter Critten describes as a 'transforming experience'.[1]

In this chapter we shall review the second generation technologies and the more recent emergent ones and examine their potential.

With the developing technology comes an initiative to expand the roles of the larger public libraries into open learning centres with facilities of this nature. This initiative is still being piloted, and just what the facilities will look like remains to be seen. But managers will not be a prime audience.

There are nowadays various exhibitions, centres and conferences devoted to a variety of media to help potential users and buyers explore the field and choose what is appropriate. Some companies offering such services are listed in Appendix 1, 'Sources of Management Development Products and Services'.

PERSONAL COMPUTERS

Personal computers are becoming ever cheaper, more powerful and smaller. Notebook computers are proving increasingly popular with learners. They are mostly used in a stand-alone mode and left a matter for personal choice by the learner. But they open the door to the possibility of networked facilities, as in computer-mediated communications, discussed later in this chapter.

One of the problems with computers – especially for older managers – is that many learners lack affinity with these tools; they may not even recognize their own computer illiteracy. Until trust is built they may be unwilling to try them out, and will not voluntarily buy one.

Yet the way the world of business and management is developing, the computer-shy probably need to overcome their discomfort in order to succeed in their jobs, more than they do to succeed with their courses of study. So some arm-twisting or making the use of a PC a precondition for study might be doubly beneficial.

This contrasts with the markedly different attitudes and skills of new entrants to the workforce, who do not suffer from the same 'hang-ups'. Younger people are more visually-oriented, PC literate and unafraid of change.

FAX

Another significant development is the burgeoning home fax market. As evidence of this, BT plans to abandon its separate fax directory and include people's fax numbers along with their phone numbers. The fax phenomenon will speed up interaction with tutors over work assignments. And it opens up the possibility of multi-learner teleconferencing facilities using a combination of phone and fax.

SATELLITES

The use of satellites seems increasingly likely as a means of beaming European distance learning into our homes. British Aerospace already has a licence from the Department of Trade and Industry to operate a broadcasting service. But the start-up and running costs are high, beyond the cost of developing suitable programmes. And cooperation is needed between the relevant countries if an economically viable audience is to be built. This seems some way off.

VHS VIDEO

Videotape-based learning programmes are popular and widely available, playable on an ordinary VHS video-recorder. Compared with laser disc-sourced material, their technological drawback is slow access to other areas of the tape – just as with music on audio-cassettes compared with CDs. They are therefore linear in presentation and not interactive like the laser disc programmes. Multi-media outlets may sell these programmes, but they are not at the heart of multi-media learning technology.

Some of the subjects are, however, given very sophisticated treatment and are cleverly designed learning experiences (see 'Supported video packages' in this chapter).

COMPUTER-MEDIATED COMMUNICATIONS (CMC)

The earlier-mentioned technologies are currently available. Their advantages are well understood, even if not always widely available or cost-justified. Computer-mediated communications (CMC), on the other hand, can be regarded as still being experimental and technology driven. In other words, what technology can do is still running ahead of whether it is likely to prove sufficiently enhancing for a viable market to develop. Henley Management College has been at the forefront of experimenting with this medium since 1988 with their HELP system (Henley Extended Learning Programme).[2]

A conferencing facility, CMC is defined by Robin Mason in the *British Journal of Educational Psychology* as:

> a method of interactive communication using the written word typed into a computer terminal. The computer stores the inputs of the conference members and allows any member to read and add to the conversation at any time.[3]

Whereas video-conferencing, by either land lines or satellites, can be used for teaching where the tutor is remote but the audience is together, CMC-conferencing works directly into individual learners' home-based computers.

Thus CMC is of potential use to home-based learners with PCs and remote tutors and administrators for transmitting written information in all directions – that is, learner to fellow learner, not just learner to tutor and administrator. It may therefore offer some help with the practicality and feeling of isolation of such learners. It may also speed up response times.

The system helps open learning providers deliver the following facilities:

○   Electronic mail
○   Course information
○   Conferencing on course assignments
○   News updates
○   Access to databases such as library services

Some of these facilities are fairly straightforward and are what David Birchall labels 'electronic tutorials' in writing about the *third generation* of distance learning.[4] But the technology offers the prospect of facilities that might better be called an 'electronic learning environment'. The idea here is to simulate some of the interactive processes which classroom-based tutors enjoy. Protagonists also claim tutors gain a level of satisfaction normally absent as a result of distant relationships with learners.

The medium is also seen as an aid to cooperative learning. Where in the traditional model, learning is thought of as largely one-way, relying on a teacher to impart knowledge, cooperative learning emphasizes active learning through group interaction. Information exchange becomes opinion exchange.

The lack of a live and spontaneous setting can be beneficial to the process. Users can take time to reflect and compose their responses. And the dialogue is archived, allowing for participants to review the transcript later.

Figure 12.1 contains a summary of the pros and cons from Henley's experience.

It is still too soon to assess whether CMC will remain an adjunct to a largely unchanged distance learning methodology, or lead to the latter's wholesale review.

FIGURE 12.1 COMPUTER-MEDIATED COMMUNICATIONS: BENEFITS AND DISADVANTAGES

Features of CMC	Benefits	Disadvantages
Computer based.	More immediate than other distance learning methods.	Difficulties with access. Computerphobes will avoid.
Time independent.	Time to compose responses.	Non-verbal behaviour absent.
Location independent.	Encourages spread of responses.	Identity of group may become vague.
Many-to-many facilities.	Collaboration brings attitude change.	Some personalities may become dominant.
Text based.	Written responses conducive to learning.	May encourage self-consciousness.

Its protagonists favour the more revolutionary scenario, not least because they see it shifting resources from paperwork-based administration to tutoring.

ACTIVITY 12.1

Assess the extent to which the practical considerations mentioned about PCs, fax, satellite dishes, VHS video-recorders and CMC apply in your own case. You may then find it helpful to consider the questions in Figure 12.2.

FIGURE 12.2 PRACTICAL QUESTIONS ABOUT USING TECHNOLOGY

1. What minimum existing IT know-how etc. are you assuming on the part of learners?
2. What IT know-how or equipment are you planning to stipulate as a requirement?
3. What additional provision will you need to arrange for learners?
4. What advice and guidance will you need to offer learners on using technology?
5. How can you best exploit IT to free up tutor and learner time which would otherwise be spent in administration and paper-chasing?

COMPUTER-BASED TRAINING (CBT)

Sometimes computer-based learning is given other names and accordingly other initials, such as computer-based learning (CBL), but the abbreviated form indicated above is the most common.

The medium's advantages include the high potential for interaction, learner sequencing, random tests and immediate feedback. An often neglected facility is to use the computer to manage the learning process (CML), which tests learner readiness, and maintains records. And using the medium helps develop keyboard skills, a side benefit.

Programmes are widely available on floppy disks and can run on a PC, thereby facilitating home use. There are many programmes available for managers on CBT for an average price of around £100.

The medium is somewhat limited in its features, although the latest versions of CBT offer some sound and limited graphics, in addition to text. For full action video effects and sound you need the more recent laser-based products.

INTERACTIVE VIDEO (IV)

More realistic than CBT, interactive video (IV) links video and personal computer technology with a monitor. The video input is typically achieved through the medium of large 12" diameter video discs, about the size of LPs. These are very costly to press; a typical programme price is in the order of £1000–£3000, and is influenced by the number of discs. And the special players are expensive to purchase. But the results in full-action video and sound are most effective.

The interactive nature of the medium allows the learner to make responses when presented with multi-choice questions. Depending upon the learner's decision, the computer chooses the next appropriate 'frame'. So the learner moves through the material by a variety of routes dependent upon their level of understanding. The learner often cannot proceed unless an acceptable answer is given, using a keyboard, mouse, or touch-sensitive screen. A recent development is the use of a hand-held laser scanner used on a workbook linked to the screen.

Because of more recent developments with compact discs, IV is in decline. Few programmes are now being written for this medium. It is possible that some of the existing IV library might be converted to other media.

CD-ROM

CD-ROM (standing for read-only memory because it cannot be recorded upon) employs compact disc technology and is a vast reservoir of data. In text form it has a capacity equivalent to 275,000 pages of A4 text, which is 400–1000 times greater than floppy disk, a magnetic medium. Basic CD-ROM has little video capability and suffers from slightly jerky pictures. An improved format is better able to handle true multi-media seamlessly – photographs, animated footage and graphics, video sequences, audio and straight text, readable by a laser. CD-ROM capability is fast developing, and will soon lead to improved full-screen, high-colour and high-definition motion video, rivalling that of IV.

To the learner, the programme facilities are similar to those described for IV, with programmes generally a little less expensive; the average price for a CD-ROM programme is around £1000.

Many people already have the disc drives attached to their computers for non-training purposes. For those with the facilities at home, this medium provides flexibility away from work or an open learning centre. However, many employers who provide the programmes for CD-ROM drives prefer not to let them out of their sight. CD-ROM is a boom market generally, and is the fastest expanding learning technology.

INTERACTIVE CD

Interactive CD (CD-I or CD-i) is pioneered and promoted by Philips. Like CD-ROM, it uses compact discs to achieve a rather similar effect. A benefit of CD-I is that it does not need a computer. In the absence of a keyboard, learners move through the programme at their own pace and indicate their responses by using a mouse or remote control handset pointer.

A disadvantage of CD-I is that it does need a special player costing around £400, which is then plugged into an ordinary television. These players are now available in miniaturized form and are portable. An additional use is for demonstrators of products who visit people's homes.

CD-I programmes are more expensive than CD-ROM ones, in the range £1250–£3750. There are far fewer currently available for managers on the market, and far less is being written for this medium than for CD-ROM. The screen quality is not as good as that of CD-ROM, but the technology is still in its infancy.

SOFTWARE

Technology apart, IV, CD-ROM and CD-I have a number of features in common from the learner's and learning standpoint. The choice of programme is more important than the particular hardware 'platform' behind it. The hardware should be transparent and come to be taken for granted, so that the learner can concentrate entirely on the subject material.

To give a flavour, a few titles currently available are shown in Figure 12.3.

FIGURE 12.3 SAMPLE OF TITLES CURRENTLY AVAILABLE

CBT	**CD-ROM**
Leading Effectively	Business Meetings
Defining Goals and Objectives	Time Management
Conducting Successful Meetings	Presentation Skills

IV	**CD-I**
Appraisal Interviewing	The Complete Manager
Selection Interviewing	Figure It Out
Effective Teamwork	No Need To Shout

A package may have a number of components. *The Complete Manager*, for example, includes the following:

Course guide

Provides an overview of the programme and helps users to plan their route through it.

Handbook

Provides background reading and an ongoing reference on each of the eighteen topics.

Guide to qualification

Provides a step-by-step description of the process that candidates need to follow in order to present evidence of their competence for assessment for a NVQ Level 4 Certificate in Management.

The workbooks

A separate workbook accompanies each of the three parts of the programme, providing space for keeping notes and guiding users through each step in the learning process.

The CD-I discs

Three discs provide a stimulus for users to examine each topic in the programme and help them see how management skills are applied in a wide variety of circumstances.

Some programmes come with a trainer's/facilitator's guide or additional materials. For example, *Finance for Non-Finance Managers* comes with a 'ratio and variance fact sheet' and a calculator. Some allow learners to choose from a number of modes. *The Complete Manager* provides the following modes:

Browse mode

This mode is for learners who wish to dip into the package without following a formal study plan.

Knowledge mode

This mode is for learners who are primarily interested in building their knowledge and understanding of management.

Skills mode

This mode is for learners who wish to go one step further, to build their practical management skills.

Qualification mode

This mode is for learners who want to have not only understanding and skills, but also a formal qualification which recognizes their all-round competence.

TAILORING

While programmes are available off-the-shelf, their producers are able to tailor the accompanying printed materials to suit the needs of employers. For a price, CD-I manufactures will tailor the compact disc. In the case of IV and CD-ROM which use computer software alongside the laser disc, some programmes come with a 'tool kit' to enable the trainer to customize the software on site.

PURCHASING

There are a small number of suppliers of multi-media products. Some supply hardware, and some supply courseware or programmes. Some of the latter are linked to publishers and therefore sell only their own productions. Some companies, such as Flex Training Ltd., promote themselves as 'one-stop shops' selling a wide range of producers' software, coupled with independent advice at no additional cost. Some are linked with hardware suppliers, such as MultiMedia Training who supply combined ('bundled') hardware and software packages across the range of suppliers' products. It is possible to have an evaluation on your premises or to view them at one of the vendors' centres prior to purchase. Factsheets are often available to describe the courseware, which may be either bought or rented.

SUPPORTED VIDEO PACKAGES

There are several companies competing in this developing market. Serious management videos sold alone, without back-up materials, are increasingly rare, especially where the subjects are complex and deal with more than individual managerial skill. While the technology is not advanced, the context frequently is, and the trend is to support videos with individual study guides and, in some instances, facilitators' guides for group use.

The BBC is at the forefront in this field, through its arm, BBC for BUSINESS. This subsidiary develops and markets a range of video-based products, including 'Management and Supervisory Skills' and 'Management Issues and Concepts', aimed at several audiences. Another product range of special interest here is known as 'Executive Development', previously marketed under the title 'Executive Video Seminars'. Now the range has been extended to embrace a variety of non-seminar products, including a set of Open University distance learning videos known as 'Mastering Business'. We shall look at the non-OU products first.

BBC'S 'EXECUTIVE DEVELOPMENT' VIDEOS

This is an imaginative, internationally-based, initiative which, in conceptual terms, stands at the most sophisticated end of the development spectrum. Unlike stand-alone videos on management topics (of which there are hundreds available) most products in this range are designed to be part of an active two-way learning and planning process based around an in-company seminar. The videos are intended to be catalytic and serve as an input to that process rather than being the heart and purpose of it.

The most complex packages include a number of videos, a facilitator's guide, several participants' guides and overhead transparencies. The facilitator's guide acts as 'a bridge between the ideas presented in the video and your own organisation', and can be used either by an external facilitator or a company manager.

Research shows that, in practice, most organizations fail to use training video packages in the way that designers originally intended, possibly because of the demands they place on facilitators. Therefore the design of packages increasingly assumes that they will be used in a stand-alone mode. This explains why later releases tend to come with fewer copies of the video and with individual participants' study guides, rather than with facilitators' or presenters' guides. This trend matters little with individual-based topics, such as those dealing with leadership skills for example; but for organization-based subjects such as improving customer service, much opportunity for applied learning is lost.

There are many titles including *Leadership, Corporate Culture and Perform-ance, Transformation* and *The Learning Organisation*. The BBC has produced some of these video-packages in association with other publishing houses. In other cases the BBC acts as a distributor. Notable presenters include world authorities such as Dr Richard Pascale, Rosabeth Moss Kanter and Michael Porter.

Some of these topics are fairly mainstream manager and management develop-ment issues. For others the focus is the strategic development of the organization or business. But it is a false division to isolate the OD topics and place them beyond our interest here. Though not directly concerned with an individual manager's personal development, they are very much concerned with the organization's collective management.[5]

This important distinction between developing the management *game* and the management *players* is dealt with at length in my companion volume *Developing Corporate Competence – A High-Performance Agenda for Managing Organ-izations*.[5]

While not cheap to buy (business videos never are), when spread across the participants, the cost compares very favourably with alternative ways of spending the training budget. And it is up to the company to see that the packages are used properly and that it gets a return on its investment. With the possibility of building company change plans directly into a group learning process, the potential return is closer to the outlay than it is for most learning processes.

BBC'S 'MASTERING BUSINESS' SERIES

The 'Mastering Business' series of videos is a sub-brand of 'Executive Development' marketed by BBC for BUSINESS. They consist of edited versions of videos used on the Open University's distance learning MBA courses. They are designed 'to develop understanding, knowledge and competence for effective management performance'. Each package comprises a video and an individual study guide. The subjects are grouped under four headings: internationalization, information tech-nology, human resource development and people in changing organizations.

Although their origin lies in MBA course material, the videos are deemed suitable for a spread of middle and senior managers. This is claimed to be made possible by the design of the study guide which provides 'multi-level access'.

Similar to the videos for group use, the subjects lie mostly at the OD/strategic end of the development spectrum, being designed to introduce core business ideas and strategies into an organization'. They are not about individual manager skill development. The guide is intended to help users apply the ideas and strategies to their own organizations. This raises the crucial issue of how best to capitalize on individual learning for application to the organization and the business. Most companies naïvely expect to experience beneficial organizational change as a result of individually targeted learning. In reality this is generally a false hope, unless a skilled facilitator is used on behalf of the organization as client (not the individual learner) to help apply the learning to the business.[5]

EXECUTIVE BUSINESS CHANNEL

The Executive Business Channel (EBC) was originally launched in association with BBC Select. As initially conceived, the service broadcast programmes over the airwaves at night into managers' homes or company offices. Subscribers used a decoding facility to unscramble the signal so it could be viewed on video (hence the 'channel'). Although ingenious, subscribers preferred to receive their videos through the post, and transmissions were abandoned in this form. The EBC subscription service continues to operate, albeit using old technology – i.e. the postman!

The service comprises both video programmes and the printed word. Programmes come with purpose-written printed materials which take the form of workbooks, trainers' notes and OHP masters, and specially designed assignments.

Subjects include many popular themes – several in the form of 'mini-series' – such as *Valuing People*, *Total Quality Management*, *Improving Performance*, *Mentoring*, *Customer Care* and *Investing in People*.

Programmes are produced weekly, with fifty programmes over the course of a year, each of a half-hour's duration, building a substantial and growing library over time. Alternatively, individual videos and back-numbers may be purchased from the catalogue.

There are three possible ways of using these programmes and learning workbooks. Managers may choose to use them as individual study opportunities. Or trainers can make use of them during formal sessions to emphasize particular points or to add interest and variety. The third option is to structure complete sessions around the programmes, using the back-up material to the full. For group use by subscribers, the materials come with a liberal Licence to Copy.

EBC has teamed up with Management Development Partnership and the University of Nottingham to provide a Certificate in Management, to MCI management standards M1 at NVQ Level 4 for a range of clients including the Royal Mail. Likewise there is a partnership planned with Robert Gordon University to offer a Certificate in Project Management at the same level.

ACTIVITY 12.2

If you are planning to make use of any of the media discussed in this chapter, you may wish to consider these issues:

- Does the proposal utilize an appropriate mix of media for the type of subject matter?
- Are the proposed media justified and cost effective?
- Are the proposed media practical and user-friendly for your intended audience?

REFERENCES

1. Peter Critten (1986) 'Open Learning – An Opportunity for Growth or a Case of Paradigm Lost?', *Journal of European Industrial Training*, **10** (6).
2. Philip Stiles, Amy Jameson and Alex Lord (1993) 'Teaching Business Ethics: An Open Learning Approach', *Management Education and Development*, London: Association for Management Education and Development, **24** (3).
3. Robin Mason (1988) 'Computer Conferencing: A Contribution to Self-Directed Learning', *British Journal of Educational Psychology*, **19** (1).
4. David Birchall (1993) 'Third Generation Distance Learning', *Journal of European Industrial Training*, **14** (7).
5. William Tate (1995) *Developing Corporate Competence: A High-Performance Agenda for Managing Organizations*, Aldershot: Gower.

POSTSCRIPT

❖

Along with its companion volume *Developing Corporate Competence: A High-Performance Agenda for Managing Organizations*, this book constitutes a clarion call for improved manager and management development – more multi-faceted in approach, more in touch with the daily realities and dilemmas which managers face, more directed at real business and organization problems, more cognizant of organizational irrationality, more integrated with other disciplines, more allied with other interventions, more future-oriented. What does the present scene have to offer such a demanding agenda?

Is the answer to be found in lasers and satellites delivering open learning into the home? Will competences prove to hold the key to nirvana? Examples like these are, of course, only potential solutions to assumed business needs and wants. Perhaps we spend too much time buying and using products, and not enough in diagnosing, understanding and sharing real organizational problems. A reasonable conclusion is that diagnostic organization skills are one of our most pressing development needs.

ENDURING FASHION

All but cynics are attracted to the idea of a Eureka-style breakthrough, the insight that has at last found 'the best way' – the best way to develop, the best way to manage, and so on. Fashions and bandwagons are by definition catching. Panaceas are seductive. Whilst we may sometimes be naïve to fall for them, arguably we need them. They replenish the vacuum caused by the natural decay of the previous idea.

Perhaps we also need a certain amount of hype – distastefully transparent though it is. How else can we expect to generate the energy to get ideas off the ground and fuel their evolution before detractors seek out their weak spots as the ideas progress through their natural life cycle to maturity and into decline?

There is nothing wrong with the endless invention, reinvention and search for the managerial equivalent of the philosopher's stone. The problem arises when the best way becomes the only acceptable way. The best way removes choice, produces political pressures and drives out alternatives. The best way becomes divorced from circumstance and context. And, paradoxically, the best way diminishes our requirement for learning and understanding, since we no longer need to make a choice to ensure a fit between solution and problem.

Shelves are filled with books about these fashions: Management by Objectives, quality circles, BS 5750, business process re-engineering, and so on. Are competences another? And if here to stay a while, how can we retain plurality in the system? Paradoxically, plurality demands competences too! And what about open learning? Might this too prove ultimately to be a passing fad? If the basic ideas are essentially sound, we must hope they endure. How can this be assisted?

Not by dogma and arm-twisting. Nor by clever packaging. The former brings resentment and strengthens the resolve of critics. Management competences and NVQs might suffer that fate, however political and powerful they are in the short term. The 1992/93 President of the IPM, no less, felt bold enough in office to voice doubt over NVQs' long-term presence in the system. Yet the basic idea has considerable merit.

As to packaging, we risk becoming bored by ideas if presented as clever delivery methodologies. Open learning, in its narrowest definition of unsupported distance learning, could suffer that fate.

What we need to do is to seek out and promote the ideas, their strengths and values, and then allow others to make free-will matches against their own needs and assessments.

It may sound rather negative, but we must hope that none of the initiatives described in this book take such a strong hold that they blind us to their limitations and cloud our vision of alternatives. All have a powerful contribution to make in the right setting with judicious application. But let's keep a sense of proportion. The boom-and-bust history of education – like the economy – suggests we might become too carried away with fashion and reap a reaction and disillusion. Let's hope moderation prevails.

A COMPETENT FUTURE

MCI's apparent decision to put all its eggs in the competence basket is therefore both helpful and unhelpful. If it had not chosen this high-risk championing strategy, managerial competences would not have taken off so strongly. Many thousands of companies would not have enjoyed a resurgence of work-oriented training. Provided that MCI remains flexible and regularly revisits its definitions, generic competences will continue to meet many companies' and employees' perceived needs.

But, for their own part, consumers and users need to judge how well the competence approach matches their own managers' experience and suits their organization. That means its business, structure and specialisms, philosophy, vision, culture and phase of company development.

The negative aspect of excessive zeal over competences is that there are many other dimensions of management development – quite regardless of what you think about competences – which are being neglected or squeezed out. They need championing too. Some of these are discussed in the companion volume to this book.

LESS TRAINING

One of the trends of the 1990s is that less emphasis is being placed on jobs as the building blocks of organizations. This could shift attention towards people's inherent competencies and qualities, rather than competences measured in the job.

If you share that view, and if you hold some of the reservations about competences discussed in this book, then the manager development process you might value most – particularly at the higher levels – may come closer to a broad and liberating 'education', rather than job 'training' whose purpose is conformity. What we increasingly need in my opinion are personal competencies which managers can bring and adapt to whatever they are called upon to do – whether for their current or future employer, or for themselves – and with little ability to predict. In this point of view, the quality of the learning experience matters more than the demonstration of (someone else's definition of) management competence.

In the debate on the key to Britain's future, most institutions and commentators are nailing their colours to the mast of training. The National Advisory Council for Education and Training Targets (NACETT) and the Management Charter Initiative (MCI) are now in discussion about setting training targets for managers on top of those for the rest of the workforce. The Institute of Management argues that 'for a developed country like the UK, it is clear that future prosperity will depend on knowledge and skills'. For the bulk of the workforce, they may possibly be right. But for managers, I personally don't think they are; this kind of ability is only one small part of the story. The danger is that the listeners may think that's all there is to it.

Ask the average manager what they need most: more skills or the opportunity to practise those they already have? I bet a great many would say the latter; their organization puts obstacles in the way of applying and realizing the potential already there. Management development needs to do some investigating there.

This nation's leaders seem to be afflicted with three blindspots:

1. They cannot see beyond the individual as the unit of hoped-for productivity gains. But teamwork and systems have more to offer.
2. They appear to want quantity irrespective of quality. We need to show more concern for developing wholesome organizational units.
3. They have forgotten the law of cybernetics which states that an organism needs a plural inside if it is to be able to manage a plural outside, i.e. its environment.

More than mass training for efficiency, organizations need wiser strategies and more confident managers who can challenge their bosses and the status quo. For developers, it requires developing the organization climate as well as individuals and teams. For managers, it requires education more than training. For government, it means encouraging variety, and backing off pressures to conform.

'Training' and 'education' are in danger of going the same way as 'less' and 'fewer'. A valuable distinction risks being lost. If you ask people whether it is OK to say 'less prunes and fewer custard', most recognize that it seems better the other way round. Likewise, 'I can educate you, but you have to train yourself!' feels instinctively wrong. When people are helped to see the difference in the concepts, they can accept it.

These are not nice distinctions: they are fundamental. And they need pointing out. Mostly what we get from officialdom, from politicians and from those who should know better is a blurred mass. Education should put more emphasis on the self, and training on what someone else wants done to you. Some sources of provision are more suited to education than training, or vice versa. The mistake is to assume that a single source has to satisfy both purposes. Even the modern universities are in danger of moving from being *seats of learning* to *training machines*. We can have both. Training doesn't have to be at the expense of education.

There was a time when we criticized classroom experience for being too centred on the teacher. What we needed, we said, was to concentrate on the learner: learner-centred education, learner-centred training, learner-centred development. We once thought this was a two-ended continuum; it had to be more of one of these or the other. We hear less of that now. What we have now is more of another dimension: employer-centredness. But was this more suited to the 1980s – another pendulum swing too far?

A WAY FORWARD

Some trainers and educators may believe that by teaching competences they are teaching the whole of managing and management. Patently, that is not so. Maybe a mistake made by the competence critics is to assume that all advocates of the competence approach are equally single-minded. The former development director at MCI openly conceded that other forms of management education were equally relevant as his own competence-based approach. Are you surprised?

We need two changes in approach. First, open acceptance of the horses-for-courses argument. Second, more guidance about how to choose. My own view is that the competence approach can only usefully address one need for managers; namely, the basic-level foundation of skills. But that is not to decry its importance. However, it is upon this floor that the real artistry of managing has to be added and has to be allowed to learn and grow by other means, since much of it is incapable of definition and is unteachable.

It would help if the government and its agencies would acknowledge limited aspirations for the competence movement so far as managers are concerned. The present picture is one of the competence advocates 'going for broke'. They have already become victims of their own propaganda – having generated demand and made so many converts, it is difficult for them to backtrack to a more limited, though still valuable role. Yet that may be what is needed.

MANAGERS – LIABILITIES OR ASSETS?

In purely accounting terms managers are a cost, and the various stakeholders have a right to expect a reasonable return – to be able to tell managers what is expected of them, and to be able to ensure that they are trained to have the necessary competence to deliver against their accountabilities.

But managers, like employees generally, are an asset and a resource, as Peter Drucker pointed out as long ago as 1946. Employing managers is therefore an opportunity – an opportunity for the organization to allow the managers to be more than mere functionaries, to be themselves, unique beings with their own ideas and the need to find meaning for their own endeavours in their own way. These are skills they can't be told, can't be trained to do, and can't have measured. The range of training, development and education – whatever the content and however designed and assessed – must accommodate these multiple perspectives.

We have two alternatives:

O   **Training**: you know (or think you know) what you want from your managers and you go about getting it.

O   **Development**: you develop your managers' awareness about their business, its chosen direction, its customers and its environment. You develop their self-awareness and curiosity, and you give them access to resources. You then set them free. Free to follow their instincts. Free to be themselves. Free to use their energies. Free above all to develop.

APPENDIX 1: SOURCES OF MANAGEMENT DEVELOPMENT PRODUCTS AND SERVICES

AirteQ Ltd
Media House
Presley Way
Crown Hill
Milton Keynes
Buckinghamshire MK8 0ES
Tel: 01908 570100
Fax: 01908 261979

Provides CD-ROM titles in areas which include HR, management skills and quality. Sells authoring tools for training managers to design and build CBT applications. Products include FastraQ 9000 (to apply ISO 9000).

BBC for Business
Woodlands
80 Wood Lane
London W12 0TT
Tel: 0181 576 2361
Fax: 0181 576 2867

Produces and distributes training videos in association with other publishers including the Open University, some with self-study resources and trainers' resource materials, in the fields of management and supervisory skills, management issues and concepts, executive development and mastering business.

BOLDU Ltd
St. George's House
40-49 Price Street
Birmingham B4 6LA
Tel: 0121 359 6628
Fax: 0121 359 6624

Home of what they describe as the 'national open learning library'. Information, advice and consultancy on open learning. Establishment of open learning centres. Distributors for established producers of open learning materials. Development and management of open learning systems. Writing and editing of bespoke open learning materials.

CC Information Systems
Broadfields House
Broadfields
Headstone Lane
Harrow
Middlesex HA2 6NZ
Tel: 0181 421 2999
Fax: 0181 421 4431

Supplies hardware and distributes *Business in Sight* series on IV.

Connaught Training Ltd
Gower House
Croft Road
Aldershot
Hants GU11 3HR
Tel: 01252 331551
Fax: 01252 344405

Publishes and distributes open learning programmes, films, videos, games and trainers' resource packs.

COTU
Coventry Training Services
    Ltd
Butts
Coventry CV1 3GD
Tel: 01203 526709
Fax: 01203 526789

Involved in the development and delivery of a range of open and flexible learning products for industry and education, including general and sector-specific management development materials. Also provides a consultancy service.

Cumbria Open Learning
Management House
72 Kingstown Broadway
Carlisle CA3 0HA
Tel: 01228 512539
Fax: 01228 590988

Provides open learning advice, support and consultancy. Agents for all open learning producers. Writes, produces and commissions customized training materials. Trains trainers, open learning practitioners and assessors.

Development Processes
    (UK) Ltd
The Granary
50 Barton Road
Worsley
Manchester M28 4PB
Tel: 0161 728 3700
Fax: 0161 728 3440

Consultancy and assessment services. Developers for MCI management standards. Publications include a Portfolio Development Guide and Mentoring Guide. Modular open learning programmes. Titles include *The Manager's Route to Competence* and *The Local Government Manager's Route to Competence*.

Durham University
    Business School
Mill Hill Lane
Durham City DH1 3LB
Tel: 0191374 2219
Fax: 0191374 3389

Offers a distance learning MBA using their own commissioned materials.

Educational Media Film &
    Video Ltd
235 Imperial Drive
Rayners Lane
Harrow
Middlesex HA2 7HE
Tel: 0181 868 1908/15
Fax: 0181 868 1991

Produces and distributes, for sale or hire, management videos with support materials. Titles include *The Paradigms of Performance, Performance Management.*

Executive Business Channel
Shaw House
18 Shaw Road
Stockport
Cheshire SK4 4AE
Tel: 0161 442 2225
Fax: 0161 432 5536

Sale of videos. Subscription service available for weekly supply. Titles include *Managing Meetings, Developing a Business Plan, Report Writing, Team Briefing*.

Fenman Training
Clive House
The Business Park
Ely
Cambridgeshire CB7 4EH
Tel: 01353 665533
Fax: 01353 663644

Produces and distributes videos, for sale or hire, plus free postal previews, in interpersonal and general business skills. Titles include *Setting Objectives, Managing for Customer Care*. Also trainer-led, text-based activity packs and session shakers.

Flex Training Ltd
9–15 Hitchin Street
Baldock
Herts SG7 6AL
Tel: 01462 895544
Fax: 01462 892417

Distributes a wide range of management and interpersonal skills training resources, most available for hire and sale. Media include CBT, CD-I, CD-ROM, IV, video, workbooks and trainers' guides. Independent advice and preview centre. Provides information and consultancy in setting up and running open learning schemes and resource centres.

Gower Publishing Ltd
Gower House
Croft Road
Aldershot
Hants GU11 3HR
Tel: 01252 331551
Fax: 01252 344405

Publishes books and self-study packages on business and management, and trainer-led resource material on management skills.

HDL Training & Development Ltd
Craigmore House
Remenham Hill
Henley-on-Thames
Oxon RG9 3EP
Tel: 01491 571552
Fax: 01491 579843

Provides open learning programmes. The *First Line Management Programme* to identify and implement work-based improvements. Diploma, Certificate and Supervisory Certificate in Management programmes. *Tomorrow's Manager, New Career Manager, The Line Manager as Developer*, etc. Investors in People workshops.

Heriot-Watt University
The Esmée Fairbairn Research Centre
Edinburgh EH14 4AS
Tel: 0131 451 3090
Fax: 0131 451 3002

Offers a distance learning MBA using their own materials published for them by Pitman.

ICDP Europe Ltd
Rosemount House
Rosemount Avenue
West Byfleet
Surrey KT14 6LB
Tel: 01932 354525
Fax: 01932 354585

Publishes and distributes generic management courses on CD-I. Titles include *Credit Where Credit's Due* (APL), *The Complete Manager, Developing Competence, No Need to Shout*.

The Industrial Society
Robert Hyde House
48 Bryanston Square
London W1H 7LN
Tel: 0171 262 2401
Fax: 0171 706 1096

Provides advisory and training services, including consultancy work, various publications and training videos.

Insight Consultants Ltd
Sheerspeed House
Heathpark Way
Honiton
Devon EX14 8BB
Tel: 01404 46878
Fax: 01404 46879

MCI licensed centre. Distributes MCI products. Trains assessors. Assesses portfolio evidence. Provides flexible learning programmes.

Keytime Management
   Development
72 Victoria Road
Burgess Hill
West Sussex RH15 9LZ
Tel: 01444 235141
Fax: 01444 870004

Provides a time manager system for *Managing Time for Better Results*. Modules include Delegation and Objective Setting.

Kogan Page
120 Pentonville Road
London N1 9JN
Tel: 0171 278 0433
Fax: 0171 837 6348

Publishes a wide range of management development titles including open learning books called Management Action Guides written by Manchester Open Learning. Also books on NVQs, competences, assessment, APL, strategic management, etc.

Lancaster University
University House
Lancaster LA1 4YW
Tel: 01524 65201
F2Y: 00524 843087

Offers company MBA programmes. Close academic-industry links.

Lasermedia UK Ltd
Media House
Arundel Road
Walberton
Arundel
West Sussex BN18 0QP
Tel: 01243 533003
Fax: 01243 555020

Publishes and markets own technology-based training. Develops and produces custom-built and generic interactive TBT. Distributors for other publishers' products, e.g. in project management, team development, negotiation skills and PC skills.

The Learning Business Ltd
Park House
25-28 Shrivenham
   Hundred Business Park
Watchfield
Swindon
Wiltshire SN6 8TZ
Tel: 01793 783300
Fax: 01793 783558

Distributors of open learning programmes at NVQ Levels 4 and 5. Producers of bespoke programmes in text, audio, video, CBT, or multi-media.

Leicester University
   Management Centre
University Road
Leicester LE1 7RH
Tel: 01162 523952
Fax: 01162 523949

Offers distance learning MBA, Diploma and Certificate programmes using their own materials.

Lifeskills International Ltd
Wharfebank House
Ilkley Road
Otley
West Yorkshire LS21 3JP
Tel: 01943 851144
Fax: 01943 851140

Developers of generic learning materials and special learning packages for client organizations. Developers of employee development and internal marketing strategies.

Training Direct
Longman House
Burnt Mill
Harlow
Essex CM20 2JE
Tel: 01279 623927
Fax: 01279 623795

Provides training resources. Sells and hires video films, IV CD-ROM multi-media courseware and print-based resource packs. Free previews.

Management Development
   Partnership
Plas Menai
Caernarfon
Gwynedd LL55 1UE
Tel: 01248 671617
Fax: 01248 671610

Offers a Certificate in Management course, using Executive Business Channel videos, in conjunction with Nottingham University, accredited as an NVQ Level 4 programme. Similarly offers a Certificate in Project Management with Robert Gordon University. Works with clients to develop in-house competences.

Management Learning
  Resources Ltd
PO Box 28
Carmarthen
Dyfed SA31 1DT
Tel: 01267 87661
Fax: 01267 87315

Distributes learning resources, tools, instruments, questionnaires, books, games, etc by mail order.

Manchester Open Learning
Lower Hardman Street
Manchester M3 3FP
Tel: 0161 833 9858
Fax: 0161 834 5051

Provides client-customized, tutor-supported, accredited open learning programmes to meet training and development needs within organizations.

Maxim Training Systems
  Ltd
61 Ship Street
Brighton
East Sussex BN1 1AE
Tel: 01273 204198
Fax: 01273 738829

Sells generic and bespoke CBT based programmes. Titles include *Performance Troubleshooting, Keeping Staff Informed, Pushing for Profit, Managing the Reprimand.*

Melrose Film Productions
16 Bromells Road
London SW4 0BL
Tel: 0171 627 8404
Fax: 0171 622 0421

Produces and distributes training videos (some include workbooks), CD-I and management games. Titles include *Liberation Management, The Management Revolution.*

MOST Management
  Training
Bloomfield Road
Tipton
West Midlands DY4 0AH
Tel: 0121 557 3280
Fax: 0121 520 0053

Publishes generic and customized open learning workbooks and materials at M1(S), M1 and M2. The *Progressive Manager* series. Runs tutor-led courses at these levels

MTS Publishers Ltd.
Oakwood
Spa Road
Melksham
Wiltshire SN12 7NP
Tel: 01225 790998
Fax: 01225 790998

Publishes video courses. Titles include *Financial Management, Real Management by Results*, etc by Peter Drucker.

MultiMedia Training Ltd
Marcom House
1 Heathlands
Heath Gardens
Twickenham
Middlesex TW1 4BP
Tel: 0181 744 1624
Fax: 0181 744 1175

Sells and hires multi-media hardware and courseware. Demonstrations, evaluations and library service.

NEBS Management
76 Portland Place
London W1N 4AA
Tel: 0171 278 2468

Provides programmes to help individual managers improve competence by emphasizing practical work-based activity.

NETG Applied Learning
1 Hogarth Business Park
Burlington Lane
Chiswick
London W4 2TJ
Tel: 0181 994 4404
Fax: 0181 994 5611

Provides integrated training solutions, primarily in IT subjects. Also distributes CD-ROM packages produced by Tarragon Training.

The Open College
St Paul's
781 Wilmslow Road
Didsbury
Manchester M20 8RW
Tel: 0161 434 0007
Fax: 0161 434 1061

Publishes open learning programmes, including *Effective Mentoring, Moving into Management – A Course for Women, Managing Change – Working Effectively*. Operates flexible learning network.

The Open Learning Centre
24 King Street
Carmarthen
Dyfed SA31 1BS
Tel: 01267 235268
Fax: 01267 238179

Markets open learning to industry. Consultancy and support services available.

Open Mind
Delphi House
Deanfield Avenue
Henley-on-Thames
Oxon RG9 1UE
Tel: 01491 411061
Fax: 01491 411531

Distributes videos, CBT, CD-ROM and CD-I open learning courseware.

Pergamon Open Learning
Linacre House
Jordan Hill
Oxford OX2 8DP
Tel: 01865 310111
Fax: 01865 310104

Publishes open learning programmes for supervisory and management development. Compiles and publishes the annual *Open Learning Directory*.

PictureTel UK
258 Bath Road
Slough
Berkshire SL1 4DX
Tel: 01753 673000
Fax: 01753 673010

Video-conferencing for distance learning.

Pitman Publishing
128 Long Acre
London WC2E 9AN
Tel: 0171 379 7383
Fax: 0171 240 5771

Publishes the Heriot-Watt distance learning MBA material. Management books from Ashridge with *Financial Times*. Business books.

Resource Development
  International
10 Mercia Business Village
Westwood Heath
Coventry CV4 8HX
Tel: 01203 422422
Fax: 01203 422423

Produces distance learning materials. Writes tailored programmes. Offers international consultancy. Handling agents for Leicester University's distance learning MBA, Diploma and Certificate programmes.

Staffordshire Open
  Learning Unit (SOLU)
The Chetwynd Centre
Newport Road
Stafford ST16 2HE
Tel: 01785 52313
Fax: 01785 57736

Runs Learning Technology Centre for demonstrations, previews. Supplies equipment and courseware. Develops in-house programmes. Consultancy. Produces generic and bespoke materials. Establishes learning resource centres.

Tarragon Training
  International
71 Epping Road
North Ryde
NSW 2113
Australia
Tel: +61 2 887 3988
Fax: +61 2 887 1780

Produces CD-ROM packages for distribution through several UK outlets. Titles include *Participating in Project Teams, Coaching in the Workplace, Negotiating for a Positive Outcome, Making Your Time Count*.

TDA Consulting Ltd
4 Thameside Centre
Kew Bridge Road
Brentford
Middlesex TW8 0HF
Tel: 0181 568 3040
Fax: 0181 569 9800

Tailored training design and delivery. Consultancy. Creative publications/media design for communication and training purposes. Career management counselling services.

Graham Thompson
2 Caldy Road
Alsager
Stoke-on-Trent ST7 2BB
Tel: 01270 872976

Produces and distributes Practical People Development modules for developers and trainers to use. Titles include *Managing Change, Leadership, Delegating, Decision Making*.

The University of Reading
The Management Unit
Building L22
London Road
Reading
Berkshire RG1 5AQ
Tel: 01734 318180
Fax: 01734 316539

Offers open learning MBA, Diploma in Management, Certificate in Management using materials published by HDL Training & Development. Offers an in-house Supervisory Certificate in Management.

Video Arts Ltd
Dumbarton House
68 Oxford Street
London W1N 0LH
Tel: 0171 637 7288
Fax: 0171 580 8103

CD-I and off-the-shelf and bespoke video training programmes with support materials. Titles include *Chairing Meetings, Report Writing, Meetings Bloody Meetings, The Dreaded Appraisal*. Agents for Tom Peters' and Ken Blanchard's video packages.

Viewtech Film and Video
161 Winchester Road
Brislington
Bristol BS4 3NJ
Tel: 01272 773422
Fax: 01272 724292

Sells or hires management videos, many from the Harvard Business Review Series: *The Middle Manager as Innovator, Responding to Organisational Change, Service Management*, etc.

Wolsey Hall Oxford Ltd
66 Banbury Road
Oxford OX2 6PR
Tel: 01865 310310
Fax: 01865 310969

Helps organizations design and deliver open learning programmes. Develops materials in print, audio, video, CBT and multi-media. Programmes can lead to Certificate and Diploma in Management level qualifications (including NVQs).

Xebec MultiMedia
  Solutions
2nd Floor, Critchley Site
Bath Road
Woodchester
Stroud
Glos GL5 5EY
Tel: 01453 836135
Fax: 01453 832241

Develops and publishes the *Business Sense* series on CD-ROM. Titles include *Leading Teams, Business Meetings*.

XOR
29 Charlotte Road
London EC2A 3PB
Tel: 0171 613 2660
Fax: 0171613 2670

Provides a range of services to support the creation of multi-media applications. Offers a CD-ROM title *Essential Interviewing Techniques*.

APPENDIX 2: SOURCES OF ADVICE, INFORMATION AND MEMBERSHIP

Association for Management Education and Development
14–15 Belgrave Square
London SW1X 8PS
Tel: 0171 235 3505   Fax: 0171 235 3565

Institute of Administrative Management
40 Chatsworth Parade
Petts Wood
Orpington
Kent BR5 lRW
Tel: 01689 875555   Fax: 01689 870891

Institute of Management
Management House
Cottingham Road
Corby
Northants NN17 1TT
Tel: 01536 204222   Fax: 01536 201651

Institute of Personnel and Development
IPD House
Camp Road
Wimbledon
London SW19 4UX
Tel: 0181 971 9000   Fax: 0181 963 3333

Institute for Supervision and Management
Mansell House
22 Bore Street
Lichfield
Staffs WS13 6LP
Tel: 01543 251346   Fax: 01543 415804

Management Charter Initiative
Russell Square House
10–12 Russell Square
London WC1B 5BZ
Tel: 0171 872 9000   Fax: 0171 872 9099

There are several valuable sources of information and advice specifically on open learning. Some offer membership, giving access to newsletters, workshops, etc. None cater exclusively for managers and supervisors.

THE OPEN LEARNING FEDERATION

The Open Learning Federation is a practitioner support group offering individual and institutional members advice and guidance on all aspects of open learning. Its main objectives are to foster and promote policy in the development of open and flexible learning systems, to help and advise the training of tutors and counsellors and to review and promote the use of self-development materials in appropriate learning situations. The Federation operates on a regional basis mainly through regional events and a member self-help consultancy service. It also publishes the *OLF Newsletter*, regional newsletters and occasional papers.

The Open Learning Federation
c/o Sam McKeown
Competence Assessment Training Services (CATS)
26 Tenterden Drive
London NW4 1ED
Tel/Fax: 0181 203 9200

THE BRITISH ASSOCIATION FOR OPEN LEARNING

The British Association for Open Learning was formed through the merger of the National Learning Association and the Supervisory and Management Open Learning Federation a few years ago. BAOL represents the interests of organizations whose core activity is open or flexible learning. Membership benefits include national representation on lead policy-making and funding bodies, development of quality standards and codes of practice and forums for the exchange of ideas and information. BAOL publishes *Open Learning Today*.

The British Association for Open Learning
Suite No. 16, Pixmore House
Pixmore Avenue
Letchworth
Herts SG6 1JG
Tel: 01462 485588   Fax: 01462 485633

THE NATIONAL OPEN LEARNING LIBRARY

The National Open Library represents the largest one-stop free preview centre in the UK. Over 6500 open learning packages are available for callers to view on site at Birmingham. Information, advice and consultancy available.

The National Open Learning Library
c/o Birmingham Open Learning Development Unit Ltd (BOLDU)
St. George's House
40–49 Price Street
Birmingham B4 6LA
Tel: 0121 359 6628   Fax: 0121 359 6624

OPEN LEARNING SYSTEMS NEWS

Open Learning Systems News is published by the Gilwern Social Science Enterprise. Its purpose is to provide subscribers with the latest information about developments in open and flexible learning and supported self-study by acting as an information exchange. Covers applications of learning organized through computer control (e.g. multi-media).

Open Learning Systems News
11 Malford Grove
Gilwern
Abergavenny
Gwent NP7 0RN
Tel: 01873 830872

THE OPEN LEARNING DIRECTORY

The *Open Learning Directory* is updated annually and is expanding rapidly with the growth of open learning. The 1995 edition contains 680 pages, covering 2500 materials and 250 support organizations. Many are relevant for managers. The directory also offers advice and explanations.

The Open Learning Directory
Lineacre House
Jordan Hill
Oxford
OX2 8DP
Tel: 01865 310111   Fax: 01865 310104

OPEN LEARNING FOUNDATION

Works in close association with universities (mainly ex-polytechnics) to write, design, produce and assist with the use of open learning materials, including management especially in health service and social services sectors.

The Open Learning Foundation
3 Devonshire Street
London W1N 2BA
Tel: 0171 636 4186   Fax: 0171 631 0132

DATAMAIL DISTRIBUTION LTD

Distribution of 'matching databases' produced by the Employment Department on diskettes, designed to find open learning materials which fulfil the training needs for particular NVQs.

Datamail Distribution Ltd
4 Rookery Lane
Thurmaston
Leicester LE4 8AU
Tel: 01533 697081   Fax: 01533 697271

INDEX